Latino Students in American Schools

Historical and Contemporary Views

Edited by
Valentina I. Kloosterman

Foreword by Virginia Gonzalez

PRAEGER

Westport, Connecticut
London

Library of Congress Cataloging-in-Publication Data

Latino students in American schools: historical and contemporary views / edited by
  Valentina I. Kloosterman ; foreword by Virginia Gonzalez.
    p.   cm.
  Includes bibliographical references and index.
  ISBN 0–89789–898–2 (alk. paper)
  1. Hispanic Americans—Education.   2. Hispanic Americans—Education—Social
aspects.   I. Kloosterman, Valentina I., 1968–
  LC2669.L384   2003
  371.829'68073—dc21   2003046313

British Library Cataloguing in Publication Data is available.

Library of Congress Catalog Card Number: 2003046313
ISBN: 0–89789–898–2

First published in 2003

Praeger Publishers, 88 Post Road West, Westport, CT 06881
An imprint of Greenwood Publishing Group, Inc.
www.praeger.com

Printed in the United States of America

The paper used in this book complies with the
Permanent Paper Standard issued by the National
Information Standards Organization (Z39.48–1984).

10 9 8 7 6 5 4 3 2 1

Copyright Acknowledgment

The editor and publisher are grateful for permission to reproduce the following copyrighted
material:

Chapter 3 originally appeared as Lilia Bartolomé, "Beyond the Methods Fetish: Toward a
Humanizing Pedagogy," *Harvard Educational Review*, 64:2 (Summer 1994), pp. 173–194.
Copyright © 1994 by the President and Fellows and Harvard College. All rights reserved.
Reprinted with permission.

I dedicate this book to my mother, Rebeca Ventura de Kloosterman, for being a wonderful role model and permanent inspiration in my life; and to the memory of my father, Dirck Henry Kloosterman, for teaching me what the words social justice, determination, and courage are all about. He is a true hero. This book is for the millions of Latino children who are eager to learn, to be loved, and to be understood in our schools today.

Dedico este libro a mi madre, Rebeca Ventura de Kloosterman, por ser un gran modelo de persona e inspiración permanente en mi vida; y en memoria de mi padre, Dirck Henry Kloosterman, por enseñarme lo que las palabras justicia social, determinación, y coraje realmente significan. Es un verdadero héroe. Este libro es para los millones de niños latinos que están ávidos de conocimiento, de ser amados y comprendidos en nuestras escuelas, hoy.

Contents

Foreword

We often find many books on the history of American education, and sometimes the education of Latinos will be mentioned only tangentially from a mainstream perspective. However, with *Latino Students in American Schools: Historical and Contemporary Views*, Valentina Kloosterman dedicates an entire volume to the education of Latinos. This proves a unique contribution to the literature because not only is it very rare to find a historical account of how Latino students experience the American school system, it is even more rare to find an *authentic* Latino perspective. Kloosterman brings together a very well selected group of experts who articulate complementary perspectives as researchers, educators, and school administrators. The blend of the editor's and the contributing authors' professional expertise and personal connections to the topic results in a unique contribution to the field of education.

This volume helps readers understand that Latino students have been present in North America for many centuries. Understanding that states such as New Mexico, Texas, and California have three to five decades of Latino history brings continuity to the contemporary educational issues of culturally and linguistically diverse students. A historical account helps educators make important conceptual connections between the socio-historical, political, economic, cultural, and linguistic issues associated with the quality and characteristics of the educational programs offered to Latino students in the United States. The hot political debate on what language or languages to use to educate Latino students in public schools is not a new issue; on the contrary, it has a long socio-historical context. The use of schooling and the English language as a social institution to *Americanize* Latino students is also not a new strategy; it existed before the

United States conquered this territory. By gaining a historical perspective, readers are able to realize that there is continuity between the new Latino immigrants who are currently learning English as a second language and the Latinos with multiple generations in the United States who have experienced the language and cultural barriers since the 1700s and 1800s. In addition, this book points out that Latinos are *not* a racial group but a *Creole* blend of multiple cultures and races that add diverse shades to the *new face of America*.

I have learned a great deal from reading this unique, innovative volume edited by Valentina Kloosterman. I extend my sincere congratulations to her for taking the initiative of providing a *fresh* approach to the education of Latino students. Kloosterman has brought together a select group of writers to produce a complete historical and contemporary view of Latino students in American schools, from preschool to higher education. The topic of contemporary Latino education is uniquely embedded within a historical account, not easily available in the literature. All authors bring an advocacy perspective and enrich the topic discussed with their own personal and empathic perspectives. I invite readers to enjoy this unique collection of beautifully written contributions of outstanding scholars and educators.

Virginia Gonzalez, Ph.D.

Preface

Nos desdeñamos u odiamos porque no nos compredemos, porque no
nos tomamos el trabajo de estudiarnos.
                                    —Santiago Ramón y Cajal, 1852–1934

It is difficult for me to articulate only one reason for wanting this book to
become a reality. As I continually grow as a professional and, more importantly, as a person, I encounter situations and meet people, children,
adults, and elders, who force me to reflect upon the ways in which I can
contribute to this society. The notions of social justice and determination,
as well as a high value for education, have been ingrained in me from the
beginning by my parents. I am fortunate for having the opportunity to be
nurtured in a family in which these values have always been present. When
I chose education for my profession, I felt the need to join scholars such
as Henry Trueba, Jonathan Kozol, and Harry Passow to give voice to the
millions of children who are provided with a substandard education. I hope
this book, which addresses the condition of Latino students in U.S. schools,
will prove a step toward this end.

It is unquestionable that the United States is a diverse and pluralistic
society. Its citizens differ in culture, ethnicity, language, sexual orientation,
and religion. Since the foundation of this country, these differences have
influenced the expression of values, norms, and traditions of its immigrant
groups. Although they are often clustered in one large ethnic denomination,
we must remember that Latinos, also labeled *Hispanics*, express unique
differences in their cultural and linguistic backgrounds. Not only do Latinos come from diverse countries of origin, they differ in their traditions,

immigration circumstances, socio-economic and educational levels, and degrees of language proficiency. The Latino population is often identified as a so-called *minority* group. However, since the term *minority* has implied several negative socio-educational connotations, this book employs the term *culturally and linguistically diverse* (CLD) when referring to a *minority* group or individual.

Although Latinos are the fastest growing population in the United States, they remain among the most educationally disadvantaged. More than ever before, it is critical for schools to develop comprehensive pedagogical and culturally sensitive approaches to provide and improve learning opportunities and outcomes for Latino students. Unfortunately, a number of barriers prevent this from occurring. In this book, the socio-educational condition of Latino students is analyzed through the various educational levels, as well as bilingual education, special education, gifted education, migrant education, urban education, and teacher preparation.

As we address Latino students' socio-educational needs, I emphatically believe that we are *years* behind. We must act *now*. I for one am tired of the educational demagogy surrounding *elite* educational circles and political arenas. I challenge scholars and politicians to cease simply talking about the *reality* of Latino students and begin to experience firsthand the abhorrent situation that many Latino students in this country face. Simply put, diversity is not yet a moral value ingrained in our collective consciousness. If it were, the acceptance of and respect for differences would not be *the* challenge for the U.S. school system today. Thus, there is a need to promote a better understanding of people's differences and commonalities. What a child brings to school in terms of cultural background, knowledge, experience, and ability is an essential starting point for providing a caring and meaningful education. For a Latino child "to be told, whether directly or indirectly, explicitly or implicitly, that your language [and culture] and the language [and culture] of your parents, of your home and of your friends is non-functional in school is to negate your sense of self" (Cummins & Swain, 1986, p. 101). More than ever before, educators need to become aware and deeply knowledgeable of their Latino students' expressions of cultural, ethnic, and linguistic backgrounds; focus on the dynamic interaction between them, their students, and their students' families; and reflect on their own values and cultural backgrounds, as well as the moral educational principles guiding their schools and classrooms. Only then will equitable and challenging educational opportunities be provided, and the quality of education improve.

As a democratic society, the United States of America needs to self-evaluate its educational system and answer the following questions. *What current educational paradigm is in place in our school system today? Who is creating and supporting the current educational paradigm? What kind of knowledge is valued in school? Who is benefiting from it?* Our answers to these questions are directly related to how we define ourselves as an American people. We must challenge not only the current educational paradigms deeply rooted in our schools but also the elite academic and political agencies that create, sustain, and support those paradigms while resisting, rejecting, and impeding the creation and implementation of new ones in order to maintain the socio-educational status quo.

It is my hope that readers will find this book informative and important. If the book prompts readers to reflect, question, and even argue about the many issues addressed, it will have achieved its goal. I believe that no child should be condemned to a substandard and indifferent education; and no child should be prevented from developing to his or her full potential. Our Latino children are waiting for social justice and a quality education. Let us not disappoint them!

ORGANIZATION OF THE BOOK

This book is organized in 11 chapters. Chapter 1 discusses the origins and evolution of Latino education in the United States from the Spanish-Mexican era to the present. Those in control of education have sought to use it to establish the political and cultural dominance of their own group and promote the subordination of racial and ethnic groups and the elimination of their cultural differences. The subordinate groups, in turn, did not passively accept the education provided for them by the dominant rulers. This chapter provides a broad sketch of the complex interactions between education and Latinos.

Chapter 2 presents a framework of the condition of Latino children in early childhood programs across the nation. Latino families now live, work, and learn in every arena in America, from rural hamlets to dense urban areas. As these families become integral members of communities, their history, language, and culture have a direct impact on America's daily life. For early childhood education, the challenge is how to best serve this growing population. The chapter also presents professional understanding and strategies on how to appropriately work with Latino families and young children.

Chapter 3 explains the asymmetrical power relations of society that are maintained in schools and the deficit view that educators uncritically and often unknowingly hold about culturally and linguistically diverse students. The chapter also provides recommendations about how to redesign teacher education in order to promote prospective teacher ideological clarity and understanding of the myriad ways in which the prevailing power hierarchy in U.S. society is reinforced in schools and perpetuates the underachievement of Latino students.

Chapter 4 examines the many obstacles to achieve educational equity and excellence that Latinos face at the middle and high school level. This chapter documents the educational trends in reading, math, and science and presents demographics on issues of access, academic achievement, and student dropout. Conditions hindering the development of Latino youth and quality of education these students receive are also presented.

Chapter 5 analyzes the complex conditions influencing Latino students' participation and success in higher education. It describes how the characteristics of higher education institutions positively or negatively influence Latinos' completion of a degree. This chapter also offers suggestions for building home–school partnerships and increasing the likelihood of Latino students' entering and completing post-secondary programs.

Chapter 6 discusses what is currently known about the diversity of communication skills of bilingual Latino students and the programs that have been implemented to address their unique needs. It provides an overview of the linguistic diversity of the Latino population and the socio-cultural and socio-linguistic experiences Latino children encounter prior to entering formal education.

Chapter 7 focuses on Latino students in special education, specifically those who are English Language Learners. This chapter addresses the critical components of service delivery for Latino students in special education; the prevention of academic problems; the provision of early intervention for struggling learners; and appropriate assessment avenues regarding special education referrals.

Chapter 8 addresses the main causes for Latino students' underrepresentation in gifted programs. The chapter provides a brief historical overview of the most important events affecting the field of gifted education in regard to the inclusion of diverse learners. The core of the chapter is the discussion of socio-cultural as well as educational aspects contributing to or hindering the development of talents in Latino students. Findings from a study conducted on high-ability Latino students are highlighted.

Chapter 9 discusses the social, economic, and academic obstacles that migrant families and their children confront on a daily basis. The chapter offers strategies to support and enhance Latino migrant students' schooling while traveling from one harvest site to another. The empowerment of Latino migrant parent participation in the school system is also discussed, as are the challenges migrant students face at the secondary and higher education levels.

Chapter 10 uses a critical lens to describe the educational experience for Latino students in urban schools, with especial attention on the schooling of Latinos in Los Angeles. The chapter also highlights the work of a social justice teacher education program that prepares teachers to teach in urban schools. The chapter concludes with a recommendation for the development of a Latino educational initiative that is broad-based, inclusive, and culturally responsive.

Chapter 11 begins by presenting a brief history of preservice teacher education in the United States, as well as some of the more visible reform efforts in recent years. Especially highlighted is the fact that even though important and potentially far-reaching reform has been proposed and implemented in teacher education, the preparation of teachers for service in a multicultural society in general and for service of Latino students in particular has been glaringly and painfully absent. The chapter also presents practical ways in which preservice teacher education programs can serve Latino students.

REFERENCE

Cummins, J., & Swain, M. (1986). *Bilingualism in education*. New York: Longman.

Acknowledgments

My deepest appreciation goes to the authors for their hard work, knowledge, and dedication to this project. Without their commitment and motivation, this book could not have been possible. My sincere appreciation goes also to Dr. Virginia Gonzalez, Professor at the University of Cincinnati, for her Foreword, which saliently captures the message of this book. I am also sincerely thankful to Greenwood Publishing Group reviewers and editors, especially Marie Ellen Larcada and John Donohue, for their editorial contributions. I am also deeply grateful to my family, *mi familia*, in Argentina and the United States for sharing with me their daily accomplishments, struggles, laughter, and sadness in this journey called life. Finally, I would like to express my profound gratitude to my husband for his invaluable support and assistance in preparing this book, but most importantly for challenging me with his questions and thoughts throughout the process. Many thanks to all. *Muchas gracias a todos.*

Chapter 1

Contested Learning: Latino Education in the United States from the 1500s to the Present

Guadalupe San Miguel, Jr.

INTRODUCTION

This chapter discusses the origins and evolution of Latino education in the United States from the Spanish/Mexican era to the present. It examines the various ways in which formal and informal education emerges in what is now the continental United States and how it has related to and impacted the Latino groups residing within its boundaries over the past five centuries. This history is intended to be a broad sketch of the complex interactions between education and Latinos. Much of this history, especially of the educational experiences of groups such as Puerto Ricans, Cubans, and Central and South Americans, is yet to be written. This chapter uses the term *Latino* as an umbrella group for several nationality groups such as Mexicans, Puerto Ricans, Cubans, and Central and South Americans. The term *ethnic Mexicans* is used to refer to all individuals of Mexican origin, whether citizens of the United States or not. Other terms such as *Mexicans* and *Mexican Americans* are also used interchangeably with ethnic Mexicans. The term *Anglo* is used to refer to White Americans of European descent.

The methodology used in this chapter is similar to the one used by San Miguel and Valencia to study the history of Mexican American education (San Miguel & Valencia, 1998). These scholars use two approaches to analyze this history. The first approach—the plight of Latino education—focuses on the development of education, on how it responded to Latino students, and on how these students fared in it. The second approach—the struggle aspect of Latino education—explores the manner in which Latinos responded to the types of education offered them. Using these two approaches, a historical sketch is provided for a better understanding of the educational experiences of Latino students in the United States for the past 500 years.

During these five centuries education was both an instrument of hegemony and subordination and an important site of contestation. In other words, those in control of education sought to use it for two major purposes: to establish the political and cultural dominance of their own group and to promote the subordination of racial and ethnic minority groups and the elimination of their cultural differences. The subordinate groups, in turn, did not passively accept the education provided for them by the dominant rulers. They responded to these efforts in several creative ways. First, they subverted, selectively accepted, or modified the intended purposes of education. Second, they contested, questioned, challenged, subverted, or rejected the conformist and marginalizing intentions of the dominant rulers and sought to use education to promote its own identity and its own advancement in the existing society. The result was conflict and tensions in the educational arena.

EDUCATION IN THE SPANISH-MEXICAN ERA, 1519–1848

The original Spanish influence extended from the Carolinas and Florida, down through the Gulf Coast, and on to the western part of the United States. By the end of the Spanish period in the early 1800s the vast majority of Spanish subjects were concentrated in Indian-controlled lands of what we know today as the American Southwest: California, Arizona, New Mexico, Colorado, and Texas. During these three centuries of Spanish and Mexican rule, education occurred in informal and formal settings, but the former was the general norm. Among the most important institutions providing informal education were the missions, the presidios, and the civilian settlements. Education, in this case, was primarily for the Indian population. Its purposes were to replace the Indian identity with a Spanish one and to teach them acceptance of their social subordination (Menchaca, 1999; Van Well, 1942). This was done by teaching them literacy, music, Catholic doctrine, la doctrina, and Spanish manners and destroying or suppressing their indigenous religious and social beliefs (Spell, 1927; Weber, 1992).

By the early nineteenth century, civilian settlements such as Santa Fe, Los Angeles, and San Antonio became increasingly important in education because of the decline of missions and presidios. Unlike earlier decades, education during these decades shifted toward the children of the Spanish settlers. In this case, it became an instrument for transmitting the social and cultural status of the dominant population and for teaching adult life skills necessary for survival and success in the new Spanish-Mexican social order. Formal instruction also occurred in the frontier. The increasing needs of the Spanish/Mexican population for literacy, religion, and social control served as motivating factors for the establishment of frontier schools. These types of learning institutions originally were established only in the missions, but beginning in 1793, constitutional and statutory efforts were made to establish them throughout the settlements. Because of financial inability and political conflict, only a few were established during this period. These schools were held in temporary facilities and staffed by teachers with minimal training and inadequate instructional materials. Many of these teachers also had low pay, were resented by the local citizens, and were burdened with petty supervisors (Tyler, 1974). Most of these schools did not last long and closed within a year or two after their founding.

Indian Responses to Colonial Education

Although education for Indian groups throughout the Southwest was aimed at developing a subordinate group, they responded in diverse ways to its conformist and dominating purposes. Some Indian groups such as the Pueblos in New Mexico militarily resisted Spanish rule of any sort and engaged in significant battles over control of the Southwest (Hackett, 1970). Others resisted the imposition of a Spanish identity by refusing to go to the missions, running away from these institutions and from the missionaries, and murdering individual missionaries or making their lives unpleasant (Weber, 1992). Still others welcomed education and selectively accepted Spanish customs and Catholic ideals and incorporated them into their own belief systems. A few willingly learned to read and write in the Spanish language and used their education to inform others about the Spanish form of government. These agents of literacy known as doctrinaires, *doctrinarios*, in New Mexico also used their knowledge to negotiate their survival in the existing social order. Some Indian slaves, for instance, used their literacy to gain access to Spanish society, something denied to most Indians, and to profit from economic activities in the frontier. A few used the knowledge gained from Spanish education to contest official church policies, petition Spanish authorities for defense of their own Indian communities, apply for land grants, or challenge government edicts prohibiting sale and export of wool and sheep for community consumption (Gallegos, 1992).

EDUCATION AND EARLY ANGLO RULE IN THE SOUTHWEST, 1836–1890

During the first several decades of Anglo rule in the Southwest, education still took place in informal and formal settings, but the latter assumed a more important role. In this period, education developed in a political and economic context of Anglo control. Between 1836 and 1855, the United States conquered Mexico and annexed, among other states, Texas, Arizona,

California, and Colorado. During the next several decades, Mexicans remaining in the area became a subordinate group with little political, economic, and social power. This is especially the case for the White Mexican elite who lost their land, their political positions, and their economic dominance. By the latter part of this period most of the Mexican elite joined the other non-White subordinate groups in the existing society (Acuña, 1988; González, 1999; Griswold del Castillo & De León, 1997). Because of these new political and economic realities, formal education became increasingly important in the new American Southwest.

New Developments in Education

During the first two decades of Anglo rule, from 1836 to the early 1850s, formal education occurred in schools established by the Catholic Church and ethnic Mexicans. Soon thereafter, however, public officials and Protestant groups began to establish schools for Mexican children. Each of these groups had its own reasons for establishing or expanding schools. Ethnic Mexicans, both elite and non-elite, as well as Catholic officials supported or encouraged the establishment of schools in order to maintain their religious, secular, and linguistic traditions, learn American customs, and more readily integrate into the developing social order (San Miguel, 1999). Anglo political and religious leaders, on the other hand, established public and Protestant schools in order to assimilate or evangelize and convert the large numbers of groups identified as *foreigners*. In the new American Southwest, this meant Native Americans, Mormons, and Mexicans (Szasz, 1988). Toward the latter part of the century Protestant missionaries established schools in order to create a new generation of bilingual leaders. These institutions, especially secondary schools, aimed at providing the future ethnic Mexican leaders with the skills and knowledge necessary for participation in an evolving social order (Atkins, 1980).

Despite the variety of reasons given for the establishment of schools, education served different purposes for Anglos, Mexicans, and Catholic officials. For Anglos, it was an instrument for ensuring or asserting their emerging social, economic, cultural, and political hegemony; for Mexicans and Catholic officials, it was an instrument for maintaining their precarious and declining social, economic, cultural, and political status in the Southwest (San Miguel, 1999). The importance of education for the survival and mobility of the ethnic Mexican population is expressed in an 1851 editorial by the *Los Angeles Star*, a local newspaper supportive of Mexican Americans in that region. "Unless educated," the editorial noted, "[Mexicans] will inevitably sink to the status of house servants and vaqueros, which would be a pity, since there are many bright though undeveloped talents among them" (*Los Angeles Star*, 1851, p. 2). The following year, the same newspaper issued the community an *invitation to learning* after the

Mexican-dominated city council agreed to a partial subsidy for the education of poor Spanish-speaking children in three parochial and private schools. This invitation reminded the Mexican community of the advantages of education and also encouraged local officials to establish their own public schools.

In addition to assuming a larger role in the social order, schools became instruments of cultural conformity. Most of the schools—whether public, Protestant, or Catholic—taught the 3Rs (reading, 'riting, and 'rithmetic) and some religion. But many of them, especially the elementary schools, began to focus increasingly on trying to eliminate non-English languages, cultures, and communities from their operation. Many schools, for instance, eliminated the use of Spanish and of Mexican history and culture in the schools. School officials, in many cases, believed that the native language and culture of Mexican children should not be used in the schools because they were incompatible with or inferior to American values and speech patterns (Banker, 1993; Getz, 1997). Many of these educators and schools also vehemently opposed the involvement of the Mexican population and of Catholic officials in the governance, administration, and operation of schools. Another way in which the schools tried to eliminate differences and promote cultural conformity was by encouraging the assimilation of the ethnic Mexican population, for example, by inculcating an idealized American identity and discouraging or stamping out the community's own religious, cultural, and linguistic values (Szasz, 1988).

Not all schools sought cultural conformity. Some of them utilized Spanish, Mexican history, and the cultural heritage in order to facilitate the community's integration into mainstream *American* society. Others allowed the ethnic Mexican community and Catholic officials to participate in the governance, administration, and operation of the schools. These efforts, however, were usually limited primarily to Catholic schools or else based on political expediency. Once Anglos consolidated their political control of the schools, especially public education, diversity gave way to conformity. The most contentious battles occurred in the New Mexico territory because of the large size of the Mexican population and the influential role of the Catholic Church (Everett, 1984).

Mexican Responses to Education

Ethnic Mexicans responded in various ways to the establishment of Anglo-controlled Catholic, Protestant, and public schools in the Southwest. They supported or attended these institutions, but they subverted their religious or conformist intentions and used them to promote pluralism in the larger society (Szasz, 1988). With respect to Protestant education, for instance, Yohn (1995) describes the experiences of Catholic, *Hispano* (i.e., ethnic Mexican) youth in New Mexico who converted to Protestantism or who benefited from the Protestant schools. Yohn argues that these students selectively accepted the Protestant value of education, but not its religious beliefs. In other words, Hispano students sought schooling to learn English, not moral instruction or patriotism, and to seek upward mobility in an Anglo-dominated society. These youth also never abandoned their Mexican heritage. They used their ethnicity to reshape the Protestant missionary effort by encouraging more favorable attitudes toward Catholicism and by fighting against unfair stereotypes and discrimination within the Protestant churches and schools. Hispano students then selectively took from the mission schools and forged their own ethnic Presbyterian culture and redirected missionary priorities.

In a few cases, ethnic Mexicans opposed the establishment of schools or the enactment of policies that were viewed as detrimental to their cultural and political interests. Milk (1980) describes how during the early 1850s the Mexicans in New Mexico, distrustful of Anglos and the impact they were having on their language and culture, opposed the establishment of a publicly funded, English-only public school system for economic and cultural reasons. They also opposed the enactment of English-only school laws during the 1890s because of their suspicion that the schools aimed at promoting English at the expense of Spanish. Instead of English-only laws, they supported the enactment of bilingual school policies. Their intent, although unsuccessful, was to reject the conformist goals of school officials and to ensure that their heritage was reflected in the schools.

LATINOS AND THE EXPANSION OF AMERICAN EDUCATION, 1890–1960

During this period, learning occurred in many settings, but public education became the dominant means for acquiring knowledge in the United States. In the latter part of the nineteenth century and during the next 60 years, public education changed dramatically—largely in response to the tremendous social, economic, political, and cultural changes under way in American life. Between 1890 and 1960, education was extended to individuals from all racial, national, gender, and age groups; governance structures were altered to benefit middle-class individuals, and innovations in educational administration such as testing were introduced. The curriculum was diversified to meet the varied needs of the heterogeneous student population, educational programs were standardized, and instructional methodology was revolutionized through the introduction of a new *American* psychology based on *scientific* principles of learning and a variety of assessment tools (Johanningmeier, 1980). Furthermore, one-room schools in rural areas were consolidated into larger units for efficiency, and schools became articulated from elementary to the post-secondary grades.

The Latino population also changed and became more diverse during the twentieth century. Of particular importance were the origins of a Cuban migration to Florida and the significant growth of Puerto Ricans and their settlement on the East Coast and in the Midwest (González, 2000). The number of Mexicans likewise increased during this century, but they tended to settle in the Southwest, the Midwest, and the Pacific Northwest (García, 1996). These Latino groups were diverse in many ways. The two major groups of this period, ethnic Mexicans and Puerto Ricans, however, tended to be politically powerless, economically impoverished, and socially alienated. Most of them lived in highly segregated communities, tended to speak Spanish as a group, and lived in dismal housing conditions. Mexicans and Puerto Ricans were predominantly a cheap source of labor for American industry (Meier & Stewart, 1991). Cubans shared many cultural and linguistic similarities with ethnic Mexicans and Puerto Ricans, but they were racially and occupationally distinct and numerically small during this historical period. Their numbers did not increase significantly until after 1960 (González, 2000; Masud-Pilot, 1996).

Emerging Patterns of Latino Education

The subordinate position and the culturally distinct status of ethnic Mexicans and Puerto Ricans posed significant challenges for public schools over the decades. Schools, for the most part, were unable to meet these challenges. They ignored the multiple needs of this heterogeneous student population or else, because of assimilationist ideology and deficit thinking, interpreted them in such a way that the differences brought by these children had to be eliminated (San Miguel & Valencia, 1998; Vaca, 1971; Valencia, 1997). In many cases, the schools responded not to the genuine needs of this diverse group of children but to those of other stronger political and economic interests who sought to use schools as instruments of cultural conformity and of social and economic subordination. Because of these contextual realities, more school access was provided to Latinos, but the quality and quantity of that education were inferior.

The education of Latinos was structurally exclusive of the community and the children. In the latter part of the nineteenth century and early twentieth century, as the number of Latino school-age children increased, Latino representation in governance structures such as local or county school boards eroded and nearly disappeared. Racism, politics, and demographic realities influenced these developments (González, 1990). Latinos, for the most part, were not elected to school board positions in significant numbers until the post–World War II years. Latino administrators, teachers, and other professional staff in the schools also were removed from these positions or else rarely hired for them. In the early 1900s, for instance, George Burch, superintendent of the Guadalupe County schools in New Mexico, complained that Spanish American teachers were using a *little too much* Spanish in their teaching. He recommended that districts with a large number of non-English-speaking students hire teachers without any knowledge of Spanish at all "to prevent them from lapsing into Spanish" (Getz, 1997, p. 23). Some school districts began to hire Latino teachers after 1949, but at a snail's pace. The earliest report calling for the recruitment of Spanish-speaking teachers to instruct Puerto Rican children on the East Coast was in 1949. This was followed by several additional reports a few years later. On the basis of these reports, the New York City Board of Education appointed 10 Puerto Rican teachers as Substitute Auxiliary Teachers (SATs) and assigned them to schools with the greatest concentrations of Spanish-speaking students (Sánchez Korrol, 1996). Latino children also were provided limited and inequitable access to the elementary, secondary, and post-secondary grades (González, 1990; Weinberg, 1977). In addition, Latino children were educated in separate and unequal school facilities. The phenomenon of Latino school segregation began at the turn of the century in the Southwest and soon expanded to other parts of the country that had significant numbers of Latino children (San Miguel, 1987).

Latino schoolchildren were provided with an imbalanced and subtractive curriculum. Instead of being provided with a rigorous academic curriculum, Latino children were classified as either intellectually or culturally deficient and given larger doses of non-academic instruction. At the elementary level, they were placed in slow or low-ability groups. At the secondary level, the handful of students who had not dropped out were often placed in non-academic, vocational, or general programs on the basis of racially and culturally biased standardized test scores (González, 1990). Most scholars misinterpreted the low test scores of Latino children and argued that biological or cultural factors were to blame (Valencia, 1997). Based on test scores, students were classified as either intellectually or culturally deficient and placed in *developmentally appropriate* ability groups or curricular tracks. The placement of Latino children in these types of curricular tracks led to an imbalance in the curriculum and to fears among parents and community activists that Latino children were being tracked toward the lowest rungs of the socio-economic ladder (Sánchez Korrol, 1996). Schools for Latino children, in other words, were now being used as instruments of economic subordination.

Latino children were also provided with a subtractive school curriculum characterized by the elimination of their language, history, and culture from the content and instruction of public education. Spanish was eliminated through the enactment of increasingly stronger English language laws and through its prohibition in the schools. Latino history and culture, in turn, were excluded from the curriculum as indicated by the presence of Anglocentric instructional materials and perspectives in American history textbooks (Leibowitz, 1970; San Miguel & Valencia, 1998). Curricular, instructional, and school language policies then were aimed at meeting the cultural conformist intentions of the public schools.

Furthermore, Latinos experienced a pervasive pattern of poor school performance as indicated by low intelligence quotient (IQ) and achievement test scores, relatively high dropout rates, and low educational attainment over time. During the early decades of the twentieth century, the majority of educators tended to blame the children's genes for this pattern of underachievement (Valencia, 1997). After World War II, they blamed an inferior culture for poor school test scores and high dropout rates (Vaca, 1971; Valencia, 1997). While the majority of educators tended to blame Latinos for the pattern of underachievement, a few of them sought more complex explanations. Individual scholars such as George Sánchez, Lloyd Tireman, and Herschel Manuel, for instance, blamed the school, state legislators, and the federal government for this pattern. These scholars were school warriors and challenged the dominant ideas and explanations about the poor school performance of Latino children in the schools.

George Sánchez became one of the most important champions of Mexican American civil rights and of quality education in the United States. Sánchez's views during the 1930s consistently pointed to the impact of environmental factors on the performance of Spanish-speaking children on intelligence tests, on academic achievement in general, and on social and political life. He questioned the racial interpretation of intelligence testing and argued that environmental factors, especially language and family life conditions, were to blame for low test scores. The school system was to blame for failing to educate Spanish-speaking children and the government for failing to assist Spanish-speaking individuals in adapting to American life. Most mainstream educators and school officials, however, ignored the important findings of Sánchez, Manuel, and Tireman indicating the need to consider environmental factors in school performance. For the most part, they continued to blame Latinos for the pattern of underachievement (Carter, 1970; Valencia, 1991).

Not all Latino students did poorly in school. Contrary to popular and scholarly opinion, a small but significant number of Latinos experienced school success (San Miguel & Valencia, 1998). The pattern of school success, however, has rarely been studied by scholars or acknowledged by educators. Although much more research on those who succeeded needs to be done, evidence suggests that a significant group of Latinos completed both secondary and post-secondary school during the years from the 1890s to 1960. In the late 1920s, approximately 10% of the ethnic Mexican school-age population in Texas completed high school (Manuel, 1930). Several studies of religious schools such as St. Michael's Catholic school in Santa Fe, Central High Catholic School in Los Angeles, and Menaul High School in Albuquerque have been graduating Latino students since their establishment in the late nineteenth or early twentieth century. In most cases, these schools had high standards of academic excellence and found ways of incorporating their cultural heritage into the curriculum (Becklund, 1985). It is quite possible that these types of successful schools existed in other parts of the country containing significant numbers of Latino students.

A few studies also indicate that while the number of Latino students attending college in the early twentieth century was extremely small, usually less than 1%, the existence of such college students indicates an unexplored tradition of school success (Muñóz, 1989). Educators, for the most part, tended to view successful students as exceptions to the general rule. School achievement was interpreted as being due to personal factors such as initiative, determination, and natural brightness. The consequences of this pattern of school performance in general and of underachievement in particular led to limited economic mobility, stunted political participation, and restricted social development. In other words, it led to the social and economic subordination of the growing Latino population.

Emerging Forms of Latino Responses

The use of schools for cultural conformity and social and economic subordination led to the emergence of a complex pattern of contestation and adaptation within the Latino community. Latinos, in other words, struggled against all forms of discrimination in public education and challenged, contested, or adapted to school policies and practices detrimental to their cultural, political, and academic interests. This set of responses was influenced by structural developments such as increased occupational mobility and stability, a shifting consciousness from immigrant and migrant to ethnic American, and increased numbers. Between 1890 and 1930, contestation and resistance were sporadic, locally based, and mostly limited to Mexican communities in the Southwest. During these years, a few activist scholars and community groups spoke out against discrimination in education, against the lack of equal educational opportunities, and against the cultural conformist intentions of the curriculum. Other individuals and groups took the initiative to develop their own schools or to encourage their children to attend private schools of all sorts (Stevens, 1999).

From 1930 to 1965, efforts to resist conformist, exclusionary, and discriminatory school policies became more systematic and organized throughout the country. The quest for educational equality took various forms and is reflected in three major reform strategies. A major strategy was to oppose certain discriminatory policies and practices. This quest for educational equality focused primarily on contesting six specific policies— testing, unequal funding, segregation, biased historical texts, language policies, and discrimination in higher education (Alvarez, 1986; Gonzales,

2001). Another strategy focused on supporting pluralist and quality educational policies. During these decades Latinos and committed Anglo educators developed innovative school-wide reforms aimed at improving school achievement, curricular innovations aimed at promoting the community's cultural heritage in the schools, instructional changes allowing the use of Spanish in elementary school instruction, and reforms encouraging the hiring of Spanish-speaking teachers for Spanish-speaking students (Bachelor, 1991; Sánchez Korrol, 1994).

The emphasis on the tradition of parents' sending their children to private schools or of developing community-based instruction for their own purposes was another major strategy (San Miguel, 1987). The little evidence we have at this point is mostly from the Southwest, but more likely than not the practice of establishing Spanish-language community schools was widespread and fairly common in those areas containing significant numbers of Latinos. In the late 1890s, for instance, ethnic Mexicans opened a community school in Hebronville, Texas, a small rural community in the southern part of the state. This school, in existence until the early 1930s, opened with an enrollment of over 100 children and was maintained by the Mexican community of Jim Hogg County. The Mexican community founded the Colegio Preparatorio in Laredo, Texas, in 1906 and the Escuela Particular in 1909 in Zapata County, also in south Texas. In July 1910, the latter community school held a public examination and a school festival, *fiesta escolar*, for the community. An additional private school taught by María Rentería was opened in Laredo, Texas, in 1911 (Hernández, n.d.).

LATINO EDUCATION IN THE CONTEMPORARY PERIOD, 1960 TO THE PRESENT

In the contemporary period, from 1960 to the present, public education became more responsive to the academic, cultural, and linguistic needs of the Latino population even as the political context became increasingly conservative over time. The Latino community, in turn, significantly increased and became more diverse. In addition to Mexicans and Puerto Ricans, it included a significant number of Spanish-speaking immigrants from Cuba, Central America, and South America (Griswold del Castillo & De León, 1997). Cuban migration to the United States began earnestly in 1959 and increased during the 1960s and 1970s (Boswell, 2000). Central and South American migration increased significantly in the 1980s and 1990s (González, 2000). Political conflict, poverty, and social unrest in the home countries, global economic fluctuations, and changes in U.S. immigration policies contributed to this increase in immigration from Latin America.

Changes and Continuities in Public Education

During the latter decades of the twentieth century, significant school reforms benefiting Latinos were made. At the elementary and secondary level, some of the most blatant forms of discriminatory practices were eliminated in the 1960s and 1970s. Schools also developed a variety of remedial, vocational, and academic courses; provided increased resources to low-performance schools; established a host of parental involvement programs; and implemented decentralization experiments, bilingual education classes, and affirmative actions programs (Carter & Segura, 1979; Sánchez Korrol, 1996). In the 1980s and 1990s, school-wide and district-wide reforms aimed at improving the pattern of underachievement in minority schools and new types of parental and community involvement programs were initiated (McAdams, 2000). At the post-secondary level, minority recruitment programs for students and faculty were implemented, ethnic studies programs and classes developed, and student support services provided (Olivas, 1989). As a result of these changes, Latino children gained parity in access to the elementary and secondary grades and significant access to the post-secondary grades. They also improved their school performance and graduation rates and enrolled in larger numbers in universities and in graduate and professional schools (College Board, 1999; Darder, Torres, & Gutierrez, 1997; Tashakkori & Ochoa, 1999). Latinos, in turn, were elected or appointed to school decision-making positions and hired as administrators and teachers. They thus became an increasingly important part of the governance, administration, and operations of public education (Fraga, Meier, & England, 1997).

Despite these advances, some significant patterns of educational inequality remained. Latino children continued to attend increasingly separate and unequal schools, to score low in standardized tests, to be placed in low-ability groups, to underachieve, and to be underrepresented in important decision-making positions in education (Haro, 2001; Orfield & Monfort, 1992). Lingering racism, an influx of immigrant children from war-torn countries in South America, a growing Latino *underclass*, and a sputtering economy contributed to the maintenance of these patterns.

Intensification of Latino Responses

During the latter decades of the twentieth century, the struggle for equality escalated as indicated by an increase in Latino involvement in school reforms. Latinos engaged in several major actions during this period (San Miguel, 1996). First, they lobbied federal, state, and local agencies to develop policies aimed at eliminating discrimination in the schools, improving the educational opportunities for Latino studies, and gaining recognition of their political, linguistic, cultural, and academic needs (ASPIRA, 1968;

Gerry, 1974; Office of the Mayor, 1967). Second, they filed countless federal lawsuits against school segregation, the testing and placement of culturally distinct children in classes designated for the *educationally mentally retarded*, unequal funding of public schools, and the exclusion of undocumented immigrant children from the public schools (Cárdenas, 1974; San Miguel, 1987). They also initiated legal challenges to discrimination in school board elections, at-large elections, and employment hiring practices (Vigil, 1992). Third, they participated in many federal and state legislative efforts for bilingual education, equitable funding, and desegregation (Valencia, 1991). Fourth, they engaged in many political struggles against exclusion and discrimination in the schools. At the elementary and secondary level, they struggled for equal treatment in the schools and against Anglo control of schools, an Anglo-centric curriculum, and the exclusion of Spanish in the schools. They also supported the hiring of Latinos as administrators, teachers, and counselors and the establishment of culture and history classes. Additionally, Latino activists established or participated in a variety of community and school-based organizations such as Parent-Teacher Associations or parental involvement programs. Once in these organizations, they supported the establishment and development of bilingual education, compensatory education, and other special educational programs (Fuentes, 1984; Rodríguez & Sánchez Korrol, 1996; San Miguel, 2001). At the post-secondary level, they protested the lack of access to higher education and supported the recruitment of Latino students to the undergraduate, graduate, and professional schools. They promoted the hiring of Latino faculty and the establishment of ethnic studies programs and joined the professional staffs of these schools and initiated curricular, instructional, and administrative changes from within (San Miguel, 1996; Tashakkori & Ochoa, 1999).

During the late 1970s and 1980s, an increasing number of Latinos began to defend existing programs and policies against the threats made by conservative forces in the United States to dismantle many of the programs they had promoted. They defended bilingual education programs from attacks, opposed the dismantling of desegregation efforts, and supported affirmative action and ethnic studies programs at the post-secondary level (Acuña, 1998; Díaz Soto, 1997). Threats to minority gains in elementary, secondary, and post-secondary education increased significantly in the 1990s. Between 1994 and 1998, for instance, two propositions in California and one major federal court decision in Texas threatened to limit immigrant access to K–12 education, culturally diverse groups access to bilingual education in the elementary grades, and Latino access to institutions of higher learning (San Miguel & Valencia, 1998). As in earlier decades, Latinos pressured these agencies, developed legal arguments to challenge these propositions, and even marched and demonstrated against them in the streets. In addition to conducting a struggle for equality, Latinos sought access to quality instruction in non-public schools. They continued enrolling in Catholic and Protestant schools, or else they established their own private or charter schools. In Houston, for instance, the community established a Mexican American university in 1970 and an alternative junior and senior high school in 1979. The former was known as the Hispanic International University. Its purpose was to offer an academic program that would relate to the personal, cultural, and professional needs of the Mexican American community. Its name was changed in the mid-1980s and soon closed its doors. The alternative school, known as the George I. Sánchez Junior and Senior High School, continues to exist as a charter school and is an extremely popular institution in the Latino community of that city.

CONCLUSION

The history of Latino education is intimately related to the changing social, economic, and political context of the United States and is directly impacted by immigration and migration from Spanish-speaking countries in the Caribbean and Latin America. More importantly, this history shows how education became a political instrument for the establishment and maintenance of power. From the 1500s to the early 1800s, the white Spanish and Mexican elite used education to establish a socially and racially stratified system that would increase its political, social, and cultural hegemony at the expense of the Indian and mestizo population. In the nineteenth and twentieth centuries, Anglo elites promoted education in order to maintain and strengthen their own political and cultural power at the expense of the subordinate Latino population. The history of Latino education also shows that while learning has been used for political purposes, it was an important site of contestation. Structured learning became a crucial public space in which the community contested, challenged, selectively accepted, or subverted the conformist and dominating intentions of the dominant group in the society. Latinos, in other words, did not passively accept the type of education offered by the dominant rulers. They desired and fought for an education reflective of their cultural and linguistic heritage and in concert with their own political, economic, and social aspirations and interests.

In many ways, then, education became a site where statuses and identities were negotiated, contested, and constructed in a society undergoing significant change. This centuries-old phenomenon of struggling against cultural conformity and social/economic subordination and for pluralism, social acceptance, and mobility will undoubtedly continue. Although the obstacles are formidable and the conditions look bleak in the foreseeable future, the Latino community's resolve to challenge those in power and to construct its own status and identity suggests that its resoluteness will continue, and even escalate, in the years to come.

REFERENCES

Acuña, R. F. (1998). *Sometimes there is no other side: Chicanos and the myth of equality*. Notre Dame, IN: University of Notre Dame Press.

Acuña, R. F. (1988). *Occupied America: A history of Chicanos* (3rd ed.). New York: HarperCollins.

Alvarez, R. (1986). The Lemon Grove incident: The nation's first successful desegregation court case. *Journal of San Diego History, 32*(2), 116–135.

ASPIRA. (1968). *Hemos trabajado bien: A report on the first national conference of Puerto Ricans, Mexican Americans, and educators on the special needs of urban Puerto Rican Youth*. New York: Author.

Atkins, C. (1980). Menaul school: 1881–1930 . . . not leaders merely, but Christian leaders. *Journal of Presbyterian History, 58*, 279–297.

Bachelor, D. L. (1991). *Educational reform in New Mexico: Tireman, San José, and Nambé*. Albuquerque: University of New Mexico Press.

Banker, M. T. (1993). *Presbyterian missions and cultural interaction in the far Southwest, 1850–1950*. Chicago: University of Illinois Press.

Becklund, L. (1985). Catholic high school backers sue LA diocese to halt school sale. *Los Angeles Times, 1*, 6.

Boswell, T. D. (2000). The Cuban Americans. In J. O. McKee (Ed.), *Ethnicity in contemporary America: A geographical appraisal* (pp. 95–116). Lanham, MD: Rowman and Littlefield.

Cárdenas, B. (1974). Defining equal access to educational opportunity for Mexican American children: A study of three civil rights actions affecting Mexican American students. Unpublished. University of Massachusetts.

Carter, T. P. (1970). *Mexican Americans in school: A history of educational neglect*. New York: College Entrance Examination Board.

Carter, T. P., & Segura, R. D. (1979). *Mexican Americans in school: A decade of change*. New York: College Entrance Examination Board.

College Board. (1999). *Report of the national task force on minority high achievement*. New York: College Board.

Darder, A., Torres, A., & Gutierrez, H. (Eds.). (1997). *Latinos and education: A critical reader*. New York: Routledge.

Díaz Soto, L. (1997). *Language, culture, and power: Bilingual families and the struggle for quality education*. Albany, NY: SUNY Press.

Everett, D. (1984). The public school debate in New Mexico, 1850–1891. *Arizona and the West, 26*(2), 107–134.

Fraga, L. R., Meier, K. J., & England, R. E. (1997). Hispanic Americans and educational policy: Limits to equal access. In F. Chris García (Ed.), *Pursuing power: Latinos and the political system* (pp. 279–285). Notre Dame, IN: University of Notre Dame Press.

Fuentes, L. (1984). The struggle for local political control. In Clara C. Rogríguez, V. Sánchez Korrol, & J. O. Alers (Eds.), *The Puerto Rican struggle: Essays on survival in the U.S.* (pp. 111–120). Maplewood, NJ: Waterfront Press.

Gallegos, B. P. (1992). *Literacy, education, and society in New Mexico, 1693–1821.* Albuquerque: University of New Mexico Press.

García, J. R. (1996). *Mexicans in the Midwest, 1900–1932.* Tucson: University of Arizona Press.

Gerry, M. H. (1974). Cultural freedom in the schools: The right of Mexican American children to succeed. In A. Castañeda, M. Ramírez III, C. E. Cortés, & M. Barrera (Eds.), *Mexican Americans and educational change* (pp. 226–254). New York: Arno Press.

Getz, A. M. (1997). *Schools of their own: The education of hispanos in New Mexico, 1850–1940.* Albuquerque: University of New Mexico Press.

Gonzales, F. (2001). *Forced sacrifice as ethnic protest: The Hispano cause in New Mexico and the racial attitude confrontation of 1933.* New York: Peter Lang.

González, G. G. (1990). *Chicano education in the era of segregation.* Philadelphia: Balch Institute Press.

González, J. (2000). *Harvest of empire: A history of Latinos in America.* New York: Penguin.

González, M. G. (1999). *Mexicanos: A history of Mexicans in the United States.* Bloomington: Indiana University Press.

Griswold del Castillo, R., & De León, A. (1997). *North to Aztlan: A history of Mexican Americans in the United States.* New York: Twayne Publishers.

Hackett, C. W. (Ed.). (1970). *Revolt of the Pueblo Indians of New Mexico and Otermin's attempted reconquest, 1680–1682.* Albuquerque, NM: Coronado Historical Series.

Haro, R. (2001, December). The dearth of Latinos in campus administration. *Chronicle of Higher Education.*

Hernández, F. (n.d.). The Mexican schools. Unpublished. [in author's possession].

Johanningmeier, E. V. (1980). *Americans and their schools.* Chicago: Rand McNally.

Leibowitz, A. H. (1970). *Educational policy and political acceptance: The imposition of English as the language of instruction in American schools.* Washington, DC: Center for Applied Linguistics.

Manuel, H. T. (1930). *Education of Mexican and Spanish-speaking children in Texas.* Austin: University of Texas Press.

Masud-Pilot, F. (1996). *From welcomed exiles to illegal immigrants: Cuban migration to the U.S., 1959–1995.* Lanham, MD: Rowman and Littlefield.

McAdams, D. R. (2000). *Fighting to save our urban schools . . . and winning! Lessons from Houston.* New York: Teachers College Press.

Meier, K. J., & Stewart, J. P. (1991). *The politics of Hispanic education.* Albany, NY: SUNY Press.

Menchaca, M. (1999). The Treaty of Guadalupe Hidalgo and the racialization of the Mexican Population. In J. F. Moreno (Ed.), *The elusive quest for equality* (pp. 3–29). Cambridge, MA: Harvard Educational Review.

Milk, R. (1980). The issue of language in education in territorial New Mexico. *Bilingual Review, 7*(3), 212–221.

Muñóz, C. (1989). *Youth, identity, power: The Chicano movement.* New York: Verso.

Office of the Mayor. (1967). *Puerto Ricans confront problems of the complex ur-*

ban society: A design for change: Proceedings of the Puerto Rican community conference. New York: Office of the Mayor.

Olivas, M. (1989). Latino college students. New York: Teachers College Press.

Orfield, G., & Monfort, F. (1992). Status of school desegregation: The next generation. Alexandria, VA: Council of Urban Boards of Education.

Rodríguez, C. E., & Sánchez Korrol, V. (Eds.). (1996). Historical perspectives on Puerto Rican survival in the United States. Princeton, NJ: Markus Wierner.

Sánchez Korrol, V. (1996). Toward bilingual education: Puerto Rican women teachers in New York City schools, 1947–1967. In A. Ortiz (Ed.), Puerto Rican women and work (pp. 82–104). Philadelphia: Temple University Press.

Sánchez Korrol, V. (1994). From colonia to community: The history of Puerto Ricans in New York City. Berkeley: University of California Press.

San Miguel, G. (2001). Brown, not white: School integration and the Chicano movement. College Station: Texas A&M University Press.

San Miguel, G. (1999). The schooling of Mexicanos in the Southwest, 1848–1891. In J. F. Moreno (Ed.), The elusive quest for equality: 150 years of Chicano/ Chicana education (pp. 31–52). Cambridge, MA: Harvard Educational Review.

San Miguel, G. (1996). Actors not victims: Chicanas/os and the struggle for educational equality. In D. R. Maciel & I. D. Ortiz (Eds.), Chicanas/Chicanos at the crossroads: Social, economic, and political change (pp. 159–180). Tucson: The University of Arizona Press.

San Miguel, G. (1987). Let all of them take heed. Austin: University of Texas Press.

San Miguel, G. (1986). Status of the historiography of Mexican American education: A preliminary analysis. History of Education Quarterly, 26, 523–536.

San Miguel, G., & Valencia, R. R. (1998). From the Treaty of Guadalupe Hidalgo to Hopwood: The educational plight and struggle of Mexican Americans in the Southwest. Harvard Educational Review, 68(3), 353–412.

Spell, L. (1927). Music teaching in New Mexico in the seventeenth century. New Mexico Historical Review, 2(1), 27–36.

Stevens, J. D. (1999). The Menaul School: A study of cultural convergence. Unpublished. University of Houston.

Szasz, F. M. (1988). The Protestant clergy in the Great Plains and Mountain West, 1865–1915. Albuquerque: University of New Mexico Press.

Tashakkori, A., & Ochoa, S. H. (Eds.). (1999). Education of Hispanics in the United States. New York: AMS Press.

Tyler, D. (1974). The Mexican teacher. Red River Valley Historical Review, 1(3), 207–221.

Vaca, N. (1971). The Mexican American in the social sciences, 1912–1970 (Part 2, 1936–1970). El Grito, 16, 17–51.

Valencia, R. R. (1997). The evolution of deficit thinking: Educational thought and practice. Washington, DC: The Falmer Press.

Valencia, R. R. (1991). Chicano school failure and success: Research and policy agendas for the 1990s. London: The Falmer Press.

Van Well, M. S. (1942). The educational aspects of the missions in the Southwest. Milwaukee, WI: Marquette University Press.

Vigil, M. E. (1992). MALDEF: Chicano advocate for educational, economic, and political reform. In M. Romero & C. Cordero (Eds.), *Community empowerment and Chicano scholarship* (pp. 231–244). Berkeley, CA: National Association for Chicano Studies.

Weber, D. J. (1992). *The Spanish frontier in North America.* New Haven, CT: Yale University Press.

Weinberg, M. (1977). *A chance to learn: The history of race and education in the United States.* Cambridge: Cambridge University Press.

Yohn, S. M. (1995). *A contest of faiths: Missionary women and pluralism in the American Southwest.* Ithaca, NY: Cornell University Press.

Chapter 2

Faces of the Future: Latino Children in Early Childhood Education Programs

Luis A. Hernandez

INTRODUCTION

In visiting a child care or preschool setting in any American community at the beginning of the twenty-first century, we are looking at the faces of a future generation of doctors, teachers, restaurant workers, politicians, and police officers. These infants, toddlers, and preschool-age children in Early Childhood Education (ECE) programs reflect future America. These faces also reflect the vast demographic changes occurring in our society. Many of the new faces are Latino children whose families have a long history in this country or are recent newcomers. These new faces also embody a more diverse world of origin, as well as a world of various cultural backgrounds and languages.

This chapter examines the relations and dynamics between Latino children and their families and the world of early care and education programs. As professionals in the field, we can gain a deeper sense of community by understanding the history and origins of the families with whom we share the care and education of their children. Our knowledge of the theories and research in brain and language development, learning, and our awareness of cultural dynamics guide our work with Latino children. Quality early childhood education programs for infants, toddlers, and preschool-age children help all families create a path toward school achievement.

A NEW AMERICAN GENERATION

Children who attend a high-quality ECE program are less likely to repeat grades, drop out of school, require special education, or experience legal trouble (National Research Council, 2000). The long-term positive impact proves a benefit for the well-being of our society. The dramatic increase of Latinos across the country has brought the Spanish language and culture into areas and communities where it previously had not been heard. In addition, a new group of people who look and conduct themselves differently are now working alongside and living next door to people who speak only English and who have lived in these communities for generations.

Latino history is intertwined with the early history of the United States. Until the last few decades, Latinos in the United States had lived in select urban areas and along the border states in the Southwest. Families in parts of New Mexico and Texas trace their families back 15 generations. Today families may have arrived in the United States as recently as the latest flight from Santo Domingo or an overnight border crossing. Part of knowing the history of Latinos in America is understanding the history of the nation itself. The journeys of Spanish explorers, such as Fernando De Soto and Ponce de Leon, chronicle early colonies in Florida, on the coast of Georgia, and along the Mississippi as far north as Memphis. The West with its strong Spanish history includes the extraordinary journeys to the fabled City of Gold *Coronado* high in the mountains of New Mexico. While the descendants of some of these explorers created important places like Santa Fe and the California missions, others remained in isolation in mountain hamlets in the vast New World.

Across the country, the early Latino culture evolved from the Louisiana bayous to the Sierra Nevada, intermingling with Native peoples, African slaves, and other European immigrants. It was once easy to identify places where the people with Spanish or Latin American backgrounds lived in the United States. Those with a Mexican background primarily lived in the western states; Puerto Ricans lived in New York; and Cubans in Florida. Today, Latino Americans live in all 50 states and come from all of Latin America. In some cities and counties, they have become the majority population, achieving high degrees of economic and political power. In other places, Latinos have become a significant presence in communities with no previous historical reference.

While some newly arrived Latinos are in the United States fleeing political upheavals such as Cubans or Salvadorans, others have come to fulfill their own American Dream of opportunity and freedom. The American economic expansion during the 1990s drew more immigrants to the United States to fill jobs in agriculture, poultry and meatpacking, construction, restaurants, and other service industries. The faces of the new Latinos also reveal a more diverse people. Latinos can be any mixture of races and ethnicities. People of Mexican heritage, often referred to as *mestizos*, have a mix of Spanish and Native Meso American blood. African heritage can be found in people with a Caribbean background such as Dominicans and

Puerto Ricans. More recent arrivals may include Mayan people from Central America.

A group that merits special reference and understanding is the children of Puerto Rico. The U.S. Census Bureau does not include data on residents of Puerto Rico in its general 50-state Latino data analysis. As an island with a Commonwealth status, Puerto Rico shares common norms of American political, economic, and social structures. Still, an assessment of the social and economic status of children in Puerto Rico indicates that this segment of the population faces extreme poverty and problems associated with being poor. Officially, 55% of the island's families live below the poverty level (Rodriguez, 1999). As in the United States, only a small number of all eligible children under the age of five participate in ECE programs due to limited federal funding. However, unlike Latino families in the continental United States, families in Puerto Rico can rely on ECE programs that share a common language and culture.

MAKING A DIFFERENCE: QUALITY AND COST

Quality factors hinge on the economics of ECE. Infant and toddler care is a delicate and intensive interpersonal process. It requires a low adult–child ratio of 1 to 4 in most states, with a recommended one adult to three infants in accredited programs. A low adult–child ratio means proper individual attention in learning experiences, menus, diapering, and equipment. Taking care of babies is an expensive proposal. The Early Head Start program, considered the premier federally funded infant/toddler program in the United States, serves a limited number of pregnant women, babies, and toddlers to the age of three. Still, the average annual cost for Early Head Start services is $9,000 to $10,000 per child. This is an unattainable figure for most working-class families and beyond the reach of poor families. A preschool program of excellence is also an expensive proposition because it requires low ratios and small group size, available resources and equipment, and well-qualified and well-compensated teachers.

The cost of care and the education of our youngest children are a major crisis in the United States. Programs providing even the most minimal factors in quality settings are beyond the financial reach of most families. It is a marketplace of the haves and have-nots. The primary cost of care and education falls within the responsibility of families, even with some minimal support in tax credits. Again, primary responsibility for ECE programs lies with federal and state governments. Only about 40% of poor children attend state-supported ECE programs because there is insufficient funding for all possible eligible children (Shore, 2000). More working families could certainly benefit from some type of financial assistance. For all families with young children under the age of five across the country, 60% attend either preschool or some form of child care (Shore, 2000).

In comparison to other advanced nations, there is no political consensus to develop and fund educationally enriching experiences. This is due to the fact that high-quality ECE programs require major funding. A significant roadblock to this consensus is the lack of national or shared standards across the nation. For example, while 15 states have curriculum standards for state-sponsored preschools, only 6 require that preschools follow any type of guideline. Together with a lack of trained and properly compensated teachers and other ECE professionals, a lack of consistency in programs across the country leads to wide disparity in quality. Insufficient funding for ECE programs creates havoc and confusion for many families across the country. Lacking a national will for fully funded early childhood education programs that propel children toward success will only result in unequal availability in every community in the United States.

DIVERSITY WITHIN A DIVERSE GROUP

Latino children in the United States are as varied and complex as the families they represent. Some children come from traditional families where the mother stays at home. This tradition also supports more conventional child-care arrangements such as children's being taken care of by a relative or a neighbor. Another important factor is the Latino family propensity to have extended families, such as a grandmother, living at home (Hernandez & Charney, 1998). This helps to explain in part the low reliance on child-care centers and preschools. Latino cultural care preference is the tendency to select family child-care, either an informal arrangement with a neighbor or in a formal licensed setting. In other cases, especially for mothers working in agriculture, their children are in organized care provided by migrant service providers.

Higher-income Latino homes tend to use ECE programs for their children more than do lower-income Latino families (El Valor Corporation, 2001). Due to these differences in family patterns, employment, and community availability, Latino enrollment in early childhood programs differs from that of other national groups. For example, in 1996, only about 26% of Latino three-year-olds were enrolled in early learning centers in comparison to 60% of Black children (National Council of La Raza, 2001). Current demographic forecasts project high growth rates for Latino children, as a result of both continuing immigration patterns and a higher fertility rate than the rest of the population. By 2030, Latino children will constitute 25% of the national school-age population (U.S. Bureau of the Census, 2000). These changes are critical because they mean that the challenges confronting Latino children and families have significant implications for early care and education programs and the public education school system.

FAMILIES AS PARTNERS IN LEARNING

As it is true for families across the globe, the notion of children's being cared for by others outside the immediate family is a rather new concept in human social and economic evolution. The notion of an organized system of care and education is relatively new, and it can be jolting for new immigrant families. For professionals, creating a foundation of trust and bond with a Latino family provides reassurance that the child will be safe, loved, and cared for in a warm environment of learning. As strangers to this family, teachers and other caregivers must navigate a new territory of understanding family composition, cultural variables, language uses, and relationship building. As partners in a child's success, families and teachers can create goals that enhance an infant's development, foster learning experiences in a variety of appropriate ways for toddlers, and extend literacy efforts for preschoolers in ways that are respectful of each family's capacity. The relationship of home and center is a cornerstone in any quality program, more so for families that may be new to the community and whose English is limited.

While Latino families want success in their child's school readiness, other factors can be more important. The child's health and well-being are also key for readiness. For many children, living in poverty or in areas of environmental contamination decreases the possibility for a true physical readiness for learning. Despite difficult home and community circumstances, children acquire learning traits by experiencing the first years of their lives in a home environment where they can receive individual attention and nurturing from family members. Unfortunately, for many Latino children, the high levels of poverty impede such ideal conditions.

The poverty rates of Latino families are a major factor in ECE options and choices. Latino children are poor in disproportionately large numbers, and younger children under the age of 5 are poor more often than older children. While Latino children are likely to live in two-parent families, the proportion of Latino children under 18 living in single-mother homes continues to increase. In 2000, over 27% of Latino children lived in a single-mother household (Federal Interagency Forum on Child and Family Statistics, 2000). Children growing up in single-parent families are more likely to be poor. This contributes to specific challenges in a child's overall development, since single mothers tend to have limited education or work experience. Additionally, enrollment in ECE programs is related to the mother's education and income. Only 52% of all poor families use ECE programs (Fuller, Halloway, & Liang, 1996).

Eligibility and enrollment in quality programs depend largely on the financial resources of families as well as available public assistance. The intent of the publicly funded programs, primarily federal allocations, is designed for the poorest of the poor with a special focus on families transitioning from public assistance programs. Funding is also available for migrant families working in designated agricultural activities. The primary responsibility for ECE programs lies with federal and state funding, and that responsibility is enormous. The majority of these funds fall under child-care subsidized programs administered by state agencies. The other option is the Head Start program operated by the federal government. Accessibility to these programs can be challenging to some Latino families due to complex eligibility requirements as well as fears about immigration status. Despite the growing presence of Latinos in ECE programs, they are not equally enrolled in federal- or state-funded programs. Many programs have poor recruitment efforts or see language and cultural difference as a challenge and barrier in reaching Latino families. Latino family income levels and parental educational attainment also impact enrollment in ECE programs.

LANGUAGE AND CULTURE IN THE LIVES OF YOUNG CHILDREN

In early care settings the nurturing and safety of young children are of primary concern, but language and culture provide the heart of a program. For infants and toddlers, this is a defining developmental stage in which the language they hear and begin to experiment with should be the language that family members also use at home. The issue of language and culture represents a balancing act for many Latino families. They understand that overall success in this society depends on the mastery of the dominant language, English. However, other factors play a role in family dynamics such as the family's sense of continuity and tradition. This may mean a connection with older generations and perhaps a geographic connection to a place of origin. For others it is the advantage and benefit of knowing and mastering two languages in an increasingly small world. Language goes hand in hand with cultural identity; it is not a stand-alone activity without context or meaning.

Language and culture carry a political weight in this society. For Latinos in the United States this is an extremely sensitive and complex subject. Professionals in the field need to sensitize themselves to current research and opinion in formulating a plan of sensible action. The first step may be to follow the lead of the families: *How important is the representation of their language and culture to them? Do they want the child to be able to communicate with the grandmother, la abuela, at home? Do they want the child to understand the songs and stories from the uncle who is visiting from Guatemala? Is it important for them to have their child speak the home language as they progress through school?* The educator's role then is to support families as they navigate in making choices for themselves and their children.

Should children with a Latino background learn English? The answer is a resounding affirmation. But the divergent and thoughtful response is that while we want children to learn English well and with confidence, we also need to be sensitive and respectful of the individual home situation. If family members have little or no English skills, we must be cognizant that when the child returns home each day, he or she still needs to bond and relate to the parents and grandparents. Again, each family must be treated with individual attention. Each family has its own constellation of language use and levels. While it is easy to assume that all families want the best for their children, the standard of best varies by different hues of choices, awareness, or preferences. But as educators of children in the most important five years of life, we need to ensure that a balance occurs between home and the early care center. Studies in this area tend to support *culturally and linguistically diverse* programming (Soto, 1991). The general intent of this term is to respect and reinforce the relationship between families and the ECE practitioners in relation to culture and language. The identifiers for children have been either as *non-English-proficient* or *limited-English-proficient*. Currently, there is a move to shift the focus on children as *English learners*. This is a subtle but important difference as we consider the fact that Latino children come to the ECE setting with a variety of language hues.

The controversy over language is a major minefield of emotions, passions, and politics. There is much controversy as to what truly works for Latino children. The camps are divided into those who champion the cause of bilingual education and those who value immersion in English as the preferred route for school success. Both camps have sets of research and analysis that prove their particular point. The battle shifts according to the national and political mood. The stakes are high; the debate affects the lives of children and their future academic success. While much of the debate centers on school-age children, the implications weigh heavily for children under the age of five. Young children should not be considered *sponges* that can readily absorb the complexities and subtleties of either their home or center language. The pressure on families is tremendous when it comes to making choices regarding the long-term implications for their child at a very young age. Early childhood professionals again need to ask themselves: *Should the toddler be spoken to only in English, even though the grandmother at home speaks no English? Should I request that the child be taught only in English, because it will guarantee school success? Or should the child be taught both languages because the parent was denied that opportunity when she was a child?*

Much of this discussion centers on how language is learned and how second language skills are acquired. Are the skills of knowing two languages, even at a young age, valued in this society? Are there other factors that view the use of Spanish as less worthy than that of other languages?

One decisive factor may be the United States' position on language differences as opposed to that of the rest of the world. Children and adults in many other nations are taught the value of knowing more than one language as a way of communication between neighbors for trade, travel, education, and celebrations. As citizens of the world, we can no longer deprive our children of the opportunity to view themselves as neighbors of the global village.

CREATING COMMUNITY QUILTS

For many Americans today, the search to connect to and establish a sense of community is a constant dynamic. Cities and towns are continually changing; this is also true of many Latino communities, whether old barrios in Los Angeles or trailer parks in northern Alabama. For ECE professionals, knowing the communities of our families is also part of our mandate in delivering quality services. Part of this work is becoming an anthropological investigator in observing and knowing families. While many of us may hold a romantic view of communities of families knowing and assisting each other, that model may not be universally true. We live in communities well defined along economic, racial, and ethnic boundaries. Their poverty or prosperity, their vacant storefronts or their overloaded malls easily identify neighborhoods. Latinos tend to settle and congregate in areas where they can feel most at home, close to churches and businesses and other services familiar to all.

In knowing the communities in which families live, the tools of social anthropology may guide the journey. Visit the local store where families shop and frequent and go to the parks where they take their kids. Drop by their local parish or temple and talk to clergy members for their insights into the families you both know. Have dinner at one of the local restaurants and savor the unfamiliar foods listed on the menu. Listen to a local radio station playing music unfamiliar to your ears. In doing this work, you may discover differences and similarities. You may also gain perspective on how Latino families raise their children and the implications for the work you do. If anything, the biggest community resource are parents themselves. To be truly relevant and useful, the ECE center needs to fit itself within the larger community quilt.

SETTINGS FOR LEARNING

As in any quality ECE setting, Latino children and families expect the same quality services as all other families. In infant and toddler centers, the program design must consider language and cultural variables. The center should provide developmental experiences that enhance the cognitive and language skills of a child. A strong language and culture framework supports family literacy experiences according to individual family strengths and abilities. In a sense, that framework honors a child's parents as primary teachers in the fullest sense. The cultural imprint starts early and sets in motion a lifelong notion of self, emotional well-being, and place in the world. The earliest months and years of life provide the connection to the roots of a family's language and culture. This starts with the songs of a grandmother, the whispers of an older sibling, the laughter of a father, the taste of a particular dish, or the warmth of a mother. For children in poverty and instability, their early experiences are their defining and lasting imprints. Whatever the path of early years, they all lead to the foundation of language and culture.

We can gain a primary assessment of the quality of a center simply by taking note of its sights, sounds, and smells. We can also observe the atmosphere of a center by asking ourselves, *Are parents welcomed and invited? Are the children and parents addressed in their home language? Do the teachers, cooks, and bus drivers relate to the children in a friendly and warm way? Are children playing with one another in happy and meaningful ways?* Social and sensory interactions are true indicators of quality in any learning setting. Conversations between members of the staff and parents should include the discipline policy for the setting, an issue that may lead to deeper discussion on how Latino parents may differ in their manner of discipline at home. Parents should also be aware of the educational goals in the ECE program, including the type of curriculum implemented at the setting, the program's approach to first and second language learning, the purpose and intent of screening and ongoing assessment, and the support of families as partners in the learning process of the child. Menus and health practices should reflect the feeding and health practices that are respectful of a child's home, especially for infants and toddlers. Daily lesson plans should reflect the child's home language in practices that are of interest and meaningful.

At times, programs with Latino children fall into patterns and practices that can be perceived as culturally expedient. For example, there is a tendency to rely on a *tourist approach* to the curriculum, using stereotypic items for different populations (Bradekamp & Copple, 1997). Hanging a Mexican sombrero in the dramatic play area does not guarantee a culturally rich experience. Just because we see them hanging at a local restaurant or brought back after a trip to Cancun does not mean sombreros are a prevalent item in most Latino homes. Big sombreros may not signify much for the young child. The sombrero is not a guarantee that the child's father has one hanging in his home. The father may have a baseball cap or cowboy hat or wool cap as does any other father in the program. Any item, food, celebration, or holidays introduced into the center should hold meaning and relevance for young children, their families, and the adults who work with them. Programs need to have a thoughtful and inclusive policy to incorporate cultural items into the overall program goal. The goal should be to enhance children's self-esteem and reinforce the connection between home and the ECE program.

CURRICULUM AND ASSESSMENT MODELS

The selection of a curriculum for an ECE program, especially those serving Latino children, should include in its criteria the appropriateness to language and culture. It should be a tool that teachers can use to foster the development and learning of children in partnership with families. A curriculum should not be a *cookbook of quick activities*, but rather a guide for teachers to create experiences in which the children can grow. For Latino children, this is key as many of them begin to learn a new language, explore learning situations, and experience success in a variety of formal and informal activities.

Considering the number of Latino children in ECE programs, few curriculum models offer solid language learning strategies or bilingual models. Head Start developed the most comprehensive selection in the late 1970s, when it funded the development and implementation of four curricula for preschool bilingual programs. These four models are *Amanecer* (Dawn), *Alerta* (Alert), *Un Marco Abierto* (An Open Framework), and *Nuevas Fronteras* (New Frontiers). The *Amanecer* model was developed by a private firm in San Antonio, Texas, and it contained a number of specific strategies in working with families, such as structuring the classroom environment to reflect the community and creating small groups for English and Spanish learners. *Alerta*, developed at Teacher's College, Columbia University in New York, focused on creating a locally designed learning and language plan based on families and communities. *Un Marco Abierto*, developed by the High Scope Foundation in Ypsilanti, Michigan, used the same principles as its better-known English model with an emphasis on a natural language acquisition model, using the preference of the children and families. This approach allowed the adults in the classroom to follow the language lead of the child, be it a Spanish monolingual approach, a bilingual approach, or English only. The University of California at Santa Cruz developed *Nuevas Fronteras*. This curriculum would be the most traditional of the four, using age-old Mexican stories and folktales in the provision of language learning in both languages. Each model had specific methodology in the expansion of the first home language and the acquisition skills in learning a second language. All models enjoyed a certain degree of success when the Head Start Bureau provided extensive support through a dissemination plan of training and technical assistance. Today a few programs still use parts of the models in their curricula.

With the rise of Latino children across the country, major publishers and curriculum developers are quickly responding to program needs. Aligned with the curriculum are the ongoing observation and assessment of children's development and learning. Assessment tools, both formal and informal, gather information and data on individual children and groups of children. At a minimum, the assessment tools should be appropriate for the children in terms of stage of development, language, and culture. The use of any such tool should ensure the quality, accuracy, consistency, and credibility of the assessment. The process should also be conducted by adults familiar with the child in an environment that is comfortable to the young child. As with all assessments, the adult collecting the data should be properly trained and provided with oversight and supervision in this work. Currently, there are many assessment tools on the market used by programs across the country. The consumer should be cautious and savvy in the selection of an appropriate tool. A simple translation of one tool from English to Spanish may not be the most appropriate one for children in a particular community.

For young children, an assessment tool is not to be used as a checklist of particular skills or milestones. Rather, the tool is only one of several indicators that can provide a wider view of the individual child. The indicators may look for progress over a year's time in listening, understanding, and speaking English. In addition to formal tools, other informal sources may include observations in the classrooms, conversations with parents, children's artwork, anecdotes from other adults, social behaviors with other children, and other factors that mark progress over time. The assessment of an individual child should provide a depth of understanding of a child's abilities and skills. Curriculum learning plans can therefore be based along this continuum.

MORE THAN THE ABCs: LANGUAGE AND LITERACY

In ECE programs, language development and literacy are considered important cornerstones for any curriculum. The focus on teaching reading in elementary schools has filtered down to the preschool years; school success is equated with reading readiness. There exists a debate between educators who emphasize teaching children to read through immersion in good books, an approach known as *whole language*, and those who believe in phonics, which drill children in sounding out letter combinations and words. Most seasoned practitioners try to balance both approaches in working with young children. Strategies that are truly based on phonemic awareness reflect the best in early childhood education, activities that are true to the heart of the field and profession. For young English learners, it can provide a sensible and responsive approach for learning a new language in meaningful ways. For quality programs, a literacy learning approach underlines the significance of a child's early years in overall development and academic success. Programs of quality base their learning on solid principles of child development philosophy and practices related to the individual's developmental level. Over the last 20 years, studies confirm the path of best practices in learning language and establishing literacy-rich environment (Tabors & Snow, 2002).

THE ECE PROFESSIONALS

The professionals in ECE programs are individuals, primarily women, who are known by a variety of titles: *teacher, provider, caregiver, assistant, paraprofessional,* and *aide.* People who carry these titles wear a number of hats and carry responsibilities that are beyond those of any particular concept of teacher. The job often means riding on the bus with the children, administering medicine with proper documentation and permission, preparing meals and snacks, tending to a sick child, talking to parents in the morning and afternoon, cleaning bathrooms, supervising teeth brushing, and taking care of the child with special needs. All that, in addition to creating wonder with amazing learning experiences, reading books that transport children to another world, having resources and materials in various activity areas, kicking balls on the playground, and singing the "Itsy Bitsy Spider" for the hundredth time with a smile.

Studies indicate that for adults in ECE programs, the amount and level of their education and specialized training received over time impact children's socio-emotional and cognitive development (Carnegie Task Force, 1994). Studies consistently affirm how adults affect and impact a child's identity, success in school, and eventual roles as citizens, parents, and future workers (National Research Council, 2000). The role of a teacher during the first years of a child's life is critical. The relationship is one of security, trust, and comfort. This provides the basis for normal development and learning opportunities. For children with limited English skills, the impact of a teacher in the learning process is even more important. These teachers can make a difference in inspiration and success or failure and detachment.

However, the lack of trained teachers, especially Latino professionals, compounded by poor compensation, creates unstable learning environments. In 2001, preschool teachers working with 3- and 4-year-olds in some states earned an average annual salary of $19,430, half of what the average kindergarten teacher earned. All states require kindergarten teachers to have a bachelor's degree and a teaching certificate, but only 20 states require similar credentials for preschool teachers (Shore, 2000). At the heart of the effort to promote quality early childhood programs is the movement to raise the qualifications of those who work with young children. Increasingly, adults in ECE programs are mandated to have higher academic qualifications that are particularly related to the children they serve. The level of professional development means a mandated associate of arts degree in ECE by 2003 for 50% of Head Start teachers (U.S. Department of Health

and Human Services, 2000). Current trends suggest the eventual requirement of bachelor's degrees with a specialization related to early childhood
education. Teachers are required to have more specific foundational knowledge of the development of children's language, thinking, and social and
effective behavior. Indeed, the instructional practices for young children
may also incorporate knowledge of mathematics, science, health, and literature, among others.

As important as earning a living wage, teachers should expect qualified
supervision in curriculum implementation. Feedback from mentors and
other ECE facilitators can guide teachers on a path of greater responsive-
ness in their work with children and families. For some Latinos in teaching
and caregiving positions, a forward step in their careers will also involve
leadership development. Leadership development is not only identifying
people deemed qualified to occupy positions of responsibility and authority
but also providing them with the skills and opportunities to do so. This is
especially important when considering the challenges and opportunities for
Latino children, families, and communities.

CONCLUSION

Knowing how to best work with children and families in a future of
ever-changing demographics, economic unevenness, and political upheavals
will require the ability to understand the world and our local communities.
Working with Latino families and children requires a sense of history and
current global events. As the increasing numbers of immigrants from Latin
America continue on their trek to their American Dream, certain principles
should shape our professional view. Every human being, whether a recent
immigrant or a sixteenth-generation citizen, is worthy of respect. Families
who sacrifice to be part of the American Dream also carry a pioneering
spirit to do better for themselves and their children. As individuals, immigrant families deserve a chance to prove themselves in their work and contributions.

A basic impulse is to deny the changes occurring in our communities or
society. The first step is the affirmation of the richness of the American
fabric in the many hues of its diversity. This idea goes well beyond the
simple *melting pot* concept but focuses more on the bounty on the American table, with its variety of people and cultures. Let's celebrate that which
is distinct and different and avoid unworthy labels of people and their
cultures. It is an affirmation of commonalities that can lead to reconcilia-
tion and a new national community. Instead of a defensive stance against
change, let's advocate basic values of justice and respect to lead the next
generation. Children in early childhood programs today will be the people
working in our communities tomorrow. To envision the future of America,
we have to see only the youngest citizens to recognize this nation's potential

and vibrancy. As the fruits of quality programs come to bear, the children will in turn define the society and culture in which we will all live. The future is based on the learning and care of today.

REFERENCES

Bradekamp, S., & Copple, C. (1997). *Developmentally appropriate practices in early childhood programs.* Washington, DC: NAEYC.

Carnegie Task Force. (1994). *Starting points: Meeting the needs of our youngest children.* New York: Carnegie Corporation.

El Valor Corporation. (2001). *National roundtable on Latino early childhood issues.* Chicago: El Valor Corporation.

Federal Interagency Forum on Child and Family Statistics. (2000). *America's children: Key national indicators of well being.* Available http://www.child stats.gov.

Fuller, B., Halloway, S., & Liang, X. (1996). *Family selection of child care centers: The influence of household support, ethnicity, and parental practices.* Berkeley, CA: Harvard University and University of California.

Hernandez, D., & Charney, E. (1998). *From generation to generation: The health and well-being of children in immigrant families.* Washington, DC: National Academy Press.

National Council of La Raza. (2001). *Beyond the census: Hispanics and an American agenda.* Washington, DC: Author. Available: www.nclr.org.

National Research Council. (2000). *Eager to learn: Educating our preschoolers.* Washington, DC: National Academy Press.

Rodriguez, G. (1999). *Raising nuestros niños: Bringing up Latino children.* New York: Fireside Books.

Shore, R. (2000). *Our basic dream: Keeping faith with America's working families and their children.* New York: Foundation for Child Development.

Soto, L. (1991). Understanding bilingual/bicultural young children. *Young Children, 46,* 30–36.

Tabors, P., & Snow, C. (2002). *Young bilingual children and early literacy development.* New York: Guilford.

U.S. Census Bureau. (2000). *The Hispanic population in the United States.* Available: http://www.census.gov/population.

U.S. Department of Health and Human Services. (2000). *Curriculum in Head Start.* Washington, DC: Head Start Bureau.

Chapter 3

Democratizing Latino Education:
A Perspective on Elementary Education

Lilia I. Bartolomé

INTRODUCTION

The task of successfully teaching Latino students represents a pressing challenge faced by public school educators across all grade levels. This chapter discusses the ideological dimensions of Latino education, particularly the significance of teacher ideological clarity, as well as three potentially promising instructional approaches for Latino and other culturally and linguistically diverse student populations. Although the focus of this chapter is on the classroom teacher and instructional practices, there is no doubt that the educational challenges facing Latino students are complex and require multi-faceted, multi-tiered, and collaborative solutions. Educational challenges range from increased segregation and substandard schooling, to the current English-only high stakes testing movement that unfairly tests Latino students who are still not yet proficient in academic English language abilities or standardized test-taking skills. Other challenges include enduring problems such as teachers' deficit perceptions and treatment of Latino and other low socio-economic status (SES) students (Flores & Díaz, 2001). In addition, the growing, yet historically ever-present, anti-bilingual education movement and anti-immigrant mood in the United States promise to revert to the *good old days* when Latinos were taught and *subordinated* via the English language and were punished when caught speaking Spanish (Macedo, 1991). Many of these educational challenges facing Latino students are not new phenomena in the U.S. educational landscape. On the contrary, issues such as segregated schooling, anti-Spanish language and Latino sentiment, and teacher deficit views and low expectations of Latino students constitute a socio-historical and ideological mainstay—a taken-for-granted *way of life*—for most Latinos in education. It is useful to keep in mind this socio-historical and ideological educational backdrop when discussing the improvement of Latino educational conditions. This chapter endeavors to resist facile attempts to find the *right* teaching recipes by first, offering a brief discussion of the current state of Latino education; second, exploring the important role of ideologically clear teachers; and third, examining three instructional approaches deemed potentially promising for elementary-level Latino students.

CURRENT STATE OF LATINOS IN ELEMENTARY EDUCATION

According to the ERIC Clearinghouse on Urban Education (2001) we know that the enrollment of Latino students at the elementary level has increased 157% in the 20-year span between 1978 and 1998 and that, currently, these students make up approximately 15% of the total elementary school-age population. By the year 2025, Latinos will make up nearly 25% of the elementary school-age population (White House Initiative on Educational Excellence for Hispanic Americans, 1999). Disparities between Latino students and non-Latino peers begin as early as kindergarten and remain throughout their schooling experience into high school and result in an approximate 30% dropout rate (Sanchez, 2002). By age nine, Latino students perform below their non-Latino peers in major content areas such as reading, mathematics, and science (ERIC Clearinghouse on Urban Education, 2001).

Because of the perception that public schools are not responding appropriately to the needs of Latino students, large numbers of Latino parents have sought alternative schools such as Catholic and charter schools for their children. In the case of Catholic schooling, the data on Latino student achievement are inconclusive. Some research suggests that Latino, African American, and other culturally and linguistically diverse (CLD) students experience greater academic success in these schools (Byrk, Lee, & Holland, 1993). Some reasons cited for the effectiveness of Catholic schools with CLD and low SES students include factors such as a small school size, a decentralized school system with the freedom to adapt instruction to particular localities, required parent participation and clear parent–school partnership responsibilities, shared home-school Christian values, explicit basic academic instruction, a caring and orderly learning environment, and committed teachers who hold high expectations for all students (Blum, 1985; Polite, 1992). It is important to note that some research reports academic benefits for African Americans but not for other CLD groups (Figlio & Stone, 1999).

Charter schools are publicly financed schools that operate independently of many of the regulations that govern most other public schools. A push to initiate them has begun as a strategy for responding to the academic needs of Latino students. Recently, the National Council of La Raza, a leading national Latino advocacy group, raised $10 million from private foundations to launch an initiative to create and support 50 charter schools around the country directed at Latino students (Zehr, 2001). Proponents attribute the need for charter schools to the failure of public schools in adequately preparing Latino students. The expectation is that these types of schools will better respond to Latino students' needs. However, Gold-haber and Eide (2002) explain that the empirical evidence of the academic effectiveness of school reforms such as charter schools is mixed. They point out that some schools of choice may be successful because they have cultures, missions, or expectations that are more congruent with CLD students' needs but that, in general, there is little evidence that charter and other alternative schools are having a clear-cut positive or negative impact on the academic achievement of students who select to attend them.

Despite Latinos' historical participation in Catholic schools and current interest in charter schools, the majority of Latino students attend public schools (Merritt, 2001). Thus, key characteristics of public education as they relate to Latino students need to be critically examined. When we look at teacher–student demographics, we find that one of the chief challenges in education is to adequately prepare the overwhelmingly White, female, and middle-class preservice teacher population that works with Latinos and other CLD students across grades levels (Gomez, 1994). While the nation's school population is made up of approximately 40% minority children, nearly 90% of teachers are White (National Center for Education Statistics, 1992). In addition, the social class differences between teacher and student continue to widen. For example, 36% of Latino children live in poverty, yet more teachers come from White lower-middle and middle-class homes and have been raised in suburban and rural environments (Zimpher, 1989). Furthermore, there are significant differences in teacher–student language backgrounds. The majority of teachers are English monolingual while there are approximately 7.5 million non-native English-speaking students in the public schools (McLeod, 1994).

THE SIGNIFICANCE OF TEACHER IDEOLOGY

Given the social class, cultural, and language differences between teachers and students and our society's historical predisposition to view Latino students through a deficit lens, it becomes especially urgent that teachers critically understand their ideological orientations with respect to cultural and class differences and to begin to comprehend that teaching is not a politically or ideologically neutral undertaking. Ideology refers to the framework of thought used by members of a society to justify or rationalize an existing social order. As mentioned earlier, it is important to accept that

Latino academic underachievement cannot be construed in primarily methodological terms dislodged from the social cultural and ideological reality that has shaped it and continues to sustain it. Even though it is important to identify promising instructional programs and strategies, it is erroneous to assume that blind replication of instructional programs or teacher mastery of specific teaching methods, in and of themselves, will guarantee successful student learning, especially when we are discussing a group that historically has been mistreated and miseducated by the schools (Donato, 1997).

The reality that Latinos, for the most part, in this society constitute a social, economic, and political low-status people is quite evident in their everyday experiences of subordination and mistreatment in schools. This ideological and *invisible* dimension of Latino education is usually ignored in favor of assuming a so-called *non-political*, technical, and myopic focus on educational programs or instructional methodologies. The belief by many educators that education is apolitical or non-political is a fallacy. All education reflects particular ideological positions. However, the tendency exists to label non-dominant culture ideological positions as *political* and dominant culture ideological positions as *non-* or *a-political*. This restricted focus also serves to obfuscate the sad fact that schools often reproduce the existing asymmetrical power relations that place non-White, non-middle-class, and non-English-speaking students at the bottom of the classroom totem pole (Anyon, 1997; Valenzuela, 1999). Instead of naming this ideological reality and explicitly identifying interventions to prevent the reproduction of harmful beliefs and hierarchies at the school level, educators generally choose to focus on the technical aspects of teaching.

The importance of preparing critical teachers with an understanding concerning the ideological dimensions of minority education cannot be stressed sufficiently. The ideologically informed way in which a teacher implements an approach or method can serve to offset potentially unequal relations and discriminatory practices in the classroom and, in doing so, improve the quality of the instructional process for both students and teachers. Reyes (1992) offers an example of what it means to critically examine potentially promising instructional methods for *hidden* discriminatory practices by studying the effectiveness of using dialogue journal writing for teaching writing to Latino elementary students. Reyes reports that the students enjoyed writing in their journals and dialoguing in writing with their teacher. However, when examining grammar and spelling instruction, the teacher indirectly addressed the student's errors when the teacher used the student's ungrammatical structure or misspelling in a correct manner in her or his response to that student. The teacher believed that by correcting the student errors in this indirect manner she avoided embarrassing the student and allowed the student to learn about grammar and spelling on her or his own. Despite the teacher's good intentions, Latino students did not grasp the implicit corrections and continued to make the same mistakes.

Delpit (1995) similarly warns teachers who blindly utilize a writing approach to teach African American and other working-class CLD students. She argues that White middle-class teachers need to be more critical and less lockstep in their use of the writing process when working with students who do not come from middle-class homes with the academic cultural capital expected in schools. Teachers should utilize promising teaching approaches but never lose sight that their primary responsibility is not to a particular teaching method but rather to preparing CLD students to effectively compete academically with middle-class mainstream peers.

Reyes (1992) and Delpit (1995) provide examples of why it is necessary for teachers to free themselves from the blind adoption of so-called effective and sometimes *teacher-proof* strategies and programs, so that they can begin a critical reflective process that allows them to re-create and reinvent teaching methods and materials by always taking into consideration the socio-cultural realities that either limit or expand the possibilities of their students' learning. Teachers should keep in mind that educational curricula and instructional methods are social constructions that grow out of and reflect ideologies that often prevent teachers from understanding the pedagogical implications of asymmetrical power relations among different cultural groups.

THE NEED FOR IDEOLOGICALLY CLEAR TEACHERS

Teacher ideological clarity refers to the process by which individuals struggle to identify both the dominant society's explanations for the existing societal socio-economic and political hierarchy and their own explanations. Ideological clarity requires that teachers' individual ideologies be compared and contrasted with those presented by the dominant society. The juxtaposing of ideologies should force teachers to understand better if, when, and how their belief systems uncritically reflect those of the dominant society and support inequitable conditions in school. It also refers to the processes by which individuals come to understand better the possible linkages between macro-level political, economic, and social variables and subordinated groups' academic performance in the micro-level classroom. Thus, it invariably requires educators to struggle to link socio-cultural structures and schooling.

It is a particularly difficult task in teacher education to deal with the ideological dimensions of education given the discipline's tendency to focus primarily on the technical issues of teaching. Teacher educators often face students who desire a bag of *surefire* teaching strategies that will magically work on Latinos and other CLD students. This tendency is particularly reflected in the field of diverse education, where much of the discussion about the preparation of teachers focuses on the best strategies to address the academic and linguistic development of culturally and linguistically *different* students. Teachers need to gain ideological clarity in order to increase their Latino students' chances for academic success. The unequal power relations among various social and cultural groups at the societal level are usually reproduced at the school and classroom level unless concerted efforts are made to prevent their reproduction.

The teacher education literature suggests that prospective teachers tend not to be particularly ideologically sophisticated (Freire, 1998). They often unconsciously hold beliefs and attitudes about the existing social order that reflect dominant ideologies such as the belief that lighter-skinned Latinos are smarter and more attractive than darker-skinned Latinos and that nonstandard language speakers are less capable than standard language speakers (Bloom, 1991). Many prospective teachers believe that our society is a meritocratic one where Whites are the major power holders in the society because they deserve to be and, correspondingly, that African Americans and other CLD groups occupy positions of low status because of their lack of ability and effort (Gonsalves, 1996).

Despite the difficulties in helping educators gain greater ideological clarity, it is necessary that they *name* their ideological beliefs and attitudes regarding the legitimacy of the greater social order and the resulting unequal power relations among various cultural groups at the school and classroom levels. In fact, educators who do not identify and interrogate their racist and classist ideological orientations often work to reproduce the existing social order (Bartolomé, 1998). On the other hand, recent descriptions of effective teachers of CLD students present them as knowledgeable and skilled, appearing to recognize the subordinate status accorded to low-SES CLD students and taking steps to validate them in school (Bartolomé & Balderrama, 2001).

Reyes, Scribner, and Paredes-Scribner's (1999) research on three high-performing Latino elementary schools along the Texas-Mexico border reports the creation of a school culture that fosters a strong belief in and commitment to the potential of all children to achieve at high levels as well as an *explicit* denial of the cultural deprivation deficit model to view their students. One key component of the conceptual framework for building capacity to succeed has to do with the schools' particular philosophical and ideological orientation. Their conceptual framework calls for a holistic mind-set, deeply ingrained in the belief that all children can succeed in school, a clear, explicit, and shared vision for the school among school personnel and parents, and the use of democratic dialogue and decision making among the various participants in the schools.

Likewise, Bartolomé and Balderrama (2001) examine the ideological beliefs of effective educators, both White and Latino, and suggest that these educators, for a variety of reasons, have developed an understanding that teaching is a political act that can either support the status quo or challenge it. Despite the educators' differing personal politics, they all rejected hurtful, dominant-culture myths, including deficit views of low-SES Latino students, uncritical acceptance of meritocratic explanations of the existing racial and socioeconomic hierarchy, and blind acceptance of the supposed superiority of mainstream middle-class culture. In addition, the educators also understood the arbitrariness and unfairness of being accorded subordinate or low status in relation to their own life experiences and their students. They clearly articulated their strategies for circumventing unfair attribution of student low status and for creating a more equal playing field for all students at school. These educators mentioned activities such as fund-raising to give their working-class students experiences similar to those of more affluent students, bringing in consultants and other experts to educate the teaching staff about various linguistic and cultural issues, and spending extra time and personal income to improve students' educational learning experiences.

The literature on effective teachers of Latino and other CLD students strongly suggests that teachers need to develop ideological clarity and understanding of the myriad ways in which the prevailing power hierarchy in our society is often replicated at the school and classroom levels and perpetuates the academic underachievement of CLD students (Bartolomé, 2002).

POTENTIALLY EQUALIZING AND EMPOWERING INSTRUCTIONAL PRACTICES

Teachers such as those discussed in the previous section possess a type of ideological perceptiveness or sensitivity that enables them to effectively create, adopt, and modify teaching approaches and strategies that simultaneously respect and challenge learners from diverse and subordinated cultural groups in a variety of learning environments. In this section, three instructional approaches—with the potential for student empowerment in the hands of ideologically perceptive teachers—are presented. The three potentially empowering instructional practices include culturally responsive instruction, strategic teaching, and heterogeneous cooperative group work.

Culturally Responsive Pedagogy

Culturally responsive pedagogy grows out of cultural difference theory, which attributes the academic difficulties of students from subordinated groups to cultural incongruence or discontinuities between learning, language use, and behavioral practices found in the home and those expected by the schools. Villegas and Lucas (2002) define culturally responsive pedagogy as an attempt to create instructional situations where teachers use teaching approaches and strategies that recognize and build on culturally different ways of learning, behaving, and using language in the classroom. For example, a number of well-known ethnographic studies document culturally incongruent communication practices in classrooms where students and teachers may speak the same language but use it in different ways (see Au & Mason, 1983; Cazden, 1988). This type of cultural incongruence is cited as a major source of academic difficulties for students and their teachers.

Despite the fact that the cultural incongruence literature, for the most part, solely focuses on working out cultural differences between mainstream teachers and CLD students, this body of work is undeniably useful in illustrating teacher strategies that have the potential to neutralize antagonistic teacher–student relations or teacher deficit ideologies. Positive academic and social benefits can result from teacher efforts to equalize relations by respecting, building on, and incorporating students' existing cultural capital. It is equally important to identify characteristics of school or academic discourses that need to be taught in an explicit and additive fashion to Latino and other working-class CLD students, who generally do not have access to academic discourses outside the classroom. Gee (1996) defines discourse as a "socially accepted association among ways of using language, of thinking, feeling, believing, valuing, and of acting that can be used to identify oneself as a member of a socially meaningful group or social network" (p. 143). This invariably involves recognition of class differences and how the dominant academic discourse often functions in ways to silence students. Educators must filter out and identify those communication and language skills that result from dominant culture practices and that are rarely made explicit to students. Educators must explicitly teach students so as to assist them in critically acquiring the codes of the dominant class. Strategic teaching, in the hands of ideologically perceptive teachers, can do precisely this.

Strategic Teaching

Strategic teaching refers to an instructional model that requires teachers to explicitly teach students learning strategies that enable them to consciously monitor their own learning. This is accomplished through the development of reflective cognitive monitoring (Jones, Palinscar, Ogle, & Carr, 1987). That is, students are explicitly taught specific strategies for reading and writing with the expectation that they will eventually learn to monitor their own learning. For example, during reading, teachers using this teaching strategy make explicit for students the structures of various text types used in school and assist students in identifying various strategies for effectively comprehending various genres. Although text structures and strategies for dissecting the particular structures are presented by the teacher, a key component of these lessons is the elicitation of students' knowledge about text types and their own strategies for making meaning before presenting them with more conventional academic strategies.

Examples of strategic learning strategies include teaching various text structures (e.g., narratives and various types of expository texts) through frames and graphic organizers. Frames are sets of questions that help students understand a given topic. Readers monitor their understanding of a text by asking themselves questions, making predictions, and testing their predictions as they read. Before reading, frames serve as an advance organizer to activate prior knowledge and facilitate understanding. Frames can also be utilized during the reading process by the reader to monitor self-learning or after a reading lesson to summarize and integrate newly acquired information. Graphic organizers are visual maps that represent text structures and organizational patterns used in texts and in student writing. Ideally, graphic organizers reflect both the content and text structure; include semantic maps, chains, and concept hierarchies; and assist the student to individualize the rhetorical structure of the text.

Although much of the research on strategic teaching focuses on native English speakers, more recent efforts to study linguistically diverse students' use of these strategies show similar success (Hernández, 1991). Strategic teaching improved the students' reading comprehension, as well as their conscious use of effective learning strategies in their native language. Students, despite limited English proficiency, are able to transfer or apply their knowledge of specific learning strategies and text structure to English reading texts. One particular strategic reading program, *Reciprocal Teaching*, designed to improve reading comprehension of elementary-aged students and emphasizing scaffolding strategies through teacher–student and student–student dialogue, appears to be quite promising despite the fact that it has not been thoroughly studied in schools serving large numbers of Latino students (Fashola, Slavin, Calderón, & Durán, 2002). This strategic learning approach, similar to the approach described above, encourages students to learn that concepts and ideas are phenomena to be generated and understood, not just facts to be passively memorized. Thus, students learn that they are active participants in their own learning. The explicit instruction and the naming of clear strategies for unlocking meaning help to demystify reading comprehension for many children not familiar with the process and to become more conscious of text structure and comprehension strategies. The characteristics of strategic instruction grow out of the premise that teachers actively and explicitly assist their students in appropriating previously unfamiliar academic discourses.

Gee (1996) reminds us that the social nature of teaching and learning must involve apprenticeship into the subject's or discipline's discourse in order for students to do well in school. Teachers act as cultural mentors when they introduce students to the classroom culture and discourse styles.

This apprenticeship includes acquisition of particular content matter, ways of organizing content, and ways of using language. These discourses are not mastered solely through teacher-centered and direct instruction but also by apprenticeship into social practices through scaffold interaction with people who have already mastered the discourse. The apprenticeship notion can be immensely useful with Latino students if it facilitates the acceptance and valorization of students' prior knowledge and the critical appropriation of new knowledge through the mentoring process. Students who come to see themselves as confident, capable, and able learners and develop the necessary cognitive and metacognitive learning skills and strategies cannot be held back—this is precisely the potential of strategic teaching.

Heterogeneous Cooperative Group Work

Heterogeneous cooperative group work has been described by Cohen (1994) as "a superior technique for conceptual learning, for creative problem solving, and for increasing oral language proficiency" (p. 6). The instructional approach can be described as students working together in groups small enough (four or five) so that each individual can equally participate on tasks that have been clearly assigned without direct and immediate intervention on the part of the teacher. In the review of effective programs for Latinos in elementary grades, research on cooperative instructional methods suggests positive effects on achievement in both elementary and secondary school (Fashola et al., 2002). The clear goal of improving children's higher-order thinking makes this program attractive for teachers of Latino students. In recognizing the ideological dimensions of schooling, it is also important to identify the potential of this instructional approach for changing status expectations of children perceived and treated as low-status by their classmates, as is often the case for Latino students. Cohen (1994) explains that in the society at large there are status distinctions and expectations made on the basis of social class, ethnic group membership, and gender. These status distinctions are often replicated at the classroom level unless teachers make conscious efforts to prevent their reproduction. For example, White students expect themselves and are expected by others to be smarter than non-White students. This model of group work can be used as a management and instructional tool that challenges students' expectations and teaches them the concept of *multiple abilities* (e.g., interpersonal intelligence, organizational ability, conventional academic ability, verbal ability, reasoning ability, and spatial and visual ability). Teachers work to convince their students that *all* students, including low-status students, possess multiple abilities and intelligences needed for successful group work. Students are taught that no person knows everything but that each person knows something useful that the rest of the group can benefit from.

To have students put into practice their changing expectations, teachers train them to take on specified roles, such as facilitator, checker, reporter, and recorder; and to learn group process skills, such as active listening, maintaining a positive group atmosphere, and ensuring equal participation. By assigning roles, explicitly teaching students to communicate with each other, and convincing them of their multiple abilities, the teacher works to prevent high-status students from constantly dominating group discussion and preventing low-status students from being further silenced and marginalized by peers during group work. In some cases, it is better for teachers to work individually with low-status students in order to increase their self-confidence and to prepare them to actively assume their role during group work. However, this level of heterogeneous cooperative group work, called *status engineering*, constitutes a very serious undertaking that should not be assumed unless the teacher is prepared to see it through. Another strategy is to create group work activities that require a type of expertise or ability already mastered by the low-status student and to then have the student teach his or her peers that particular skill. Beyond anecdotal evidence, Cohen (1994) offers improved standardized test scores as proof of the effectiveness of the heterogeneous group in improving Latino students' academic and English language skills.

The teacher's role as cultural mentor is a significant one in socially engineering learning contexts where low-status students come to see themselves as competent and able learners. Similarly, it is important that teachers confront issues of unequal status and low status in the classroom. Educators must recognize that, often, the classroom social hierarchy reflects the greater societal hierarchy in terms of student markers such as gender, ethnicity, socio-economic status, language proficiency, and special education standing. Teachers can support positive social change in the classroom by creating and utilizing heterogeneous cooperative groups for the purpose of modifying low-status roles of individuals or groups of children.

CONCLUSION

The task of effectively educating Latino students is not an easy one. The educational challenges facing Latino students and their teachers are numerous and complex. It has not been the intention of this chapter to suggest that teacher ideological clarity and empowering instructional approaches are sufficient for remedying Latino educational underachievement. A full-fledged attempt to improve the education of Latino students would require multi-faceted, multi-tiered, and collaborative mobilization that would include courageous and ideologically clear educators, parents, specialists, administrators, and policy makers at local, state, and national levels.

The intention of this chapter has been to bring to the fore of this discussion the urgent need for educators to address the ideological dimensions of Latino education and remind educators that when addressing current-day educational challenges, it is necessary to assume a socio-historical stance. In this way, we will see and *name* our historical tendency in this society of providing Latino and other subordinated student populations with substandard schooling experiences. By recognizing this invisible backdrop, educators can begin to critically examine teaching practices for their potential to create learning contexts where students empower themselves as part of the process of acquiring academic knowledge and skills. Specific teaching methods, in and of themselves, are not the significant factors in improving Latino students' academic performance. The actual strengths of the methods depend, first and foremost, on the degree to which they reflect a humanizing and empowering pedagogy that values the students' background knowledge, culture, and life experiences and creates learning contexts where power is shared by students and teachers. The critical issue is the degree to which educators hold the moral conviction that solutions lie not in methods but in ideologically clear and committed educators who seek to treat all students with the respect and dignity they deserve. Consequently, in addition to acquiring technical skills, teachers need to begin to develop the ideological clarity that will guide them in denouncing discriminatory school and classroom realities so as to instruct, protect, and advocate for their students. Simply put, teachers need to recognize the discriminatory educational practices before they can become agents of change working for more democratic practices both in the schools and in the greater society. Freire (1997) challenges educators to see the dense fog of ideology and to become courageous in their commitment to defend subordinated student populations, such as Latino students in the United States, even when it is easier not to take a stand. He says: "One has to believe that if men and women created the ugly world that we are denouncing, then men and women can create a world that is less discriminating and more humane" (p. 315).

REFERENCES

Anyon, J. (1997). *Ghetto schooling: A political economy of urban educational reform*. New York: Teachers College Press.

Au, K. H., & Mason, J. (1983). Cultural congruence in classroom participation structures. *Discourse Processes, 6*(4), 145–168.

Bartolomé, L. I. (2002). Creating an equal playing field: Teachers as advocates, border crossers, and cultural brokers. In Z. F. Beykont (Ed.), *The power of culture: Teaching across language difference* (pp. 167–191). Cambridge, MA: Harvard Education Publishing Group.

Bartolomé, L. I. (1998). *The misteaching of academic discourses: The politics of language in the classroom*. Boulder, CO: Westview Press.

Bartolomé, L. I., & Balderrama, M. (2001). The need for educators with political and ideological clarity: Providing our children with "the best." In M. Reyes

& J. Halcón (Eds.), *The best for our children: Critical perspectives on literacy for Latino students* (pp. 48–64). New York: Teachers College Press.

Bloom, G. M. (1991). The effects of speech style and skin color on bilingual teaching candidates' and bilingual teachers' attitudes toward Mexican American pupils. Unpublished. Stanford University.

Blum, V. C. (1985). Private elementary education in the inner city. *Phi Delta Kappan, 66*(9), 643–646.

Byrk, A., Lee, V., & Holland, P. (1993). *Catholic schools and the common good.* Cambridge, MA: Harvard University Press.

Cazden, C. B. (1988). *Classroom discourse: The language of teaching and learning.* Portsmouth, NH: Heinemann.

Cohen, E. (1994). *Designing group work: Strategies for the heterogeneous classroom.* New York: Teachers College Press.

Delpit, L. (1995). *Other people's children: Cultural conflict in the classroom.* New York: New Press.

Donato, R. (1997). *The other struggle for equal schools: Mexican Americans during the civil rights era.* Albany, NY: SUNY Press.

ERIC Clearinghouse on Urban Education. (2001). *Latinos in schools: Some facts and findings.* ERIC Digest, Number 162. (ERIC Document Reproduction Service No. ED 4499288)

Fashola, O. S., Slavin, R. E., Calderón, M., & Durán, R. (2002). Effective programs for Latino students in elementary and middle schools. In R. E. Slavin & M. Calderón (Eds.), *Effective programs for Latino students* (pp. 1–66). Mahwah, NJ: Lawrence Erlbaum Associates.

Figlio, D. N., & Stone, J. A. (1999). *School choice and student performance: Are private schools really better?* (Institute for Research on Poverty Discussion Paper No. 1141–97). University of Wisconsin–Madison, September 1997.

Flores, B., & Díaz, E. (2001). Teacher as sociocultural, sociohistorical mediator: Teaching to the potential. In M. Reyes & J. J. Halcon (Eds.), *The best for our children: Critical perspectives on literacy for Latino students* (pp. 29–47). New York: Teachers College Press.

Freire, P. (1998). *Pedagogy of freedom: Ethics, democracy, and civic courage.* Lanham, MD: Rowman & Littlefield.

Freire, P. (Ed.). (1997). *Mentoring the mentor: A critical dialogue with Paulo Freire.* New York: Peter Lang.

Gee, J. P. (1996). *Social linguistics and literacies: Ideology in discourses* (2nd ed.). Philadelphia: The Falmer Press.

Goldhaber, D. D., & Eide, E. R. (2002). What do we know (and need to know) about the impact of school choice reforms on disadvantaged students? *Harvard Educational Review, 72*(2), 157–176.

Gomez, M. L. (1994). Teacher education reform and prospective teachers' perspectives on teaching "other people's children." *Teaching and Teacher Education, 10*(3), 319–334.

Gonsalves, R. (1996). Resistance in the multicultural education classroom. Unpublished manuscript. Harvard Graduate School of Education.

Hernández, J. S. (1991). Assisted performance in reading comprehension strategies with non-English proficient students. *The Journal of Educational Issues of Language Minority Students, 8*, 91–112.

Jones, B. F., Palinscar, A. S., Ogle, S. D., & Carr, E. G. (1987). *Strategic teaching and learning: Cognitive instruction in the content areas.* Alexandria, VA: Association for Supervision and Curriculum Development in cooperation with the Central Regional Educational Laboratory.

Macedo, D. (1991). The tongue-tying of America. *Boston University Journal of Education, 173*(2), 9–20.

McLeod, B. (Ed.). (1994). *Language and learning: Educating linguistically diverse students.* Albany, NY: SUNY Press.

Merritt, C. (2001). Catholic schools and their response to disadvantaged populations. Unpublished manuscript. University of Massachusetts, Boston.

National Center for Education Statistics. (1992). *American education at a glance.* Washington, DC: Office of Education Research and Improvement.

Polite, V. C. (1992). Getting the job done well: African American students and Catholic schools. *Journal of Negro Education, 61*(2), 211–222.

Reyes, M. L. (1992). Challenging venerable assumptions: Literacy instruction for linguistically different students. *Harvard Educational Review, 62,* 427–446.

Reyes, P., Scribner, J. D., & Paredes Scribner, A. (Eds.). (1999). *Lessons from high-performing Hispanic schools: Creating learning communities.* New York: Teachers College Press.

Sanchez, L. (2002, August). Panel targets Latino education gap. *San Diego Union-Tribune,* p. B2.

Valenzuela, A. (1999). *Subtractive schooling: US-Mexican youth and the politics of caring.* Albany, NY: SUNY Press.

Villegas, A. M., & Lucas, T. (2002). *Educating culturally responsive teachers: A coherent approach.* Albany, NY: SUNY Press.

White House Initiative on Educational Excellence for Hispanic Americans. (1999). *Latinos in education.* Washington, DC. (ERIC Document Reproduction Service No. ED 440817)

Zehr, M. A. (2001). Hispanic group quietly initiates big charter push. *Education Week on the Web,* November 21.

Zimpher, N. (1989). The RATE Project: A profile of teacher education students. *Journal of Teacher Education, 40*(6), 27–30.

Chapter 4

The Struggle of Access: The Achievement Trends of Latino Youth in Middle and High School

Alberto M. Ochoa

INTRODUCTION

The education of middle and high school Latino students is characterized by two restricting problems, academic access to the core curriculum and access to college. Our public schools are stratified institutions in which some students are provided with *high-status* knowledge that yields social and economic control. Others are relegated to a second-class citizenship both within our K–12 public school system and in the larger society (Barrera, 1988; Darder, 1995; Kitchen, 1990; Velasquez, 1994). Today, our public schools continue to treat our Latino students as second-class citizens and fail to nurture their bicultural educational development. Maintaining a free and open democracy demands that we actively pursue equity and excellence for Latino youth, two values that require vision, resources, high biliteracy standards, accountability, public policy commitment, and community responsibility (Kozol, 1991; Macedo & Bartolomé, 1999; McCaleb, 1994).

The United States promotes values of an egalitarian society, yet in the institution of education one is faced with differentiated educational practices linked to economic and political inequality among different segments of society. The Latino student presently faces many obstacles to achieve educational equity and excellence. The premises of equality, fairness, and reasonableness that we proudly proclaim as national cultural standards require that we examine these two values and the implications that may impact our student communities. This chapter examines Latino middle and high school students, a student population at risk. It presents a demographic profile and discusses issues of access and academic achievement, student dropouts, conditions hindering the development of Latino youth, and communities' and parents' involvement.

DEMOGRAPHIC CHARACTERISTICS

The national profile on Latinos documents that while Latino subgroups vary considerably in their levels of poverty and education, the gap between Latinos overall and the general U.S. population is significant (U.S. Department of Commerce, 2000). The profile of Latinos in the United States consists of 63.4% Mexican, 14.3% Central or South American, 11.0% Puerto Rican, 7.3% other Latino, and 4.0% Cuban (U.S. Department of Commerce, 1998). With respect to educational attainment levels, no Latino subgroup is at parity with non-Latino Whites, almost 9 in 10 of whom are high school graduates (88%). For other Latino subgroups, only half of Latinos of Mexican origin (50%) have a high school diploma. This proportion ranges from two-thirds or 64% each for Puerto Ricans and Central and South Americans to 70% for Cubans.

Parents' educational attainment is a strong predictor of a post-secondary education (Darder, 1995). Using the percentage distribution of 1992 high school graduates in which neither parent had any post-secondary education, about 14% of Latinos received a high school diploma, 8% completed some college, including vocational or technical, and about 4% had a bachelor's degree or higher (National Center for Educational Statistics [NCES], 2001, p. xxi). These low levels of education are stifling the economic potential of Latinos and have contributed to the high poverty rate among them. More than three times as many Latinos (26%) are poor as non-Latino Whites (8%). Poverty is especially serious for Latino children; one-third are poor, compared to about 1 in 10 non-Latino White children. While the U.S. Census Bureau (2000) confirms that there are differences between Latino subgroups in their levels of education and income, it also shows that all Latino subgroups need to close, and have a stake in closing, the education gap that exists between the Latino community and the rest of the U.S. population. Moreover, the census data indicate that no Latino subgroup is immune from higher-than-average poverty rates (National Council of La Raza, 2000).

National characteristics of students by race and ethnicity in public schools are presented in Table 4.1, providing the pattern of Latino students growth at the K–12 level for the past 28 years. This table indicates that the proportion of ethnically diverse students in public schools increased between 1972 and 1999. K–12 Latino students increased from 6.0% in 1972 to 16.2% in 1999. In addition, the proportion of Latinos in public elementary and secondary schools increased at a greater rate than the pro-

Table 4.1
Percent Racial Ethnic Distribution, K–12

Year	White	Black	Latino	Other	%
1972	77.8	14.8	6.0	1.4	100
1977	76.1	15.8	6.2	1.9	100
1982	71.9	16.0	8.9	3.2	100
1987	68.5	16.6	10.8	4.0	100
1992	66.8	16.9	12.1	4.3	100
1995	65.5	16.9	14.1	3.5	100
1999	61.9	16.5	16.2	5.5	100

portion of Blacks (NCES, 2002). It is projected that between 1995 and 2025, California, Texas, and Florida will have the greatest state population growth gains—more than 6 million people to each state. In this period, the five fastest growing states (in rank order) are projected to be California, New Mexico, Hawaii, Arizona, and Nevada (U.S. Department of Commerce, 1995).

Examining data from California, the state that has the most Latino students in our nation, we can see some trends and challenges that are facing our youth:

1. Latino students in California will increase from 18.61% in 1985 to 53.43% in 2015, while Euro-American students will decrease from 62.22% in 1985 to 23.11% in 2015 (California Basic Educational Data Systems, 2001). Nationally, it is projected that Latinos will account for 20 percent of the U.S. population by 2020 (National Council of La Raza, 2001).

2. During the last 20 years, by the third grade, 80% of English-proficient Latino students are already underachieving in the basic skills of reading, writing, and math (California Basic Educational Data Systems, 2001).

3. Over 1.5 million students in 2001 in California were English language learners, of whom over 80% spoke Spanish. In the year 2015, over 3.5 million students will enter school with a home language other than English (California Basic Educational Data Systems, 2001).

4. In California, fewer than 21 of every 100 Latino high school graduates have taken the necessary course work to have access to the University of California or California State University systems (Latino Educational Summit, 2001).

5. Approximately 25 of every 100 Latino students drop out of school. Furthermore, over 40% of all students in juvenile court schools are Latinos. Related to this trend, profiles of arrestees indicate that 30% of all adults and 6% of juveniles are Latino (Latino Educational Summit, 2001).

In our nation, fewer than 25% of all Latino students complete high school with the necessary course work and academic rigor to have access to higher education (National Council of La Raza, 2001). For the remaining 75% of our students, underskilled Latino youth become dependent on social and economic assistance, and this disempowers them to become contributors to our society. Disempowerment is a condition that is visible as early as the third grade for our ethnically diverse students. In responding to this disempowering condition, schools tend to begin to implement promising practices to arrest the underachievement of low-income, ethnically diverse students at the junior and high school level. Unfortunately it is six to eight years too late—after the problem of underachievement began (Rumberger, 1998).

ACCESS AND ACADEMIC ATTAINMENT: ACHIEVEMENT TRENDS

In middle and high school the academic attainment of Latino students is alarming. Academic rigor in our schools is lacking for Latino students. In 1997, Latinos represented 7.5% of Advanced Placement (AP) math students and 6.7% of AP science students, while 8.2% of AP math students and 8.5% of AP science students were Black. In the same year, Whites represented 72.4% of AP math students and 72.8% of AP science students. The National Center for Educational Statistics (2001) reports that low-income children, mostly from culturally diverse backgrounds, begin kindergarten with lower reading and mathematics skills than do more advantaged children. Furthermore, the center reports that high school reading, math, and science performance is strongly associated with eventual enrollment in a four-year institution. When the achievement trends over the past 20 years are examined for Latino 13- and 17-year-olds in the three content areas, we find that their achievement is not competitive with the achievement or preparation of White students in our nation.

Specifically, the National Center for Educational Statistics (2000) in its report of reading trends (1971–1999) for 13- and 17-year-olds by race and ethnicity documents the low achievement of Latino students in our schools (see Table 4.2). While the achievement gap between K–12 White and Latino students has decreased over the years, it has remained over 23 points for both 13- and 17-year-olds. Furthermore, these trends do not provide the comprehensive profile of Latino students; the data are one-dimensional in assessing reading in both English and Spanish. The data also fail to account for the kind of reading programs or the type of literacy curriculum used in our schools or the literacy policy that guides school programs. Among the issues of concern is the posture of the educational system that fails to account for the large number of Latino students whose first language is other

Table 4.2
Reading Performance: Scale Scores of 13- and 17-Year-Olds

Year	White 13 & 17		Black 13 & 17		Latino 13 & 17	
1971	261	291	222	239	—	—
1975	262	293	226	241	233	252
1980	264	293	233	243	237	261
1984	263	295	236	264	240	268
1990	262	297	241	267	238	275
1994	265	296	234	266	235	263
1999	267	295	238	264	244	271

Table 4.3
Math Performance: Scale Scores of 13- and 17-Year-Olds

Year	White 13 & 17		Black 13 & 17		Latino 13 & 17	
1973	274	310	228	270	239	277
1978	272	306	230	268	238	276
1986	274	308	249	279	254	283
1990	276	309	249	289	255	284
1994	281	312	252	286	256	291
1999	283	315	251	283	259	293

than English. School districts in general do not view the biliteracy or the rich linguistic background of Latino students as an educational asset.

In the area of math, the National Center for Educational Statistics (2001) in its report of math trends (1973–1999) for 13- and 17-year-olds by race and ethnicity further documents the low achievement of Latino students in our schools (see Table 4.3). The science trends for 13- and 17-year-olds by race and ethnicity also document the low achievement of Latino students in our schools (NCES, 2001) (see Table 4.4).

Scale scores over 19 years suggest that while the achievement gap between Latino and White students has decreased, the gap continues to be large. This gap is a significant factor regarding why Latino students drop out (Espinosa & Ochoa, 1992; Rumberger, 1998). On an annual basis, Latino students leave school at an alarming rate. What can be generalized from these math and science trends? Latino students continue to be denied

Table 4.4
Science Performance: Scale Scores of 13- and 17-Year-Olds

Year	White 13 & 17		Black 13 & 17		Latino 13 & 17	
1970	263	312	215	258	—	—
1977	256	298	208	240	213	263
1986	259	298	222	253	226	259
1992	267	304	224	256	238	270
1996	266	307	226	260	232	269
1999	266	306	227	254	227	276

a rigorous curriculum in math and science, two essential and necessary skill areas in accessing higher education and the four major economic sectors in our society—the space, informational, oceanic, and cybernetic industries.

DROPOUT AND DISEMPOWERMENT OF LATINO YOUTH

The consequences of ignoring or articulating minor responses to high school dropout rates in this country are severe. At an epidemic level, young people, especially Latino low-income youth, are leaving the educational system and falling into life-threatening predicaments that keep them poor, dependent, and vulnerable (Ochoa, 1995). At the national level, the Center for Community Change (2001) has also documented that up to 60% of children in low-income communities leave school before graduating from high school. Each year, over the last decade, there were at least 3.4 million young people who were not in high school and lacked a high school diploma. Over the past decade, 347,000 to 544,000 10th–12th graders dropped out of high school each year (Fletcher, 2001).

Furthermore, the consequences and costs of dropping out of high school are not simply an individual decision, but also a community concern. Every community bears significant consequences. It is projected that 80% of all federal prisoners and 75% of youth involved in the juvenile court system are high school dropouts (Center for Community Change, 2001). It costs an estimated $51,000 per prisoner per year to address their incarceration, yet the reasons that young students drop out of school are multiple and complex. The more trauma and instability in adolescent lives, the more obstacles in their education and development. It is also understood that underskilled and undereducated youth will have difficulty maintaining a job. If a student drops out and stays out of the workforce for a significant amount of time, the consequence can last a lifetime.

CONDITIONS HINDERING THE DEVELOPMENT OF LATINO YOUTH

Today, the 100 largest urban school systems in our nation contain over 25% of all K–12 African American students, over 50% of all Latino students, and 50% of all Asian students. These 100 urban school districts have a substantial impact on the human capital of the nation (Pearl & Knight, 1999). Within the communities of these urban districts, one finds significant student disempowerment. Most of these students are poor and lacking the skills to succeed in school and in the workforce. An overwhelming number seek jobs in the service industry that pay minimal wages while living in a costly capitalist economy that often requires taking two or three jobs to pay for food and rent.

In response to the achievement gap, educational reforms have been proposed. Examination of the literature on educational reform during the past 20 years suggests that reforms have ranged from classroom teacher-centered instruction (Cremin, 1988; Darling-Hammond, 2000) to centralizing and decentralizing authority to govern schools (Lambert, 1995). Yet, most reforms have had little impact on the large urban centers of our nation (California Tomorrow, 1995). It is important for policy makers, educators, researchers, and administrators to understand why reforms are rarely effective. Such understanding calls for pursuing problems that match the school context and solution. This requires an understanding of national economic shifts, the demands of the workforce, and public policy directed at enhancing the skills of youth. It requires school leadership and governance that implement academic expectations, school structures that are conducive to learning, staff expertise that matches student needs, curricula designed to prepare youth for a post-industrial informational society, and social support for work-study that connects youth to the world of work and exposure to career choices.

To move the agenda of educational reform from looking at poverty as the simple solution to explain why Latino and ethnically diverse students do not achieve at the level of White students, we need to examine conditions that hinder and contribute to the success of low-income students. Seven conditions are briefly discussed that negatively impact upon the quality of education received by Latino students: school structural conditions, low standards or lack of curriculum rigor, status equalization, parent participation, lack of school accountability, absence of professional development, and biliteracy.

School Structural Conditions

School structural conditions are related to school size and zoning. Existing research that points to school size at the elementary level is highly correlated with achievement, with 650 students being the threshold for predicting student success (Espinosa & Ochoa, 1992). The majority of low-income Latino students attend schools that exceed 1,000 students. Zoning regulations serve as a driving condition of school overcrowdedness. For example, with respect to school size, research suggests that urban elementary schools that have over 650 students tend to be ethnically impacted, have the minimum basic funds, and have large categorical programs and funding that have a negative bearing on student learning and motivation (Orfield & Yun, 1999). Thus, in low-income communities one finds large schools while in middle- and upper-income communities one finds small schools below a 500 average daily student attendance. Furthermore, large schools are often segregated and overcrowded. In addition, large schools have the highest number of limited-English-proficient students. Hence, school size at the elementary level and structural conditions certainly contribute to the underachievement of students.

The types of schools Latino students attend have powerful implications regarding the beginning of their underachievement and the possible solutions. In addition, with respect to school structural conditions, their school size, teacher retention, unpredictable, year-by-year budgetary allocations, and inadequate school facilities disempower many ethnically diverse school communities. This situation creates conditions of overcrowding, absence of capital improvement, diminishing educational and recreational space, delimiting classroom and support service space, lack of school safety, high number of inexperienced staff to address the needs of students, overloaded administrative responsibilities in managing the school site, and commissioned zoning conditions that allow for overcrowded school communities (Orfield & Yun, 1999).

Low Standards or Lack of Curriculum Rigor

Educational reform in the 1980s and 1990s and the push for standards in the 1990s failed to improve the achievement of Latino students. In the 1990s, Latino 15- to 17-year-olds were more likely than Whites to be below grade level (NCES, 2001). We know that in order to take AP courses in high school, one must begin taking the prerequisite core course in 7th grade. Yet, placement in these courses is driven by test results in 5th grade and by teacher recommendations. Thus, academic rigor is a process that must be in place and ongoing from kindergarten to 12th grade. It is imperative that Latino youth be provided with school interventions that demand high standards and expectations. Latino parents need to monitor the educational services provided to their children, specifically ensuring that the curriculum is not compensatory or remedial. Monitoring grade level standards and school performance are two essential tasks for parents to undertake on an ongoing basis. It is advantageous for both the student and the community. These interventions must be carefully planned, addressing the core curricular educational needs of students and preparing them for the world of work in our information-driven society. Above all, there is a need for the early identification of academic gap as based on what standards students are expected to achieve at each grade level (Macedo & Bartolomé, 1999).

Status Equalization

In the United States, the best schools that have an ethnically diverse population do not approach the achievement of low-achieving schools that have mostly White students (Macedo & Bartolomé, 1999; Romo & Falbo, 1996). Tracking in our schools continues to be prevalent; there is an absence of status equalization in our schools. Status equalization is measured by a student sense of belonging in all aspects of the school curricular and extracurricular activities. Research on educational organizations documents that our public schools are stratified institutions (Pearl & Knight, 1999). School expectations and human capital point to the expectations of parents and school personnel as directly empowering or disempowering student school success (Stanton-Salazar, 1997). For example, school achievement expectancies channel students into five respective curricular tracks—remedial, vocational, non-college-bound, college-bound, and gifted. These tracks are designed to address the characteristics and perceived needs of children that are often determined by the zoning and housing density patterns of a school district, the low-income status of the student, language background of the community, parent occupation, welfare incidence, and transience in the community. Maintaining high expectations demands that we actively pursue equity and excellence for ethnically diverse and low-income youth (Gordon, Piana, & Keleher, 2002).

Parent Participation

While the research on parent involvement speaks to the importance of their inclusion to raise student achievement, few schools actively integrate parents (Núñez, 1994; Romo & Falbo, 1996; Wink, 2000). Parental interactions with schools are inconsistent and do not address the barriers of meaningful school participation. For the most part, schools do not inform parents about how they can be connected to the education of their children and how they can collaborate with the school. Informing parents also requires the use of multidimensional modalities of learning and communicating. The most frequently used approach in communicating with parents is via paper announcements written in a jargon that only educators understand. Also, many low-income parents work two or more jobs or have to face the hard edge of daily concerns with basic housing, medical care, food, and safety. If parent participation means engaging parents in the education of their children, it should accommodate the schedules of parents, not of schools. Thus, there is a need to provide training to Latino parents on home–school collaboration that will enable them to monitor the academic achievement of their children and collaborate with the school in their social and academic development. This training will enable parents and the school to collaborate in order to yield high aspirations, positive self-esteem, self-respect, and productivity in ethnically diverse youth who are proud of their language and culture and personal development. Lastly, teacher training programs in our universities and school districts need to ensure that their prospective teachers and personnel possess a deep understanding of the rich socio-cultural context of their ethnically diverse students, specifically their bilingual, bicultural, and bicognitive skills. Such understanding should be based not on a deficit perspective that views the student as deprived, but from an additive perspective that recognizes the richness of the experiences and skills (Valencia, 1997).

Lack of School Accountability

There is an absence of data and accountability for assessing and developing the skills of middle and high school students to have access to the core curriculum or the course requirements yielding access to higher education. The absence of a systemic school accountability process to determine instructional and school program effectiveness allows schools to perpetuate educational expectancy bands that justify low achievement and student disempowerment. For many schools, accountability means performing to the expected socio-economic background of their students. Historically, school success has been based on schools' performing to their level of expectation (Mehan, Villanueva, Hubard, & Lintz, 1996; Ochoa & Hurtado, 1987). Ethnically diverse school communities must be provided with an accountability system that is designed to provide its youth with the core curriculum that prepares them for the informational economy of the world of work, while addressing the prevention of early underachievement. We must *mandate* educational excellence at every school, through a curriculum that is driven by state core curriculum standards and highly challenging learning. While standards do not recognize the bicultural or bicognitive characteristics of Latino students, they serve as a tool to increase the rigor of what our students should be able to perform. Standards need to be actualized through multiple modes of content delivery and assessment. The teaching methods should include reflective teaching practices, various inquiry and problem-posing models, didactic instruction, a variety of discussion methods and models for large and small group discourse, Socratic seminars, group interaction, role-playing, mock trials, and simulations.

Moreover, meaningful learning and teaching require thoughtful planning consistent with and exemplifying each teacher's pedagogical values for diversity and social justice.

Absence of Professional Development

Latino students attend schools that proportionally have the least experienced teachers. In the largest and most demanding schools in many low-income school communities it is not unusual to find that over 50% of teachers have only one to two years of teaching experience. (Mehan et al., 1996; Slavin, 1996). There is an absence of and thus a need for the rigorous professional development of prospective and credentialed teachers that nurtures their development and growth and that matches the academic and linguistic need of low-income school communities. Institutions of higher education and school systems must also be accountable for preparing teachers, counselors, and administrators who can incorporate the nature of pluralism and the diversity of school communities in the overall preparation of teacher candidates (García, 2001; Wink, 2000). Schools must bring forward credentialed staff that is trained to meet the diverse academic and linguistic learning needs of students. These teachers should demonstrate knowledge of the application of socio-cultural and linguistic diversity to cognition, learning, and schooling; concrete applications and strategies for ethnically diverse classrooms; and sensitivity in working with ethnically diverse parents as equal partners in the education of youth.

Biliteracy

Culturally and linguistically diverse students in our nation, specifically Latino students, are viewed as having linguistic deficits. This is so because the language policy of our nation fails to support the development of biliteracy (Miramontes, Nadeau, & Commins, 1997). Biliteracy is the development of academic proficiency in the primary language (L1), simultaneously with the development of language and academic proficiency in the second language (L2), resulting in academic biliteracy in both languages with competence to read, write, and articulate in at least two languages. Rather than promoting the biliteracy of our students, our schools and programs work to assimilate the students into an English-only curriculum without regard to the cognitive development of our students (García, 2001). More recently, as our country continues to be more ethnically diverse, English has become a political issue calling for establishment of English as the official language of the United States. Thus, as the world economy demands multiliteracy for our youth, our educational system continues to promote monolingualism (Crawford, 1999). Furthermore, we must view our students' linguistic diversity as a strength, not a weakness, and promote multilingual competence for all youth in order to connect our communities with the rest of the world through an English Plus and not English-only policy (Baker, 2001).

CONCLUSION

The steady increase of the U.S. Latino community throughout the last several decades has been well documented. Thus, there is an increased sense of urgency for efforts that seek to address the issues and challenges facing Latinos, especially low-income Latino communities. Combined with the Asian American and Native American populations, these groups now make up nearly one-third of the American population. They represent a significant force in America's economic, social, and political future. The achievement data of Latino students clearly show that we, as a nation, need to take some steps to promote education. We have the means and the opportunity to invest in efforts now that will pay huge dividends to all Americans in the future. While we continue to track our nation's changing diversity and population and make the decisions that will affect us all in the coming century, all Americans have a stake in applying one standard and one standard only—equal opportunity for all Americans.

Yet, national reports on educational equity continue to reveal gross inequalities. Throughout the nation, public schools continue to subject African American, Latino, and Native American students to a special kind of *racial profiling*. If public schools regularly failed to serve students of color in a single aspect of their education, that would be bad enough. However, diverse students are provided with less academically challenging courses, they are punished more frequently and more harshly, and they are pushed out of school without a diploma—all in much higher proportions than their White counterparts.

Thus, only when we recognize the real need for an educational system responsible for all our children will we commit the human and economic resources to make schools places where all of our children have opportunities to learn the kinds of skills in math, science, language, thinking, and problem solving that are demanded today. The United States and its school communities cannot afford to relegate any of its youth to the periphery of educational opportunity. Our communities must insist on sound, effective, efficient, and relevant preschool to university teacher education programs. With the achievements of science and social commitment of educators, we must demand quality education for all students, specifically at the middle and high school level and up to the university level. It is imperative that we intervene on behalf of our youth in order to transform their social, economic, and political opportunities and quality of life.

REFERENCES

Baker, C. (2001). *Foundations of bilingual education and bilingualism*. Clevedon Avon, England: Multilingual Matters.

Barrera, M. (1988). *Beyond Aztlan: Ethnic autonomy in comparative perspective*. Notre Dame, IN: University of Notre Dame Press.

California Basic Educational Data Systems. (2001). *CBEDS data 2001*. Sacramento, CA: California Department of Education.

California Tomorrow. (1995). *The unfinished journey: Restructuring schools in a diverse society*. San Francisco, CA: Author.

Center for Community Change. (2001). *Saved by an education: A successful model for dramatically increasing high school graduation rates in low-income neighborhoods*. Washington, DC: Author.

Crawford, J. (1999). *Bilingual education: History, politics, theory, and practice* (4th ed.). Los Angeles: Bilingual Educational Services.

Cremin, L. (1988). *American education: The metropolitan experience, 1876–1989*. New York: Harper & Row.

Darder, A. (Ed.). (1995). *Culture and difference: Critical perspectives*. Westport, CT: Bergin & Garvey.

Darling-Hammond, L. (2000). *Studies of excellence in teachers*. Washington, DC: National Commission of Teaching in America's Future.

Education Trust. (1996). *Education watch: The education trust community guide*. Washington, DC: Author.

Espinosa, R., & Ochoa, A. M. (1992). *The educational attainment of California youth: A public equity crisis*. San Diego, CA: San Diego State University.

Fletcher, M. A. (2001). Progress on dropout rates stalls. *Washington Post*, March 3, p. A1.

García, E. E. (2001). *Hispanic education in the United States: Raíces y alas*. New York: Rowman & Littlefield.

Gordon, R., Piana, L. D., & Keleher, T. (2002). *Facing consequences: An examination of racial discrimination in U.S. public schools*. Oakland, CA: Applied Research Center.

Kitchen, D. (1990). Educational tracking. Unpublished. San Diego University, Claremont Graduate School.

Kozol, J. (1991). *Savage inequalities: Children in America's schools*. New York: Harper Perennial.

Lambert, L. (1995). *The constructivist leader*. New York: Teachers College Columbia.

Latino Educational Summit. (2001). *Educational summit report 2001*. San Diego, CA: San Diego County Office of Education.

Macedo, D., & Bartolomé, L. (1999). *Dancing with bigotry*. New York: St. Martin's Press.

McCaleb, S. P. (1994). *Building communities of learners: A collaboration among teachers, students, families and community*. New York: St. Martin's Press.

Mehan, H., Villanueva, I., Hubard L., & Lintz, A. (1996). *Constructing school success: The consequences of untracking low achieving students*. New York: Cambridge University Press.

Miramontes, O., Nadeau, A., & Commins, N. (1997). *Linguistic diversity and effective school reform: A process for decision making.* New York: Teachers College Press.

National Center for Educational Statistics. (2002, March). *Mini-digest of education statistics 2001.* Washington, DC: U.S. Department of Education.

National Center for Educational Statistics. (2001). *The condition of education 2001.* Washington, DC: U.S. Department of Education.

National Council of La Raza. (2000). *NCLR President Report on the Hispanic Census Profile.* Washington, DC: National Council of La Raza.

National Council of La Raza. (2001) *NCLR Hispanic fact sheet.* Washington, DC: National Council of La Raza.

Núñez, R. (1994). Schools, parents and empowerment: An ethnographic study of Mexican American-origin parents' participation in their children's education. Unpublished. San Diego State University, Claremont Graduate School.

Ochoa, A. M. (1995). Language policy and social implications for addressing the bicultural immigrant experience in the United States. In A. Darder (Ed.), *Culture and difference: Critical perspectives* (pp. 179–198). Westport, CT: Bergin & Garvey.

Ochoa, A. M., & Hurtado, J. (1987). The empowerment of all students: A framework for the prevention of school dropouts. San Diego, CA: Policy Studies Department.

Orfield, G., & Yun, J. T. (1999). *Resegregation in American schools: The Civil Rights Project.* Boston: Harvard University Press.

Pearl, A., & Knight, T. (1999). *The democratic classroom: Theory to inform practice.* Cresskill, NJ: Hampton Press.

Romo, H. D., & Falbo, T. (1996). *Hispanic high school graduation: Defying the odds.* Austin: University of Texas Press.

Rumberger, R. W. (1998). Achievement for Latinos through academic success. In P. Gándara, R. Larson, R. Rumberger, & H. Mehan (Eds.), *Capturing Latino students in the academic pipeline* (pp. 3–12). Berkeley: University of California Press.

Slavin, R. E. (1996). Success for all: A summary of research. *Journal of Education for Students Placed at Risk, 1*(1), 41–76.

Stanton-Salazar, R. (1997). A social capital framework for understanding the socialization of racial minority children and youths. *Harvard Educational Review, 67*(1), 1–40.

U.S. Census Bureau. (2000). *March 2000 current population survey: The Hispanic population in the United States, population, characteristics.* Washington, DC: U.S. Government Printing Office.

U.S. Department of Commerce. (2000). *Current population survey: The Hispanic population in the United States, population characteristics.* Washington, DC: U.S. Bureau of the Census.

U.S. Department of Commerce. (1998). *Poverty status of the population in 1999 by sex, Hispanic origin, and race.* Washington, DC: U.S. Bureau of the Census.

U.S. Department of Commerce. (1995). *Population projections of the U.S. by age, sex, race and Hispanic origin: 1995 to 2050.* Washington, DC: U.S. Bureau of the Census.

Valencia, R. (1997). *The evolution of deficit thinking*. Bristol, PA: Taylor & Francis.

Velasquez, P. (1994). Chicano cultural variability and postsecondary retention and development: The relationship between student and institutional characteristics. Unpublished. San Diego State University, Claremont Graduate School.

Wink, J. (2000). *Critical pedagogy: Notes from the real world*. New York: Longman.

Chapter 5

Latino Students in Pursuit of Higher Education: What Helps or Hinders Their Success?

Alana M. Zambone and Margarita Alicea-Sáez

College is for the good, American persons, but not for me. I didn't think that I could have part of the American dream.
—Student testimony to the Hispanic Dropout Project, 1998, p. 11

INTRODUCTION

In U.S. culture, education is one of the major ways that individuals gain access to power and opportunity. Latino citizens, however, are less likely to earn a higher education degree than any other group in the United States. This means that their income potential and opportunity to contribute to governance and the larger culture are severely curtailed by their lack of post-secondary education. Limited educational attainment diminishes Latino citizens' quality of life. Moreover, the communities in which they live and the country as a whole lose the benefit of their full participation. Education, particularly higher education, has proven to be an important factor in furthering racial harmony and social integration across race, class, and geographic location. Because power and success are so closely linked to educational attainment, our notion of American society as equitable is severely challenged when a significant population group has limited educational achievement. Furthermore, it signifies that the American Dream is not only elusive but illusive.

The factors that restrict Latino students' success in higher education are complex. They include the ways in which educational institutions serve and support Latino learners, as well as attitudes and expectations on the parts of educators and the general society. This chapter provides an overview of the conditions that positively and negatively influence Latino youths' success in higher education programs. It is not designed to be a comprehensive review of research, model programs, and outcomes. Rather, it contextualizes the factors that mitigate Latino youths' realization of higher education success, particularly opportunity, support, and school–family partnerships. The first section provides an overview of the current state of higher education attainment for Latino citizens. The second section explores the dynamics that influence both admission to and completion of college and suggests some ways to better support Latino students in these efforts. The third section considers the relationship between school–family partnerships and success in higher education and offers some strategies for strengthening that partnership on behalf of Latino students. Future direction for research and conclusions are discussed in the final section.

LATINO CITIZENS' EDUCATIONAL ATTAINMENT AND ITS IMPACT

During the twentieth century, realization of the American Dream became inexorably linked to educational attainment. Yet, the percentage of Latino students who attend four-year colleges has not changed in the past 20 years. While 27% of the U.S. population hold four-year degrees, only 11% of Latinos 25 years of age or older have graduated from college (National Center for Education Statistics [NCES], 2002; President's Advisory Commission on Educational Excellence for Hispanic Americans [PACEEHA], 1996).

Many researchers and policy makers cite the negative impact of Latinos' low graduation rates on personal and national income. Young men who earn a bachelor's degree have incomes 150% higher than those with high school diplomas, and young women's income is twice as high with college completion (NCES, 2002). Limited educational attainment not only restricts income potential but also has far-reaching implications for our workforce. A review of demographic research indicates that over the next 25 years the number of White working-age adults will dwindle, while the number of Latino working-age adults will increase (Fry, 2002). This means that employers will have to fill their personnel needs from the population of young Latino citizens—additional justification for immediate action to improve their success in higher education.

Negative economic impact is only one of many reasons to be alarmed about the current state of educational opportunity and success for Latino youth and adults. With limited education, Latinos face vulnerability for the risk factors that are associated with low socio-economic status, including physical and mental health and cognitive, behavioral, and social concerns. Equally compelling, a group's limited educational achievement bounds the full range of benefits the nation can realize from their participation. The issues influencing Latino students' participation in higher education are directly linked to the educational opportunities and successes they experience from the beginning of their formal education. Other chapters in this book discuss the outcomes and implications of preschool, elementary, and secondary education for Latino students. The reader who is concerned about higher education for Latino students must be cognizant of the full educational context in order to understand and positively influence educational opportunities and outcomes in higher education.

FACTORS INFLUENCING SUCCESS IN HIGHER EDUCATION

Successful completion of a post-secondary program involves a multi-stage process that begins with gaining entry into an institution of higher education. The *Report on White House Strategy Session on Improving Hispanic Achievement* (U.S. Department of Education, 2000a) states that among young adults ages 18–24, only 27% of those who are Latino enroll in higher education, compared to 37% overall. This report further notes that Latino students constitute only about 6% of the students at four-year schools and 11% of the students in community colleges. The number of Latino students who go on to post-secondary education after successfully completing high school has not increased over the last 25 years. Between 1974 and 1999, the number of Latino students who enrolled in college the October after high school graduation decreased by 4.6%. The percentage increased during this time period by 19.1% for White students and 11.7% for African American students (NCES, 2002). Yet, an analysis of U.S. Census Bureau data from 1997 to 2000 reveals that the percentage of Latino American high school graduates of all ages who enroll in college is higher than the national average and every other ethnic group except Asian Americans (Fry, 2002).

To understand the apparent discrepancies in the data, we must consider both the percentage of Latino students who successfully complete secondary education and the age at which they enroll in some form of higher education. While in 2001 a higher percentage of Latino youth completed high school than in the previous 30 years, their graduation rate was only 63.2%, while the rate for the total population was 87.7% (NCES, 2002). Furthermore, statistics indicate that few Latino students enroll in higher education while they are of traditional college age. Examining higher education in two phases—gaining admission into college and completion of a two- or four-year degree—provides a format for exploring the specific issues and concerns that influence Latino students' success in post-secondary education.

Gaining Admission into Higher Education

The initial phase of higher education begins in middle or high school when students solidify their intent to go to college and begin the selection and application process. *Where are you going next year? Any word yet? What did you say in your essay? How'd your scores turn out?* These questions are heard annually in high schools throughout the country. They convey some of the excitement and anxiety felt by many high school seniors. The conditions that make these conversations possible include middle or high family income, friends who plan to enroll in college, rigorous academic preparation, and high parent education levels. Approximately 40% of Latino children are living below the poverty level, a figure that has steadily risen from 33% in 1985 (Federal Interagency Forum on Child and Family Statistics, 1998). Latino students are less likely to have friends who plan to go to college and access to a rigorous curriculum because they are more likely than White students to be enrolled in segregated schools with insufficient resources (White House Initiative on Educational Excellence for Hispanic Americans, 1999). A review of the educational and economic status of Latinos to date indicates that many students are likely to be the first in their family to pursue higher education. Given their numerous challenges, Latino students merit particular attention and support to ensure their successful participation in higher education.

For students who will be the first in their family to pursue higher education, school is their primary source for college-related information. The huge barrier of the cost of higher education necessitates guidance and assistance to access financial aid. Most high schools provide some form of guidance and career counseling to assist and advise students toward their career paths. But what happens if students do not know what their options might be? What happens when students with average to good grades are unsure about what questions to ask? What happens to students who do not see themselves as *college material*? Students who have grown up assuming that they are going to college, many of whom also know the school they want to attend, are familiar and accessible. Their families know what is expected and what is needed in order for them to attend college. These families and students know who to talk to and what questions to ask of school administrators. But what about Latino students, particularly those who are either at risk educationally or at a lower socio-economic level? Who ensures that these students access the assistance they need? In order to facilitate their admission to college, the U.S. Department of Education (2000b) recommends that schools begin to seek out and provide guidance and counseling to Latino students in middle school in order to make sure that students complete the courses that are required for college admission; get families involved in the education process; and regularly provide information and advice on the importance of "maintaining high grades, engaging in co-curricular activities, and mapping a plan to select a college, gain admission, and finance a college education" (p. 83).

Successfully Completing a College Program

Latino college students are less likely to attain a college degree than their White and African American peers. Furthermore, Latino college students are the only group whose rate of completion did not increase between 1988 and 2001 (NCES, 2002). The outcomes of numerous studies attempting to explain the failure of Latino youth to complete college can be broadly differentiated into personal attributions and institutional characteristics, including relationships between school personnel and students. To understand how these factors influence their success, we must consider the individual's traits in the context of the institution's environment and programs. We must also consider the cultural and historical contexts of Latino learners' educational experience from preschool through higher education, particularly the ways in which it shapes their participation in college preparation curricula, development of positive self-concept, and access to support and guidance.

Personal Attributions encompass an individual's context and experience, as well as personal characteristics such as cognitive and psychosocial traits. Contextual factors include educational history and socio-economic status, including time between high school graduation and matriculation to higher education, and full-time or part-time attendance. Successful participation in a rigorous secondary program is the strongest predictor of attainment of a bachelor's degree (Adelman, 1999). Yet, the PACEEHA (1996) notes that Latino students are often placed in general, basic high school courses. This means that they are less likely than White students to complete a curriculum that includes four years of English, geometry, advanced algebra and trigonometry, chemistry, physics, and biology. A rigorous secondary program of study not only provides the requisite knowledge and skills for college curriculum but communicates high expectations and high regard for a student's capacity to learn. It offers students an opportunity to develop a positive self-concept and gain leadership experience, both of which are correlated with good grade point averages during the first years of higher education (Ting, 1998).

Lower grades in higher education are significantly correlated with students' likelihood of dropping out (Hu & St. John, 2001). Middle and secondary course content and the skills students develop in those courses provide them with the capacity to successfully participate in higher education curricula. Success in the college curriculum requires students to comprehend and effectively use written language, apply higher-level thinking and problem-solving skills developed through advanced mathematics, and interpret data and make inferences. Because Latino students are likely to be underprepared for post-secondary education, they are at a disadvantage for success in college. While the achievement gap between White and Latino students is narrowing, Latino students continue to lag behind their White peers in literacy, mathematics, and science at age 17 (NCES, 1996).

Although class standing is a major factor in predicting academic success in the first year of college, if a student graduates at the top of her or his class from a high school with sub-standard curricula, class standing is a less powerful predictor. Students often must begin with remedial courses in a two-year college to gain the necessary skills and knowledge. These courses cost time and money, and their credits do not count toward the college degree. In 1994, about half of all Latinos who pursued higher education were enrolled in two-year community colleges (PACEEHA, 1996). While this can serve as a stepping-stone to a four-year degree, research shows that students who enroll in a two-year program are less likely to persist toward a four-year degree (NCES, 2002). While many Latino students want to transfer to four-year degree programs, barriers include the age and income requirements of the student, inconsistent and weak agreements between two- and four-year colleges, and lack of information and counseling about courses needed and sources of financial aid.

Latino students are more likely to be older than traditional college age when they enter college (Fry, 2002). This means that they are often supporting themselves and/or families and typically attend college part-time— two key factors in failure to complete a college education (King, 1999). While there are many reasons for delaying entry into college, a primary reason is cost. Many low-income students are reluctant to incur large debts and therefore resist loan programs. Many low-income Latino students do not have sufficient access to information about financial aid (Nevarez, 2001). Changes in the availability of financial aid other than loans, coupled with rising higher education costs, make it even more difficult for students to attend college without first securing employment. There is a positive relationship between hours of employment and reduction in the number of classes, access to the library, class choice, and grades, all of which further the likelihood of dropping out of higher education programs.

The psychosocial factors that are predictors of success and persistence beyond the first year include positive self-concept, realistic self-appraisal, demonstrated community service, knowledge acquired in a field, successful leadership experience, preference for long-range goals, ability to understand and cope with racism, and availability of a support person (Tracey & Sedlacek, 1987). Ting (1998) found that successful leadership experience and demonstrated community service are particularly strong predictors of success during the first year of college for low-income and first-generation students. Both of these play a role in the development of a positive self-concept and realistic self-appraisal. They also have the potential to expand the students' world as well as increase their knowledge, problem-solving ability, and network of friends and supporters.

In an exploratory study, Velasquez (1999) found that biculturalism and a sense of belonging are significant influences on Latino students' persistence in higher education. Students who are comfortable affiliating with White students and who also have positive perceptions of their primary culture and a well-developed ethnic identity are more likely to experience a sense of belonging. However, if a student's ethnic loyalty includes beliefs and attitudes that create tension between relationship-oriented goals and educational goals, particularly with regard to marriage and gender roles, realization of educational goals is more difficult (Nieman, Romero, & Arbona, 2000). Latino students' personal attributes are not the sole determinants of their attainment of higher education. Rather, Latino students' success in higher education is dependent on the interaction between the climate of the post-secondary institution and the student's experiences and traits. The more successful an institution is at welcoming Latino students and fostering a sense of belonging, the more likely the student's graduation.

Institutional Characteristics and Relationships can positively or negatively influence students' success, as indicated by the research on dropout prevention, effective schools, school restructuring, and projects such as the Hispanic Dropout Project (1998). The role of the institution in enabling students to build on or compensate for personal attributes that influence success is critical. When colleges encourage students' culture and personal identity and provide an opportunity to form supportive relationships, students can develop the sense of belonging that is necessary for persistence toward a degree. Latino students have high expectations that counselors and other sources of support are culturally sensitive and competent. When this is not the case, even students with strong academic backgrounds are more likely to drop out, and those who need assistance will not seek it (Constantine & Arorash, 2001).

On many campuses across the country, however, Latino students have difficulty finding Latino faculty and support personnel. Over 89% of faculty across the country are White (Wilds, 2000). Latino students are therefore much more likely to be required to act interracially with faculty than their White counterparts. Because faculty construct the curriculum, determine the quality of learning experiences in the classroom, and serve as mentors and advisors, the culture of higher-education institutions typically reflects a White, male, middle-class orientation (Beauboeuf-Lafontant & Augustine, 1996), leaving students feeling alienated because of their *differentness* (Gloria, Hird, & Navarro, 2001). "Minority students often contend with race-related assumptions about their academic ability, ambition, high school preparation, and faculty perceptions of minority students" (Anaya & Cole, 2001, p. 5). Those colleges whose cultures are aligned with the cultures of the Latino students report higher rates of suc-

cessful completion (Wolf-Wendel, 1998). Numerous approaches are prov-
ing effective, ranging from the Federal TRIO programs designed to
motivate and support students from middle school to post-baccalaureate
programs, to *Success for All*, which promotes school–family–community
partnerships (see U.S. Department of Education [USDOE], 2000b for profiles of numerous model programs, pp. A-1–A-34). These programs are effective, however, only when school personnel implement them within the
construct of what Freire (1995) calls "a pedagogy of hope," that is, from
a foundation of respect for the value and capacity of Latino students.

Despite legal mandates, a review of empirical research findings indicates
that racial and socio-ethnic bias and inequities persist on most campuses,
although they are less evident on racially diverse campuses (Chang, Witt-
Sandis, & Hakuta, 1999). These biases and inequities must be addressed
if Latino students are to succeed. The services and characteristics of institutions where students are successful include access to financial aid and
guidance; opportunities to build relationships with faculty; counseling and
support; instruction and other learning opportunities that match students'
learning styles and build on their strengths; and a connection between the
curriculum and students' life experiences as well as their future options.
The availability and effectiveness of these services and characteristics reflect
a belief in the capacity of Latino students and positive regard for their
culture. Without cultural acceptance and support, students will not feel as
if they *belong* and consequently will not make use of services and/or seek
assistance to facilitate their success in higher education.

The ways in which a congruent relationship between the culture of the
student and the culture of the institution influences success are complex.
Along with the likelihood of validation, cultural alignment makes it easier
for students to form high-quality relationships and experience frequent interactions with faculty outside of formal instruction, both significant variables in students' success. Latino students' positive relationships with
faculty were found to be much more important than their relationship to
other students. Research indicates that living on campus positively influences the achievement of most groups of students because, among other
reasons, it fosters students' connections to each other (Astin, 1993). Anaya
and Cole (2001) found no indication that residing either on campus or at
home significantly influences Latino students' success.

In an extensive study of predominantly White colleges and universities
that successfully graduate Latino, African American, and Native American
students, Richardson and de los Santos (1989) identified principles that
higher education institutions must embrace if they are serious about furthering Latino students' educational attainment. These can be summarized
as follows. Colleges and universities should:

1. Publicly commit to the goals of eliminating racial and ethnic disparities in degree achievement and ensuring educational opportunity

2. Back up this commitment by using the institution's discretionary funds to recruit, retain, and graduate Latino students

3. Employ Latinos in positions of leadership

4. Continually evaluate and disseminate progress toward the goals and ways in which evaluation results inform future efforts

5. Proactively provide comprehensive, integrated support services and financial aid

6. Emphasize the importance of a high quality of education and the impact on students' post–higher education opportunities

7. Reach out to community schools, agencies, and businesses to ensure adequate preparation, forge partnerships with families, provide information and guidance on financial aid and the application process, and demystify the campus and programs

8. Offer bridge programs to ensure that students have the tools and supports they need to be academically successful

9. Reward good teaching and mentoring of students and diversify the faculty

10. Actively foster and maintain a non-threatening social environment

FOSTERING FAMILY–SCHOOL PARTNERSHIPS

The decision to go to college is an outcome of students' knowledge, as well as their self-perception, particularly their sense of their own capacities, hopes, and opportunities. Students' knowledge and understanding of themselves and the world are constructed by their families, communities, and schools, each with its own cultural values, traditions, and expectations. When these values are aligned, the process of entering college begins early in a student's life, as is illustrated in the following conversations recorded by the authors in their work with diverse families and school districts across the country. The first, between Nancy and her 4th grade daughter, Amelia, shows the subtle ways in which children receive positive messages about their capacities and future possibilities when cultural values are aligned: "It's great that your teacher liked your project well enough to send it to the city science fair. If you keep up this kind of work, you'll be able to choose your college, not the other way around." To which Amelia responded, "That's sort of what my teacher said—and that maybe I'll be a scientist!" If we contrast this with another conversation overheard between Fernanda and her 5th grade son, Marcos, the issues that arise for students when there is not congruence across all of their *worlds* become evident:

"Son, I'm so proud of the way you helped your sister with her math homework! You're going to be the first person in this family to go to college!" To which Marcos replied, "If we win the lottery. But you know, the teacher said the other day when I helped her change her tire that she was glad to see I was so handy—it would be great if I went to technical school—but she never said anything about that short story I worked so hard on and I bet I'll end up with B+s again this period!" Fernanda's response was, "Well, if you want to go to technical school, that is fine—but if you want to go to college, we'll find a way, and you're smart enough!" And Marcos answered, "Thanks Mom, but I don't think I am—and B's will never be good enough anyway so it looks like maybe mechanics for me!"

These two conversations reveal the message that many Latino children may receive from their families about the importance of respecting teachers and accepting their judgments. Because many Latino caregivers generally have a deep respect for teachers, they face a difficult dilemma when teachers' judgments underestimate a student's strengths and potential. Historically, teachers' perceptions of Latino students' academic ability and worth have been anchored in a deficit-based model, influencing both the instructional methods teachers use and the messages they send to students (San Miguel & Valencia, 1998). How do Latino families provide the motivation and instill the confidence needed to apply for and successfully complete college in the face of such powerful competing messages from teachers? Cooperation between schools, family, and community plays a key role in assuring that there is the alignment of values that is important for academic attainment.

When an academically rigorous program of study is designed in partnership with the student and the family, it provides a window into the values, perceptions, and expectations of higher education, easing transition and adjustment. This is particularly important for those students who are the first in their family to attend college. Families receive the assistance needed to negotiate the complexities and idiosyncrasies of selecting and applying for admission to post-secondary programs. In addition, families can better understand the time and performance pressures students are experiencing, increasing the likelihood of support for the students. Students, their families, and their peers can begin to wrestle with the dilemma of how to stay connected while the student may be gaining knowledge and skills that can set her or him apart from family and community members.

But what happens when families are not actively present or engaged in their children's learning in a way that matches schools' expectations? Does this mean that they do not care? More often than not, Latino families are placed into this category. They are not seen or heard from, and therefore school officials pass them off as uncaring (Tinkler, 2002). This is a terrible myth whose roots require further examination. Research shows that Latino families have high aspirations for their children (Kloosterman, 1999; Shannon, 1996), care deeply about their education (Trumbull, Rothstein-Fisch, Greenfield & Quiroz, 2001), and want to participate in their children's education (ERIC Clearinghouse on Urban Education, 1998). On the other hand, research shows that teachers perceive Latino families as not caring about their children's education (Lopez, 2001). The discrepancy rests, in large part, with differing ways of defining parental involvement and the roles of caregivers and teachers.

While teachers expect families to assist with homework, participate in school activities, and ask questions about homework and grades, Latino families may feel they are encroaching on schools' responsibilities or showing disrespect. What are their reasons for not engaging in their child's education in the ways that are valued by schools? First, as children, Latinos are raised to respect those in authority. Teachers, principals, administrators, and other school system officials are held in high regard (Trumbull et al., 2001). This is especially true of families who received little formal education. Another factor is that families often feel unwelcome by the school; for example, they are often ignored when entering a school, there are likely to be no school officials who are Latino, or there is no one who can speak to them in Spanish (Tinkler, 2002). In order for school officials to attract Latino families and involve them in their child's education, they must first gain their trust. Families must feel that their culture, values, presence, and competence are recognized and respected.

If the school and family are to work together to help the student, but the family does not feel free to ask questions or does not know what questions to ask, how do they help the student determine whether college is an option? Latino families must be offered an entry point into the child's education. To ensure that cooperative relationships develop, schools must make explicit their expectations of parental involvement and accommodate parents' constraints such as language, work schedules, and educational experiences. Therefore, extending an invitation to meet with key school personnel, such as the guidance counselor, about questions or concerns regarding college entrance is an important step in building collaboration on behalf of the student. School personnel must work with families beginning in middle school to make sure the student is properly progressing. Periodic meetings with the school are needed to accomplish this. Students' program, support, and extracurricular experiences must be reviewed and adjusted so the student can explore options and meet the requirements for college.

As Latino students think about which college or university they are interested in applying to and begin inquiring about the application process, the high school guidance office or its equivalent, as the repository for college entrance applications and financial aid forms, should reach out to them. Access to financial aid in the form of scholarships, grants, and loans is critical for many Latino students and their families. They must be informed of deadlines in a timely manner and receive the guidance and support they may need to complete this potentially unwieldy process. Costs such as examination and college application fees should be distributed over time so that they do not pose insurmountable barriers for students and their families. Guidance personnel should also gather and submit, on the students' behalf, copies of transcripts, letters of recommendation, and other supporting documents necessary for application to a college or university.

Families, regardless of cultural and socio-economic background, who are unaware of the process and requisites for college admission may find this process overwhelming. A typical response to their dilemma, however, *is there is plenty of information out there; the parent and student need only to ask*. This may be true of mainstream students, but Latino students are at higher risk because, in many instances, other family members have not been through the process themselves and are unaware of where to begin. Herein lies the biggest obstacle for Latino students. If students are unsure or if their grades are not well above average, they feel that the best they can do is to take remedial courses in a community college or directly enter the workforce. Students with language barriers are at an even greater risk and feel they can never be *good enough* (USDOE, 2000).

CONCLUSION

Extensive demographic data describe many aspects of the state of education for Latino students. There continues to be a paucity of research, however, with which to deepen understanding of this group of students and their needs or the conditions and approaches that can effectively increase their successful participation in higher education. What is evident is the need to address the beliefs and assumptions about their capacity that underlie many of the current practices. Most critical—and daunting—is the need for studies of effective approaches for changing the societal and institutional biases and inequities that result in Latino students' repeatedly voiced belief that educational success is not possible. We need to understand and determine how to effectively change attitudes and beliefs about Latino students and their families that reinforce students' negative perceptions of their educational capacity. Changing policies, organizational arrangements, and educational practices will not be successful unless we can also change attitudes, perceptions, and beliefs.

Much of the literature and research on the role and importance of school climate, support services, and other factors and programs addresses Latino students as a subset of students of color. Given the magnitude of the problem, research that is focused on Latinos is needed to more fully describe their characteristics and needs in the context of the current climate, policies, and procedures of our educational institutions. Too often, research describes Latino students and their families in isolation from these contexts, contributing to the perception that their lack of educational success is an outcome of some inherent deficit rather than failure of the nation's schools and other cultural institutions to recognize and address their strengths and needs. While we can note variables that influence success, such as poverty and late matriculation, we must conduct research that will yield: (a) appreciation of the underlying complexities, (b) a useful theoretical framework for approaching education and support of Latino students, and (c) empirically sound strategies and approaches for improving educational outcomes.

We are caught in a vicious cycle of ensuring that Latinos are in positions of leadership in all aspects of society, including post-secondary institutions, while struggling to provide them with the education they need to assume those positions. It is time to stop *admiring* the problem and begin *solving* it. It is our responsibility as educators and citizens to reverse Latino students' failure to successfully complete secondary and higher education.

REFERENCES

Adelman, C. (1999). *Answers in the toolbox: Academic intensity, attendance patterns, and bachelor's degree attainment*. U.S. Department of Education. Washington, DC: Office of Educational Research and Improvement.

Anaya, G., & Cole, D. (2001). Latina/o student achievement: Exploring the influence of student–faculty interactions on college grades. *Journal of College Student Development, 42*(1), 3–14.

Astin, A. (1993). *What matters in college? Four critical years revisited*. San Francisco: Jossey-Bass.

Beauboeuf-Lafontant, T., & Augustine, D. (Eds.). (1996). *Facing racism in education* (2nd ed.). Cambridge, MA: Harvard Educational Review.

Chang, M., Witt-Sandis, D., & Hakuta, K. (1999). The dynamics of race in higher education: An examination of the evidence. *Equity and Excellence in Education, 32*(2), 12–16.

Chavkin, N. F., & Gonzalez, D. L. (1995). *Forging partnerships between Mexican American parents and the schools*. Charleston, WV: ERIC Clearinghouse on Rural Education and Small Schools. (ERIC Document Reproduction Service No. ED 388489)

Constantine, M., & Arorash, T. (2001). Universal-diverse orientation and general expectations about counseling: Their relation to college students' multicultural counseling expectations. *Journal of College Student Development, 42*(6), 535–544.

ERIC Clearinghouse on Urban Education. (1998). *Hispanic parents support their daughters' success*. NPIN Acquisition: N 001008.

Federal Interagency Forum on Child and Family Statistics. (1998). *America's children: Key national indicators of well-being*. Washington, DC: U.S. Government Printing Office.

Freire, P. (1995). *Pedagogy of hope: Reliving pedagogy of the oppressed*. New York: Continuum.

Fry, R. (2002). *Latinos in higher education: Many enroll, too few graduate*. Washington, DC: Pew Hispanic Center.

Gloria, A., Hird, J., & Navarro, R. (2001). Relationships of cultural congruity and perceptions of the university environment to help-seeking attitudes by sociorace and gender. *Journal of College Student Development, 42*(6), 545–562.

Hispanic Dropout Project. (1998). *No more excuses: The final report of the Hispanic dropout project.* Washington, DC: U.S. Government Printing Office.

Hu, S., & St. John, E. (2001). Student persistence in higher education: Understanding racial and ethnic differences. *The Journal of Higher Education, 72*(3), 265–286.

King, J. (1999). *Money matters: The impact of race/ethnicity and gender on how students pay for college.* Washington, DC: American Council on Education.

Kloosterman, V. I. (1999). *Socio-cultural contexts for talent development: A qualitative study on high ability Hispanic bilingual students* (Research Monograph 99142). Storrs, CT: The National Research Center on the Gifted and Talented.

Lopez, G. (2001). The value of hard work: Lessons on parent involvement from an (im)migrant household. *Harvard Education Review, 71*(3), 416–437.

National Center for Education Statistics. (2002). *The condition of education 2002. NCES 2002–025.* Washington, DC: U.S. Government Printing Office.

National Center for Education Statistics. (1996). *Findings from the condition of education, 1996: Minorities in higher education. NCES 1997–372.* Washington, DC: U.S. Government Printing Office.

Nevarez, C. (2001). *Mexican Americans and other Latinos in post-secondary education: Institutional influences.* Charleston, WV: ERIC Clearinghouse on Rural Education and Small Schools. (ERIC Document Reproduction Service No. ED 459038)

Nieman, Y., Romero, A., & Arbona, C. (2000). Effects of cultural orientation on the perception of conflict between relationship and education goals for Mexican American college students. *Hispanic Journal of Behavioral Sciences, 22*(1), 46–63.

President's Advisory Commission on Educational Excellence for Hispanic Americans. (1996). *Our nation on the fault line: Hispanic American education.* Washington, DC: U.S. Government Printing Office.

Richardson, R. C., Jr., & de los Santos, A. (1989). Ten principles for good institutional practice in removing race/ethnicity as a factor in college completion. In M. Odell & J. Mock (Eds.), *A crucial agenda: Making colleges and universities work better for minority students* (pp. 71–77). Boulder, CO: Western Interstate Commission for Higher Education.

San Miguel, G., & Valencia, R. (1998). From the treaty of Guadalupe Hildalgo to Hopwood: The educational plight and struggle of Mexican Americans in the Southwest. *Harvard Educational Review, 68*(3), 353–412.

Shannon, S. (1996). Minority parental involvement: A Mexican mother's experience and a teacher's interpretation. *Education & Urban Society, 29*(1), 71–84.

Ting, S. (1998). First-year grades and academic progress of college students of first-generation and low-income families. *The Journal of College Admissions,* Winter, 15–23.

Tinkler, B. (2002). *Assets for Colorado youth research report: A review of the literature on Latino parent involvement in K–12 education.* Denver: University of Denver Press.

Tracey, T., & Sedlacek, W. (1987). Predicting college graduation using non-cognitive variables by race. *Measurement and Evaluation in Counseling and Development, 19,* 177–184.

Trumbull, E., Rothstein-Fisch, C., Greenfield, P. M., & Quiroz, B. (2001). *Bridging cultures between home and schools: A guide for teachers.* Mahwah, NJ: Lawrence Erlbaum Associates.

U.S. Department of Education. (2000a). *Report on the White House Strategy Session on Improving Hispanic Achievement.* Washington, DC: U.S. Government Printing Office.

U.S. Department of Education. (2000b). *Helping Hispanic students reach high academic standards: An idea book.* Washington, DC: U.S. Government Printing Office.

Velasquez, P. (1999). *The relationship between cultural development, sense of belonging, and persistence among Chicanos in higher education: An exploratory study.* Paper presented at the Annual Meeting of the Association for the Study of Higher Education, San Antonio, TX.

White House Initiative on Educational Excellence for Hispanic Americans. (1999). *Educational standards, assessment, and accountability: A new civil rights frontier.* Washington, DC: U.S. Government Printing Office.

Wilds, D. (2002). *Minorities in higher education 1999–2000 seventeenth annual status report.* Washington, DC: American Council on Education.

Wolf-Wendel, L. (1998). The baccalaureate origins of successful European American women, African American women, and Latinas. *The Journal of Higher Education, 69*(2), 141–186.

Chapter 6

Bilingual Latino Students:
The Contexts of Home and School

Aquiles Iglesias and Leah C. Fabiano

INTRODUCTION

In his delivery of the landmark U.S. Supreme Court decision on *Lau v. Nichols* (1974), Justice Douglas reaffirmed the then Department of Health, Education, and Welfare's policy that "school systems are responsible for assuring that students of a particular race, color, or national origin are not denied the opportunity to obtain the education generally obtained by other students in the system" (*33 Federal Register 4956*; see Díaz, 2002). Central to Douglas' argument was the concern that children whose language was other than English needed to be provided a meaningful opportunity to participate in educational programs. Despite numerous attempts over the last three decades to rectify the situation, we are still confronted with many of the same issues raised by the *Lau* petitioners. Too many of our linguistically diverse children are foreclosed from any meaningful education by their inability to speak English at the level required for academic success. This is not to say we have not made significant progress in many arenas. Numerous success stories exist, but many of these are often isolated and non-sustainable events that are difficult to scale up or implement at other locations (García, 1994; Paredes Scribner, 1999). Much still remains to be done.

This chapter presents what we currently know about the diversity of communication skills of the Latino population and the programs that have been implemented to address the unique needs of their children. The chapter is organized into four major sections. The first section provides an overview of the linguistic diversity of the Latino population. Two sections, focusing on the socio-cultural and socio-linguistic experiences Latino children encounter prior to entering formal education, follow. The fourth section focuses on the educational programs in which these children participate.

LINGUISTIC DIVERSITY OF LATINOS

Latinos are not a homogeneous group; major historical, cultural, demographic, and linguistic differences exist across subgroups. Two-thirds, or 66.1%, of mainland Latinos are of Mexican descent, whereas individuals of Puerto Rican and Cuban descent account for 9.0% percent and 4.0%, respectively. Central, South American, and other Latinos account for 20.9% (U.S. Census Bureau, 2000). In addition to their customs and traditions, each new group of immigrants brings the language and dialect spoken in their country of origin. As a result, more than 46 million Americans, 17.9% of the population, speak a language other than English, with more than half of these individuals speaking Spanish (U.S. Census Bureau, 2002). Speaking Spanish is one of the major ties that bind the Latino population, and approximately three-fourths of the Latino population speaks it. The numbers of Latinos who speak Spanish, English, or both reflect the linguistic heterogeneity of the population. The U.S. Census Bureau (1995) reported that the vast majority of the Latino population consider themselves bilingual, and a small percentage is monolingual in English or Spanish. In addition, it is important to stress that the majority of Latinos are bilingual and self-reported speaking English *very well*. Only 26% of the Latino population report that they *do not speak English well* or *not at all*. Variations across Latino subgroups exist, with Dominicans and Central Americans reporting the least amount of English proficiency. Among the three largest subgroups, Cubans are the group most likely to speak only Spanish and the least likely to speak only English.

Considering that 35% of the Latino population is foreign-born and entered this country in the last three decades, it is not surprising that Spanish is the main language used in the socialization process of many Latino children. School-age children whose mothers were U.S.-born are more likely to speak English at home than those children whose mothers were foreign-born, 90% as compared to 28% (National Center on Education Statistics [NCES], 2002). These findings are consistent with the literature on language maintenance across generations that suggests a trend for language loss by the third generation (Veltman, 1988). However, the extent of language loss across generations is not consistent across socio-economic groups (Hudson, Hernández Cháves, & Bills, 1995), with the rate of Spanish language transmission being directly related to the extent to which the minority population is integrated into the mainstream culture. Thus, the most vulnerable segment of the Latino population, the poor and less educated, is the most likely to transmit Spanish to subsequent generations. The loss of Spanish could potentially be the cost of social and economic integration. However, given the strength of the Spanish media and the strong ties between speaking Spanish and Latino identity (Zentella, 1997), it is possible that the historical trend of language loss by the third generation of immigrants to the United States might reverse.

The linguistic diversity of the population results in a myriad of linguistic possibilities. Some Latinos are Spanish speakers; some are English speakers; and the vast majority fall between the two ends of the continuum. Valdes and Figueroa (1994) present a model that captures the linguistic continuum that exists across the Latino population. At either end of the continuum are monolingual speakers who have no exposure to the second language. Individuals in the center of the continuum possess linguistic competency in both languages equivalent to that of speakers at either end. Between these three points are individuals with fewer competencies in one of the languages. For all practical purposes the Latino population in the United States falls between the two endpoints of the continuum, since the endpoints can really exist only in purely monolingual environments and, as discussed below, are extremely rare, if not impossible, to find in the Latino communities. Thus, the Latino population in the United States might be best viewed as bilingual with various degrees of proficiency in English and Spanish.

Given the present and projected changes in the size, coupled with the age distribution, of the Latino population, it is in our country's best interest to ensure that this large segment of our population, especially its children, is provided the knowledge and skills needed to function productively in our society. The following sections address the two contexts, the family and the school, responsible for ensuring that Latino children possess the necessary communication skills needed to be productive members of our society. It should be noted that the discussion below focuses on the communication skills (form, content, use) of these children rather than the narrow focus on linguistic form (phonology, morphology, and syntax) that has been promulgated in most judicial and legislative mandates dealing with culturally and linguistically diverse populations. This broader view of communication has implications for how we address the issues confronting Latino children, as well as the policies and practices that need to be implemented to address their specific needs.

SOCIO-CULTURAL EXPERIENCES

All societies have loosely established routines through which children are socialized to become adults. This socialization process begins in the home via the interactions between the children and those members of their home environment. During this socialization period, children learn the cultural and linguistic norms of their community; that is, the children learn all the rules of appropriate behavior, the values and beliefs that underlie overt behavior, the linguistic system of their community, and the rules for participating in linguistic dialogue within their communities. Children's acquisition of these communication skills is gradual, and their communication systems undergo transformations as a function of the communicative demands they encounter in various social situations. The specific demands placed on children will vary across and among Latino groups.

It is difficult, if not impossible, owing to the heterogeneity that exists between and among Latino groups, to predict with any degree of certainty the specific experiences any Latino child will encounter. The specific family values and beliefs that drive socialization practices reflect, in part, the family's degree of acculturation. Although it is sometimes difficult to disentangle the source of individual behaviors, it is important to realize that during the early stages of migration, immigrant families turn more intensely to the comfort and continuity of past practices. Thus, it is highly probable that new immigrants will exhibit practices common to individuals in their country of origin, provided that these were practices in which they engaged before entering this country. Furthermore, these practices are less likely to be modified when the family has limited contact with members of ethnic and linguistic groups other than their own. For example, family members might engage in communicative interactions in which they use non-specific vocabulary (e.g., "este"/"this" while pointing to an object) or might not engage in questioning routines in which the answer is obvious (e.g., "David, what is your name?"). Unless parents are exposed to alternative interaction styles (e.g., "Do not use contextualized language and talk about the obvious"), it is highly unlikely that the children will be exposed to this type of discourse prior to entering school, a social context in which these discourse rules are critical for success.

Research on child socialization practices in Latino families can be characterized, at best, as less than adequate, consisting of isolates and often incompatible findings because of variations in sampling, procedures, lack of specific protocol, and focus. Further, the general trends are often based on a subset of an extremely diverse population (Iglesias, 2002). Rather than providing stereotypical characteristics of communicative interactions in Latino families, it might be best to provide a framework that guides behavior and provides examples of the range of possible behaviors one might expect. Doing so accommodates the array of socialization practices seen in Latino families without focusing on or denying differences that may exist among and between groups.

Either consciously or unconsciously, Latino families engage their children in interactions that prepare them to function adequately within their immediate environment. Driving these interactions are parents' values and beliefs that serve as a template that guides their actions (Iglesias & Quinn, 1997). The template can be described as a series of discrete points along a continuum from which an individual makes choices. For example, one such continuum could be the type of play in which parents engage with their children. Play may be viewed as consisting of instructional games (e.g., counting or singing the ABCs), social games (e.g., peekaboo), or an activity in which adults do not engage at all. This dimension is also related to beliefs about adult–child roles in the learning process. Parents who see their role primarily as caretakers most likely do not regard themselves as playmates for their children. Field and Winmayer (1981) studied mother–infant interactions among lower socio-economic Cuban, Puerto Rican, and South American immigrants in Miami. They found *hidden agendas* in parental styles of play. Cuban mothers, who talked the most and used polysyllabic words and long utterances, said that parents had a duty *to educate* children. Puerto Rican and South American mothers engaged in more social and interactive games in which mutual enjoyment was the primary goal. Although no interaction style is intrinsically better than another, they support different aspects of child development and could potentially influence children's ability to succeed in school (Weisner & Garnier, 1992).

The family also makes certain assumptions about the skills that will be demanded of their children outside their home and prepare their children to meet those demands. It should be noted that the cognitive, academic, and linguistic skills the parents are teaching may or may not be compatible with the demands the children will experience outside the home. For example, if the parents feel that their children are not expected to know certain skills, then the parents are less likely to engage in interactions that would foster those skills. The practice of aligning socialization practices to assumptions of future demands is not limited to Latino families. However, those families who are most marginalized from the mainstream culture are less likely to be informed of expectations of institutions outside their immediate community. These gaps between socialization practices at home and expectations in academic programs have given rise to many of our existing parent training programs.

The literature on child socialization practices suggests that the type of communicative interactions that occur in families have an effect on the discourse style and the content knowledge Latino children possess prior to entering school. The discourse skills and content knowledge acquired are independent of the specific language(s) the child is speaking. If the child's exposure has been primarily to decontextualized language, the child is likely to use decontextualized language in Spanish and English. This overlay of discourse skills and content knowledge on language proficiency has several implications for practice. From an assessment perspective, we cannot assume that the child has been exposed to the social interaction typically encountered in the testing situation. For example, several vocabulary measures require the child to label a picture of an object after a prompt ("What is this?"/"¿Qué es esto?"). A *no response* or an incorrect response according to test criteria (child giving function rather than one-word label) might be due to the fact that interaction violates the child's rule of interaction ("Don't talk about the obvious; questions are asked only when speaker does not know the answer") rather than the child's lack of knowledge of the item (Peña, Iglesias, & Lidz, 2001). From a content knowledge perspective, it is important to remember that children's experiences vary. When asked to provide the names of animals, a Latino child raised in Boise, Idaho, might say *deer, elk, moose, elefante, león,* while a child raised in Philadelphia might say *culebra, crab, caballo, spider, cat.* Ignoring for a moment the specific languages used, one can see that the specific exemplars the children used reflect their experiences. Expecting either child to provide only names of pets or farm animals might result in failure on this particular item. Despite the transparency of the inappropriateness of not taking into consideration children's experience, we continue to use static assessments that reflect children's experiences, not their ability to learn (Peña et al., 2001). From an instructional perspective, the literature on child socialization suggests that teachers should become familiar with the range of *ways of participating in different social settings.* This broader view would allow teachers to acknowledge the existence of interaction styles that are likely to function effectively in other situations. The perspective that the child needs to completely replace previous behaviors with only those that are compatible with school expectations negates the fact that other ways of interacting might be valuable and functional in other situations. "Do what an adult tells you" might be an appropriate rule in the classroom but can have negative consequences outside of school. Similarly, "Take your turn before you speak by waiting for a pause in the conversation" might be functional in the classroom but completely futile in a home environment in which getting into a conversation requires overlapping the speakers' utterances; sometimes even touching the speaker multiple times and raising one's voice are required. The issue of which specific language(s) the child is speaking (English, Spanish, or both) is important and should always be considered when planning any assessment or intervention. Equally important, however, are the content knowledge and discourse skills children bring to any social interaction. Unfortunately, most of our present policies and practices do not reflect these elements.

SOCIO-LINGUISTIC EXPERIENCES

Given the pervasiveness of English language media, the nature of Latino families, and the communities in which Latino children are raised, it is doubtful that many Latino children enter school as true monolingual Spanish or English speakers. The majority of these children are bilingual, exhibiting varying degrees of proficiency in English and Spanish. Some of the children are raised in families that report English as the only language spoken. Other children are raised in families that report speaking only

Spanish. Impressionistically, many of these children are indistinguishable from monolingual Spanish or English speakers (e.g., Spanish speakers in Mexico and European American in South Dakota). However, closer examination indicates that the language of these children differs from that of true monolinguals (García, 1994). A third group of children comes from families that report using English and Spanish. Many, but not all, of the children in these families are reported to speak English and Spanish. These children show a wide range of linguistic skills in English and in Spanish when they enter the educational system. However, their exposure and use of a language other than English makes even the most English- or Spanish-fluent members of this group different from their true monolingual peers.

Knowing where a particular child is in the bilingual continuum is not an easy task given that the communication skills the children demonstrate vary as a function of the interlocutors, the task, and the topic (Zentella, 1997). The multidimensional (form, content, and use) nature of language, coupled with the fact that we are dealing with two linguistic codes, further complicates our assessment process. Numerous definitions of bilingualism exist, each acknowledging the existence of at least two languages and differing on the extent to which the two languages must be used receptively or expressively (Bialystok, 2001). The often-used definition of bilingualism that has permeated our policies and practices is based on the concept of language dominance, two separate, independent systems competing for limited neural space and interfering with each other. To a large extent this view of bilingualism served as the basis for decisions on eligibility for services definition that emerged from the *Lau v. Nichols* decision and the assessments that were developed in order to assist school districts with compliance of the Office of Civil Rights mandates and subsequent state regulations. The assessment and identification protocols that emerged during this period were ones that focused only on whether children possess the minimal Standard English skills required to function in regular, English-speaking classrooms. Little regard was given to the extent to which the children were proficient in their first language (L1) or whether the child was proficient in a non-standard variety of L1 and/or their second language (L2).

If our objective is to arbitrarily select a point in the continuum for the sake of eligibility, then the approach of administering a language dominance test is effective and efficient. However, we must realize that this approach provides us little ecologically valuable information. It is simply a way of hastily sorting children into arbitrary categories. There is little congruency between the results of these types of assessments and the specific communicative demands placed on these children when they enter school. If our purpose is to determine the communication abilities of these children, our task is significantly different and requires an understanding of the developmental progression of the skills these children need to acquire to suc-

ceed in school. Although it is beyond the scope of this chapter to provide
a comprehensive review of the existing literature on language acquisition
in Latino children (see Goldstein, 2000), it is important to consider some
illustrative linguistic characteristics of the Spanish and English spoken by
Latino children.

The Latino population is a linguistically diverse population in terms of
dialects spoken. Dialects seen across the various subgroups differ across all
dimensions of language, with the most drastic qualitative differences in
Spanish dialects occurring in the phonology (sound, sound combinations,
and intonation) and lexicon (words and idioms of a language). Dialectal
variations also occur in the English dialects spoken by Latinos. Variations
in these dialects are due in part to the influence of Spanish, to the dialect
of Spanish that is influencing the English, and to the extent to which the
speaker is in contact with other English dialects spoken by various groups
in the United States (see Wolfram, Adger, & Christian, 1999). Knowledge
of dialectal variations spoken in a child's speech community might assist
in the determination of whether a particular construction observed is due
to the child's lack of mastery or due to the influence of the child's dialect.
For example, a child's Spanish production of *cuatro gato está aquí*/four cat
is here would be less likely to be interpreted as an *error* if we knew that
in the child's dialect word-final *s* and *n* are commonly deleted and that
once plurality is marked by a modifier (*cuatro*/four) his or her dialect allows
the deletion of plural markers.

As noted above, content knowledge reflected in the child's lexicon is
influenced by experience. It is important to be aware that to some extent
the child's cultural and linguistic background dictates the lexicon acquired.
Further, specific lexical items might be acquired in different languages as a
function of the language in which these items are introduced. For example,
although body parts are early lexical items acquired by children, our experience with Latino children suggests that these children know *pestañas*/
eyelashes very early in their development. However, it would be rare for
these children to know the Spanish word for *chin*, a word that is commonly
acquired by young children in European American households. These same
children are more likely to label the color of items in English than in Spanish. These observations are not surprising for anyone familiar with Latino
families. It is not uncommon for adults to comment on the child's *beautiful
eyelashes* and for children to acquire what parents might perceive as academic language (e.g., colors, shapes) in school. When considering lexicon,
it is also important to consider the fact that not all languages lexicalize all
qualitatively different events (e.g., while English distinguishes between *smell*
and *sniff*, Spanish does not). Before entering school, all children have acquired a rich set of communicative experiences. Adults in their families who
have attempted to prepare their children to succeed in the next stage of
their lives have guided most of these experiences. The success of the tran-

sition these children will be making is dependent, to a large extent, on the communication skills they have learned and the degree to which the programs they are entering build on their experiences.

EDUCATIONAL PROGRAMS FOR LATINOS

Programs to meet the educational needs of linguistically diverse children are not new in the United States. During the 1700s and 1800s, especially during the early 1800s, non-English and bilingual schools were accepted and common (Klos, 1971). Fueled by the large migration of non-English-speaking, non-Northern Europeans during the late 1800s and early 1900s, exclusionary legislation eventually began to appear at the federal, state, and local levels. Bilingual programs were challenged during this period, as was the teaching of any language other than English. The anti-German sentiment that swept the country during World War I made speaking English the litmus test of national loyalty. Several states passed laws that forbade the teaching of any language other than English to children below high school level. Only a few isolated programs survived during this period of xenophobia. From the 1920s until the 1960s, bilingual education virtually disappeared from the United States.

The resurgence of programs to address the needs of linguistically diverse children in the last 40 years evolved in response to the needs of an ever-increasing non-English-speaking population in the United States, the majority of whom were recent immigrants. A national climate of greater tolerance of ethnic and linguistic groups, coupled with a healthy economy that dampened opposition to immigration, provided the impetus for legislation, judicial decisions, and administrative regulations that redefined the federal government's role in the education of children who had limited proficiency in English to function appropriately in school. Both economic and political fluctuations over the last few years have further redefined existing programs.

Numerous language-support programs exist, many sharing outcome objectives but varying considerably in how they intend to achieve their goals. These programs contain explicit and implicit sets of values that influence their direction. Explicitly, all programs are designed to increase the students' English skills and in some programs their respective native language skills. In addition, all programs transmit an implicit set of cultural norms that are consistent with the values, traditions, and expectations of the economically and politically *dominant groups* in our society (Poole, 1992). The discrepancy between the cultural and linguistic norms the children bring from home and those expected in school has the potential of becoming more of an impediment than the child's inability to speak the language of instruction (Lareau, 2000). Thus, the greater the match between the student's cultural-linguistic background and the program curriculum and instructional approach, the greater the chance that a program will be successful (Iglesias & Quinn, 1997).

A variety of program models focused on linguistic skills have been implemented in order to guarantee that English language learners (only a segment of the Latino school-age population) are offered equal access to and comparable outcomes from our educational system. Unfortunately, for many English-speaking Latino students who are as likely to benefit from programs designed to meet their specific needs, specialized programs are rarely available. If their specific needs are identified, they are often served by generic compensatory programs that lack the sophisticated approaches needed to meet their unique needs. Before discussing the specific characteristics of existing programs designed to build English-language proficiency to a level at which children can compete equally with their native-English-speaking peers, it is important to consider the magnitude of the problem and the contextual factors that impinge on program availability. The 1997 School and Staffing Survey (U.S. Department of Education, 1997), based on data collected in 1993–1994, estimated that over 2.1 million students enrolled in K–12 needed special language services due to their inability to speak English. Recent figures estimate that a substantial increase has occurred in the last decade, with present size of the population being estimated at 4.4 million (Kindler, 2002). Of these, 77% were Spanish speakers. These children are represented in all states and in 46% of all school districts. Not surprising, given historical migration patterns, Latino students are concentrated in our 100 largest school districts, with 13 of these districts, such as New York City Public Schools, Los Angeles Unified School District, and Dade County School District, reporting that the majority of their students are Latinos (National Center on Education Statistics, 2002). The proportion and concentration of Latino students needing special language services are greatest in our largest school districts (U.S. Department of Education, 1997).

Although school districts are required by national and state mandates to provide programs for children who need special language services, they have the flexibility to decide on the specific approaches they use to identify the children who need services and the program they will receive. Ideally, the decisions made by school districts are child-centered and focus on what the child needs and what programs can be implemented to meet these needs. Unfortunately, this is too often not the case given the human and financial resource burdens that implementing these programs have on school districts. Implementing programs requiring specialized personnel (e.g., teachers proficient in two languages, teachers with credentials in English as a Second Language or bilingual education) or alternative assessments and curricula are not always a financially efficient solution for some school districts. For school districts, implementing these programs might result in increasing their administrative bureaucracy, overall expenditures, and the recruitment of personnel that are not always readily available. This is not to suggest that districts should not strive to implement programs that meet children's needs, but we must be realistic and recognize that contextual factors impinging on school districts might result in children's enrolling in less than ideal programs. The complexity of the decision-making process that specific school districts have to make can be illustrated in the following example. Based on school district data, a particular school in a large Latino neighborhood had projected that three kindergarten classes would be needed, two classes to meet the specific needs of children who needed specialized language instruction due to their limited English skills and one that did not. After the enrollment period, the school realized that many of the Spanish-speaking parents whose children were not proficient in English had opted to enroll their children in a recently chartered school in the neighborhood. The result was an insufficient number of children to have three first grade classes, an insufficient number of children to have two classes for the Spanish-speaking children, and an insufficient number of English-speaking children to have a class for only English-speaking students. The school opted to keep one class in which the teacher taught in Spanish and one in which the teacher taught in English. Spanish-speaking children were randomly assigned to the Spanish-English or English-only classes. Although we can conjecture on other possible solutions and consequences of these decisions, what is important to remember is that we should be mindful of the fact that, unfortunately, districts make quick decisions that are not always consistent with best practices garnered from research or specific models promulgated by districts.

It is important to note that no program is inherently better than any other, and if implemented with adequate resources, each will be successful at achieving its objectives. It is the specific final objectives, monolingualism or bilingualism, of these programs and the often associated benefits, deleterious effects, and non-effects that these programs have on children's academic achievement (August & Hakuta, 1997; Greene, 1998; Ramírez, Yuen, & Ramey, 1991; Rosell & Baker, 1996), cognitive advantage (Bialystok & Majumder, 1999), and social utility (Wong-Fillmore, 1991) that have been debated and remain controversial.

A number of taxonomies have been developed to categorize existing programs (Baker, 2001; Genesee, 1999). Each of these taxonomies classifies the programs by their intended outcome with respect to language(s) to be mastered, the languages used at different points, the student composition, and the duration of the program. These taxonomies sometimes also specify the qualifications of personnel involved, instructional materials, and cultural goals. While valuable for planning purposes, the program models do not always, except in isolated demonstration programs, represent actual practice. Fidelity to any model is difficult to maintain over time given changes in personnel, type of children served, lack of the required monitoring, and a number of other unpredicatable factors that impinge on schools and teachers. Although the evidence is primarily anecdotal, those of us who have been involved with Latino students know that lack of fidelity occurs across all program types. This is one of the reasons that the research literature on program effectiveness is in such disarray. When programs are implemented as intended, they result in positive outcomes. When they are not, we hear about the failures of the programs (e.g., immersion programs that are submersions, transitional bilingual programs in which the child never learns English). Rather than describing all possible models, three widely used and promulgated program models, *Developmental Bilingual*, *Immersion*, and *Transitional*, will be discussed. The major differences across these models reflect differences in intended outcomes with respect to language(s) mastered and variations in the timing and sequence of language used for instruction (see Baker, 2001; Genesee, 1999).

The goal of *Developmental Bilingual* programs is to help children achieve competence in English and a second language. The instructional strategies used are designed to acknowledge, respect, and build upon the language and culture of the home. The programs encourage the use of native languages as a medium of instruction and maintenance of the primary culture. Whenever possible, classes include an approximate equal number of native English speakers and English language learners. This program acknowledges that the acquisition of the second language is not hampered by the maintenance of the first language and views bilingualism from a resource perspective. A slight variation of this model is the dual immersion program in which there is a balance of language-minority and language-majority students in the classroom. As designed, students are both second language models and second language learners.

The *Immersion* model has as its main objective the acquisition of a second language (e.g., English for Spanish-speaking Latino students). The program is based on the notion that students can learn a second language as they are learning academic content and that a total immersion in that second language is the best way to achieve competence. The program was originally designed for second language learners who came to school speaking the majority language. The immersion programs vary with respect to the amount of time the student spends learning the second language, as well as when the second language is introduced. In total immersion programs, instruction during the first couple of years is exclusively in the second language. Gradually, instruction in the first language is supposed to be increased. One major variation of this model is this last component. Although the original model reintroduces the first language in later years, the model as implemented in many schools within the United States fails to do so. As a result, rather than building competence in two languages, as originally intended by the model, the model as generally implemented in the United States results in monolingual English speakers. It is also important to note that the model, as implemented in Canada, was intended for language-majority students, English speakers, to learn the country's second official language, which was spoken by the majority of inhabitants of the province in which these children lived.

The main objective of the *Transitional* bilingual education model is to employ each student's native language as a medium of instruction while he or she is being taught English. These programs combine structured-language instruction with native-language instruction, the ultimate goal being the acquisition of English. They also tend to incorporate the students' heritage into the curriculum. The transitional bilingual approach acknowledges that the acquisition of English skills, especially decontextualized academic language, takes time and that competency in L1 provides an important cognitive foundation for L2 acquisition and academic learning in general. The gradual introduction of L2 and the instruction in L1 provide the student with the comprehensible input necessary for second-language acquisition while providing the academic content in a language that the student understands (Krashen, 1996). The content acquired in L1 during the transitional period is assumed to transfer to English as the student progresses through the program. The term transitional bilingual program is presently seen as an early exit program in which students participate in the program from two to four years.

On the surface, these three models appear non-controversial; they seem to be achieving intended goals by manipulating how and when particular languages are introduced and the extent to which they are maintained. However, they have been controversial, not from a pedagogical perspective but from a political one. For some, the use of the minority language (language other than English), even if it is used for a short period of time, is viewed as fostering the minority language and not yielding adequate educational outcomes. For others, the idea of not using the home language has been reminiscent of the pre-*Lau* decision, *submersion* period when linguistically diverse children were indiscriminately thrown in English-only classes with no support and also yielding inadequate educational outcomes. Regrettably, evidence supporting both of these views exists and is used by advocates of opposing positions. Visceral reactions, rather than facts, have driven the debate. Ironically, a substantial body of literature suggests that if adequately implemented, most of the different approaches can be successful (August & Hakuta, 1997; Baker, 2001).

Students enter these programs by a variety of school-specified methods: parent recommendations, teacher observations, and home language surveys. The initial step in the process tends to under-identify those children who need additional language support. The process often relies heavily on parents' self-reports during registration, and parents who are unable to judge the English-proficiency level required to function adequately in the classroom (or who are skeptical and do not see the value of existing language-support programs) often report English as the home language. As a result, their children are placed in English-only classes where little or no language-support program is available. Although the process is sensitive to parents' needs and desires, it seems pedagogically inappropriate to place an English Language Learner in a program in which assistance is limited or non-existent. Many districts also use tests as a means of identifying and placing these learners. Even from the inception of the assessment screening process, the validity of language assessment procedures built on a divisible model of proficiency and with a heavy emphasis on the structural aspects of language could be questioned. If language competency is defined as knowledge of specific language structures (such as *wh*-questions, tense and plural markers), knowledge of those structures is measured. If, however, language competency is defined as communicative competency, which includes more than linguistic competency, the measure will be broader in scope and will reflect the communicative competency needed to function effectively in the classroom.

It is important to remember that the ultimate goal of the programs designed to meet the unique needs of Latino children, especially those who are in the process of learning English, is to ensure that they have sufficient communication skills to master the subject matter taught. We cannot, however, ignore that this learning is not occurring in a vacuum and that the conditions of the schools in which learning is occurring, the qualification of the teachers, and the support from their parents will also play a role in the children's ultimate achievement.

CONCLUSION

A great deal of the literature on bilingual education appears to be a search for the ideal program for the typical Latino child. It is not surprising that the search has led to the finding that the best programs are those in which the human and financial resources are available for qualified teachers to carry out high-quality instruction. This is consistent with our best practice research literature (Genesee, 1999). Good programs have staff members who take into consideration the specific knowledge and skills with which children enter school and build on those individual experiences in a developmentally appropriate way, with high standards for content knowledge and communication skills expected. These programs also recognize that strong parent–school partnerships are necessary since families can extend the children's learning outside the classroom. The issue of language of instruction appears not to be central to educational outcome. Language of instruction, however, is central to our society's value of other's heritage. As noted by U.S. English advocates, English is the language that binds us as Americans. While this is true, it is speaking English *y español lo que me hace a mi ser Latino y Americano.*

REFERENCES

August, D., & Hakuta, K. (1997). *Educating language-minority children.* Washington, DC: National Academy Press.

Baker, C. (2001). *Foundations of bilingual education and bilingualism.* Tonawanda, NY: Multilingual Matters.

Bialystok, E. (2001). *Bilingualism in development: Language, literacy, and cognition.* New York: Cambridge University Press.

Bialystok, E., & Majumder, S. (1999). The relationship between bilingualism and development of cognitive processes in problem solving. *Applied Psycholinguistics, 19*(1), 69–85.

Díaz, E. I. (2002). Framing an historical context for the education of culturally and linguistically diverse students with gifted potential: 1850s to 1980s. In J. A. Castellano & E. I. Díaz (Eds.), *Reaching new horizons: Gifted and talented education for culturally and linguistically diverse students* (pp. 1–28). Boston: Allyn & Bacon.

Field, T. M., & Widmayer, S. M. (1981). Mother-infant interactions among lower SES Black, Cuban, Puerto Rican, and South American immigrants. In T. M. Field, A.M. Sostek, P. Vietze, & P.H. Leiderman (Eds.), *Culture and early interaction* (pp. 41–62). Hillsdale, NJ: Lawrence Erlbaum Associates.

García, E. E. (1994). Attributes of effective schools for language minority students. In E. R. Hollins, J. E. King, & W. C. Hayman (Eds.), *Teaching diverse populations: Formulating a knowledge base* (pp. 93–103). Albany, NY: SUNY Press.

Genesee, F. (Ed.). (1999). *Program alternatives for linguistically diverse students.* Santa Cruz, CA: Center for Research on Education, Diversity, & Excellence.

Goldstein, B. (2000). *Cultural and linguistic diversity resource guide for speech-language pathologists.* San Diego, CA: Singular.

Greene, J. (1998). *A meta-analysis of the effectiveness of bilingual education.* Claremont, CA: Tomas Rivera Policy Center.

Hudson, A., Hernández Cháves, E., & Bills, G. D. (1995). The many faces of language maintenance: Spanish language claiming in five southwestern states. In C. Silva-Corvalán (Ed.), *Spanish in four continents* (pp. 165–183). Washington, DC: Georgetown University Press.

Iglesias, A. (2002). Latino culture. In D. Battle (Ed.), *Communication disorders in multicultural populations* (3rd ed., pp. 179–202). Woburn, MA: Butterworth Heinemann.

Iglesias, A., & Quinn, R. (1997). Culture as a context for early intervention. In S. K. Thurman, J. R. Cornwell, & S. R. Gottwald (Eds.), *Contexts of early intervention: Systems and settings.* Baltimore: Brookes.

Kindler, A. (2002). *Survey of the state's limited English proficient students and available educational programs and services 1999–2000. Summary report.* Washington, DC: National Clearinghouse for English Language Acquisition and Language Instruction Educational Programs.

Klos, H. (1971). *Laws and legal documents relating to problems in bilingual education in the United States.* Washington, DC: Center for Applied Linguistics.

Krashen, S. D. (1996). A gradual exit, variable threshold model for limited English

proficient children. *National Association for Bilingual Education News,*
    19(7), 1, 15–18.

Lareau, A. (2000). *Home advantage.* Lanham, MD: Rowman and Littlefield.

Lau v. Nichols. (1974). U.S. Supreme Court, 414 U.S. 563.

National Center on Education Statistics. (2002). *Characteristics of the 100 largest
    public elementary and secondary school districts in the United States: 2000–
    2001.* Washington, DC: U.S. Department of Education.

Paredes Scribner, A. (1999). High performing Hispanic schools. In P. Reyes, J. D.
    Scribner, & A. Paredes Scribner (Eds.), *Lessons from high-performing His-
    panic schools* (pp. 1–18). New York: Teachers College Press.

Peña, E., Iglesias, A., & Lidz, C. S. (2001). Reducing test bias through dynamic
    assessment of children's word learning ability. *American Journal of Speech
    Language Pathology, 10*(2), 138–154.

Poole, D. (1992). Language socialization in the second language classroom. *Lan-
    guage Learning, 42*(4), 593–616.

Ramírez, J. D., Yuen, S. D., & Ramey, D. R. (1991). *Final report: Longitudinal
    study of structured English immersion strategy, early exit and late-exit pro-
    grams for language-minority children.* San Mateo, CA: Aguirre Interna-
    tional.

Rosell, C. H., & Baker, K. (1996). The educational effectiveness of bilingual edu-
    cation. *Research in Teaching of English, 30*(1), 8–73.

U.S. Census Bureau. (2002). *Profile of selected social characteristics 2000.* Wash-
    ington, DC: U.S. Department of Commerce.

U.S. Census Bureau. (2000). *The Hispanic population in the United States: Popu-
    lation characteristics* (P20–527). Washington, DC: U.S. Department of Com-
    merce.

U.S. Census Bureau. (1995). *Statistical abstract of the United States.* Washington,
    DC: U.S. Department of Commerce.

U.S. Department of Education. (1997). *A profile of policies and practices for Lim-
    ited English Proficient students: Screening methods, program support, and
    teacher training* (NCES 97–472). Wahington, DC: Office of Educational Re-
    search and Improvement.

Valdes, G., & Figueroa, R. A. (1994). *Bilingualism and testing: A special case of
    bias.* Norwood, NJ: Ablex.

Veltman, C. J. (1988). *The future of the Spanish language in the United States.*
    Washington, DC: Hispanic Policy Development Project.

Weisner, T. S., & Garnier, H. (1992). Nonconventional family life-styles and school
    achievement: A 12-year longitudinal study. *American Educational Research
    Journal, 29*(3), 605–632.

Wolfram, W., Adger, C. T., & Christian, D. (Eds.). (1999). *Dialects in schools and
    communities.* Mahwah, NJ: Lawrence Erlbaum Associates.

Wong-Fillmore, L. (1991). When learning a second language means losing the first.
    Early Childhood Research Quarterly, 6, 323–346.

Zentella, A. C. (1997). *Growing up bilingual.* Malden, MA: Blackwell Publishers.

Chapter 7

Addressing the Needs of Latinos in Special Education

Alba A. Ortiz

INTRODUCTION

In 1998, almost 10 million students came from homes where languages other than English were spoken. These culturally and linguistically diverse groups are growing at a significantly faster rate than the overall student population and will soon represent the majority school population in more than 50 major U.S. cities (National Clearinghouse for Bilingual Education, 1995). Some diverse students have such limited English skills that they cannot profit from English-only instruction without support. These students are increasingly referred to as *English language learners* (ELLs), a term suggested by Rivera (1994) to avoid the negative connotation of *limited* as a descriptor of a student's abilities. In the 1999–2000 school year, states reported serving 4,416,580 ELLs in pre-K through grade 12 (Kindler, 2002a). This represents approximately 9.3% of the total public school enrollment and is a 27% increase over the number of ELLs reported by states in 1997–1998. California enrolled the largest number of students, followed by Texas, Florida, New York, Illinois, and Arizona, Spanish speakers comprising 76% of the population of ELLs (Kindler, 2002b).

This chapter addresses three critical components of service delivery for Latino students. The first, preventing academic problems, and the second, providing early intervention for struggling learners, are key to preventing inappropriate special education referrals. The third, ensuring that only those students with true disabilities are placed in special education, requires that special education processes be adapted to address the unique linguistic, cultural, and other background characteristics of this student population. Because they pose complex challenges relative to special education referral, assessment, and instruction, the chapter focuses specifically on Latino students who are also limited-English-proficient (i.e., Latino ELLs).

LATINOS IN SPECIAL EDUCATION

Latino students experience widespread underachievement, are retained more frequently than their White peers, and drop out of school in higher numbers (Robertson, Kushner, Starks, & Drescher, 1994). Underachieving students are typically removed from mainstream classrooms to receive basic skill instruction. This instruction generally has a less academic orientation; objectives are lower; activities lack clear purpose and focus; textbooks and related instructional materials emphasize facts and lower-level skills; and material is covered at a slower pace (Oakes, 1986). Moreover, low-performing students often spend most of their school day together, which results in de facto tracking or segregation (Knapp, Shields, & Turnbull, 1995). Over time, they come to believe that they cannot master challenging academic content, which, in turn, lowers their self-esteem and diminishes their interest in school and their motivation to do well, all of which contribute to rates of school attrition (Ortiz & Kushner, 1997). As students' academic performance worsens, these students become likely candidates for special education referral.

The representation of Latinos in special education is an issue of long standing. As early as 1968, 60–80% of the students in special education were culturally and linguistically diverse (CLD) students (Dunn, 1968). In 1973, Mercer reported that Mexican Americans were four times as likely to be placed in special education than were their White peers. *The Individuals with Disabilities Education Act* (IDEA) Amendments of 1997 drew attention to the continuing problem of overrepresentation of CLD learners in special education.

In 1998, approximately 5,900,000 children and youth were served in federally supported programs for individuals with disabilities (National Center for Educational Statistics [NCES], 1999). The majority of them were classified as having mild disabilities in the categories of learning disabilities, speech or language impairments, mental retardation, and emotional disturbances. Language development, reading, and mathematics were the areas most frequently targeted for special education instruction. Data indicated that Latinos were proportionately represented at the national level, that is, that the percentage of Latino students in special education was consistent with their representation in the general student population. However, disaggregating national data to the state and local levels is critical to understanding representation patterns. Doing so reveals that representation is affected by such factors as geographic location and language proficiency status, limited-English-proficient (LEP) versus non-LEP. In some states, ELLs were underrepresented, while in others as many as 27% of students with limited English proficiency were in special education programs (Robertson et al., 1994). The 1996 National Assessment of Educational Progress (NAEP) assessment data indicated that one in five 4th grade LEP students (20%) were classified as having disabilities (Mazzeo, Carlson, Voekl, & Lutkus, 2000).

In a five-year period, 1993–1994 to 1998–1999, special education placements for ELLs increased by 345% (Artiles, Rueda, Salazar, & Higareda, 2000). Students with limited proficiency in both the native and the second language were more likely to be overrepresented in programs for students with mental retardation, learning disabilities, and speech and language impairments. ELLs who received the least language support were more likely to be placed in special education programs. Students in full English immersion classes were almost three times as likely to be served in special education than were students in bilingual education programs.

Disproportionate representation of Latinos in special education, both over- and under-identification, can be explained by a general lack of understanding of the influence of such factors as linguistic, cultural, and socio-economic differences on student learning (Ortiz & Yates, 2001). Differences are sometimes interpreted as disabilities, as happens, for example, when students are referred to speech pathologists because they speak English with an accent. Conversely, teachers may not refer Latino students because they inaccurately attribute difficulties to lack of English proficiency. Disproportionate representation also reflects the absence of well-thought-out policies and procedures to (a) ensure that school climates are conducive to the success of Latino students; (b) guide teachers in deciding whether a Latino student should be referred to special education; (c) ensure that assessments are non-discriminatory; (d) help multidisciplinary teams interpret assessment outcomes; and (e) rule out factors, such as lack of English proficiency, cultural differences, or inappropriate instruction, as the cause of students' learning problems (Ortiz & Yates, 2001).

Today, in spite of standards-based reforms and school improvement efforts, there continues to be a significant gap between the achievement of students with special needs (e.g., those from low-income backgrounds, CLD students, ELLs, and students with disabilities and their middle-class, majority peers) (Goertz, Floden, & O'Day, 1996). Moreover, legislative and legal mandates implemented to protect the rights of culturally and linguistically diverse learners have failed to resolve issues associated with disproportionate representation in special education. A contributing factor is that educators and policy makers have essentially ignored the changing student demography and the increasing diversity of America's classrooms as they have implemented education reforms.

PREVENTION OF ACADEMIC PROBLEMS

Preventing school failure begins with creating school climates that foster academic success and empower students rather than breed failure (Cummins, 1989). Such environments reflect a philosophy that all students can learn, and perhaps more importantly, those educators are responsible for seeing to it that they do. Positive school climates are characterized by strong leadership by principals; high expectations for student achievement; a challenging curriculum; a safe and orderly environment; ongoing, systematic evaluation of student progress; and shared decision making (Anderson & Pellicer, 1998). Several other factors, though, are crucial to the academic success of CLD learners (Ortiz, 1997). All teachers who work with Latino students, regardless of their program assignment (i.e., bilingual education, English as a Second Language [ESL], general education, special education, and/or compensatory education), should understand second language acquisition, the relationship of Spanish language development to the development of English proficiency, and socio-cultural influences on student learning. In addition, they should be able to (a) assess native language and ESL proficiency; (b) provide native language (L1) and/or English language instruction; (c) conduct informal assessments to analyze current level of performance in Spanish and in English and to monitor progress, particularly in relation to language and literacy development; and (d) forge partnerships with the families of the Latino students they serve.

In schools with positive climates, special language programs enjoy the support of principals, teachers, parents, and community members. It is understood that native language instruction provides the foundation for achieving high levels of English proficiency (Krashen, 1991). Thus, using the native language is a key instructional strategy in these schools (Snow, Burns, & Griffin, 1998). It is also clearly understood that general education teachers are critical to the success of ELLs and that language and literacy development and content area instruction are a shared responsibility, not the sole purview of bilingual educators and ESL teachers.

In school environments conducive to the success of Latino students, parents are seen as effective advocates for their children and as valuable resources in school improvement efforts (García & Malkin, 1993). By being involved with the families and communities, educators come to understand the social, linguistic, and cultural contexts in which their students are being raised. Thus, educators learn to respect cultural differences in child-raising practices and in how parents choose to be involved in their children's education (García & Domínguez, 1997). They relinquish control over decision making and join parents and other community members in promoting academic progress both in school and at home (García, Wilkinson, & Ortiz, 1995).

In classrooms where ELLs are successful, teachers use instructional strategies known to be effective for CLD learners (Wilkinson & Ortiz, 1986). They draw heavily upon students' prior knowledge, linking what students already know to what they need to learn (Leinhardt, 1992). They provide multiple opportunities for students to review previously learned concepts and teach students to apply those concepts to the tasks at hand. They organize the content into themes that connect the curriculum across subject areas. Because struggling learners often lack prerequisite skills to successfully complete tasks, teachers provide individual guidance, assistance, and support to fill in gaps in background knowledge. As their skills improve, students begin regulating their own learning and assume greater levels of responsibility and independence (Burke, Hagan, & Grossen, 1998).

Early Intervention for Students Experiencing Achievement Difficulties

Most learning problems can be prevented if students are in positive school and classroom contexts that accommodate individual differences and if they receive effective instruction. Even in the most positive of environments, though, some students still experience difficulty (Ortiz, 1997). For these students, early intervention strategies must be implemented *as soon as learning problems are noted.* Early intervention means that "supplementary instructional services are provided early in students' schooling and that they are intense enough to bring at-risk students quickly to a level at which they can profit from high-quality classroom instruction" (Madden, Slavin, Karweit, Dolan, & Wasik, 1991, p. 594). Such intervention is critical; once students fall one year below grade level, it is almost impossible to close the gap.

Examples of early intervention include clinical or diagnostic-prescriptive teaching, general education peer and teacher support, and alternative general education services, such as tutorial or remedial instruction (Ortiz, 1997). Teachers who use clinical or diagnostic-prescriptive approaches teach skills, subjects, or concepts; re-teach using significantly different strategies or approaches for the benefit of students who fail to meet expected performance levels after initial instruction; and use informal assessment strategies to identify students' strengths and weaknesses and the possible causes of academic difficulties (Ortiz, 1997). Teachers conduct curriculum-based assessments (e.g., using observations, inventories, and analyses of student work) to monitor student progress and use these evaluation data to plan and modify instruction as needed (King-Sears, Burgess, & Lawson, 1999).

If clinical teaching fails to resolve students' achievement problems, teachers should have immediate access to general education support systems for further problem solving (Chalfant & Pysh, 1989). Peers or experts can work collaboratively with general education teachers to develop strategies to address students' learning problems and to guide them as they implement recommendations. For example, teachers can share instructional resources and can observe each other's classrooms and offer suggestions for improving instruction or managing behavior. ESL teachers can help their general education peers by demonstrating strategies for successfully integrating

ELLs into their classes; general education and ESL teachers can meet to coordinate language, literacy, and content instruction.

Teacher Assistance Teams (TATs), made up of four to six general education teachers and the teacher who requests assistance, design interventions to help struggling learners (Chalfant & Pysh, 1989). At the TAT meeting, team members reach consensus on the nature of the problem; determine priorities for intervention; help the teacher select the methods, strategies, or approaches to be used in solving the problem; assign responsibility for carrying out the recommendations; and establish a follow-up plan to monitor progress. The teacher then implements the plan, with the assistance of team members or other colleagues, if needed. Follow-up meetings are held to review progress toward problem resolution. If the problem is resolved, the case is closed; if not, the team repeats the problem-solving process. Research on TATs shows that general education teachers have the skills and competencies to serve students with serious learning needs and that the majority of cases considered by teams (70–90%) are resolved without referral to special education (Ortiz, 1990).

Alternative Services

General education, not special education, should be primarily responsible for the education of students with significant learning needs that cannot be attributed to disabilities. These would include, for example, migrant students who miss critical instruction over the course of the school year or immigrant children who arrive in U.S. schools without any prior education. If the general education system does not have alternatives for students such as these, it is easy for teachers and principals to conclude that it is in the students' best interest to refer them to special education (Frymier & Gansnedner, 1989). A variety of general education alternatives can be used to serve students with serious academic difficulties. These include one-on-one tutoring, family and student support groups, family counseling, and the range of services supported by *Title I* funds. Support provided students through alternative programs *supplement*, not replace, general education instruction. Interventions should be initiated as soon as a teacher notices that a student is experiencing academic difficulties, not when learning problems have become so serious that the teacher has decided that the student should be referred to special education.

Prevention and early intervention are not intended to discourage the referral of Latino students to special education. Rather, they are meant to prevent referrals of students whose problems result from factors other than the presence of a disability. It is inappropriate to attach a disability label to students who do not meet eligibility criteria. Instead, attention should be focused on adapting general education programs and services and providing alternative support systems in the context of the regular program, to ensure the academic success of ELLs. Decisions of special education re-ferral committees should be informed by data gathered through the pre-vention, early intervention, and referral processes (Ortiz, 1997). The recommendation that a student receive a comprehensive individual assess-ment indicates that (a) the teacher used effective instructional strategies; (b) neither clinical teaching nor interventions recommended by campus-based problem-solving committees (e.g., TATs) resolved the problem; and (c) other general education alternatives also proved unsuccessful. It is likely that students who continue to struggle, in spite of such extensive efforts to individualize instruction and to accommodate learning characteristics, have disabilities (Ortiz, 1997).

CONSIDERATIONS IN ASSESSING LATINO STUDENTS

Too often, special education assessments fail to produce the data needed to determine whether a Latino student has a disability. For example, re-search on Latino students with learning disabilities and communication disorders showed that few students were tested in Spanish and that when they were, inappropriate adaptations of standardized procedures, such as translating tests, were common (Ortiz, García, Wheeler, & Maldonado-Colón, 1986). Because the instruments and procedures used were not valid, it was impossible to tell whether Latino students had disabilities; qualifying them for special education on the basis of faulty data was therefore inap-propriate. More recent research has shown that, even when school districts have access to bilingual assessment personnel, identifying disabilities among Latinos is still a complex task. There are few intelligence and achievement tests in Spanish and, unfortunately, many of the few available tests often have poor psychometric properties. Moreover, most bilingual assessment personnel were taught to assess in English and left to their own devices to figure out the interaction among linguistic, cultural, and other student char-acteristics and disabilities.

Assessment Personnel

Priority should always be given to using qualified professionals in as-sessing Latino students. If they are not available in the district, the services of bilingual assessment professionals should be contracted. Assessment per-sonnel should have expertise in (a) Spanish language development and ESL acquisition; (b) the influence of such factors as culture and socio-economic status on student performance; (c) conducting assessments in Spanish and by using ESL approaches; (d) involving parents and family members in referral and assessment processes; (e) acceptable adaptations of standard-ized assessment instruments and procedures and alternatives to traditionally used procedures; (f) interpreting assessment outcomes; (g) applying eligi-

bility criteria in light of linguistic, cultural, and other background characteristics; and (h) effective instructional practices for Latinos with disabilities
(Ortiz & Yates, 2001). Everyone involved in the assessment process must
understand the professional ethics and responsibilities associated with student evaluations. Appraisal personnel should assess their knowledge base,
their own cultural values and biases, their awareness of culturally appropriate assessment practices, and their understanding of relationships with
families (Heur, 1997). If, upon reflecting on the results of a self-assessment,
they find that they do not have the requisite skills or values to effectively
serve Latino students, assessors should refer these students to other evaluators (Leung, 1996). This will minimize the possibility that an evaluator's
perceptions of the child or of the child's racial/ethnic group will negatively
affect the assessment.

While the use of interpreters in the conduct of special education evaluations is a controversial topic, making decisions about special education
eligibility with some insight into how students function in Spanish is pref-
erable to basing decisions entirely on their performance in English. However, individuals who assist with assessments must be proficient in the
student's native language and trained as interpreters (Ortiz & Yates, 2001).
Today it is unacceptable for the assessor to ask the school secretary, the
custodian, or an older sibling to provide on-the-spot interpretation for a
special education evaluation. Training of interpreters should include principles of assessment, instruction in the administration of specific instruments, arranging the testing setting and materials, interacting appropriately
with examinees, recording responses and information that may be helpful
in interpreting these, and protecting security of test materials (Muñóz-
Sandoval, Cummins, Alvarado, & Ruef, 1998). Appraisal personnel must
also be trained in how to use the services of interpreters.

Planning the Assessment

A tremendous volume of information is gathered over the course of a
student's school career. However, this information is recorded on many
different forms, forms are kept in many different files, and records are kept
in many different locations. Consequently, neither bilingual education nor
special education committees typically have the benefit of all available data
on a student when they make decisions about eligibility or program placements or when they develop instructional plans or programs. Districts
should develop forms and technology that allow student data to be cap-
tured in one place (e.g., annual language dominance assessment results,
decisions of bilingual education/ESL committees, special education recommendations). Assessment personnel should begin by reviewing existing data
to generate questions to be answered through the comprehensive evalua-

tion. Doing so moves the assessment beyond the administration of routine test batteries.

While it is beyond the scope of this chapter to review standardized instruments for assessing Latino students, guidelines to minimize bias in assessment are offered. Latino students should be assessed *in both languages*, Spanish and in English, even if there is reason to believe that the student speaks only one language. For example, a student may understand and speak Spanish but may prefer to use English only for a variety of reasons. The student's parents may understand, but not speak, English. They interact with the child in Spanish, and the child, in turn, responds in English. Because they understand each other, they communicate successfully, albeit each uses a different language. It would be inappropriate to treat this student as an English monolingual; furthermore, assessing in English only would yield an incomplete profile of language functioning.

When limited-English-proficient Latino students are assessed in English only, as occurs when assessment personnel are monolingual English speakers, the eligibility decision hinges on ruling out lack of English proficiency as the root of the problem. In these instances, the assessor must establish the student's English proficiency and interpret results in relation to the student's current functioning level. Under ideal circumstances, before referring the student, the teacher would have established the baseline, provided ESL instruction for a period of time, and documented progress. With appropriate instruction, students without disabilities will demonstrate increased proficiency. Those with disabilities will continue to struggle, despite the interventions; students who struggle, despite such interventions, are the ones who should be referred.

Whenever possible, equivalent instruments and procedures should be administered in English and Spanish. In this way, assessors are able to compare what students know in each language but also are able to describe what students know cumulatively (Ortiz & Yates, 2001). For example, a student who knows 10 vocabulary words in Spanish and 10 different words in English should be credited with knowing 20 vocabulary words. Not to do so underestimates the student's abilities. This is not to say that scores from administrations in each language should be added together but, rather, that patterns of strengths and weaknesses should reflect all that a student knows and can do, regardless of the language in which the skill is demonstrated.

The IDEA Amendments (1997) require that tests and other evaluation materials are free of racial or cultural bias, that standardized tests are validated for the specific purpose for which they are used, and that tests are administered in accordance with the instructions of test publishers. Relying on tests with questionable sampling procedures, inherent cultural specificity, and poor reliability and validity yields incomplete or inappropriate information (Leung, 1996). Given the lack of technically sound instruments for Latino students, it is necessary to identify alternative assessments and to determine acceptable adaptations of standardized procedures. Standardized achievement tests that are available in Spanish but that were normed outside the United States can be used for diagnostic purposes. On the other hand, it is inappropriate to use tests that are translated on the spot because not only is it impossible to judge the accuracy or appropriateness of these translations, but translating tests at the same time invalidates them.

It is important to bear in mind that adapted assessments and procedures have many of the same limitations as traditionally used instruments, including inadequate psychometric properties, and that they may not provide a comprehensive picture of students' skills and abilities (Damico, 1991). Thus, results from adapted or non-standard administrations cannot be the basis for determining special education eligibility. Test scores derived from inappropriate instruments should not be reported. Instead, these clinical data should be used for *diagnostic* purposes; that is, performance should be analyzed to pinpoint problem areas and to describe patterns of strengths and weaknesses. Evaluators and multidisciplinary teams should use these descriptive data, not test scores, to decide whether the student qualifies for special education. Results of standardized tests must be cross-validated with data from other sources (Leung, 1996). For example, results of formal reading assessments in Spanish and in English can be compared with those of informal reading inventories in both languages. If both norm-referenced and informal assessment outcomes are low; it is more likely that the student has a disability. If decisions are based solely on results of standardized measures, there is a lingering question as to whether low performance was an artifact of the limitations of the instruments used.

Assessment results should be considered in light of the students' school history and progress in the general education (including bilingual education and ESL) curriculum and should corroborate the concerns identified by teachers and parents at the point of initial referral. For example, if the student has a history of academic difficulties, the referral committee should have documented that these problems were not resolved, even though alternative programs and services were provided. In preparing the evaluation report, the assessor should report all adaptations of instruments and procedures and should describe the nature of bilingual assessments (e.g., an interpreter was used; instruments were translated on the spot; limits were tested by administering items missed in English in the native language). This allows consumers of assessment information to judge the appropriateness of the data.

THE MULTIDISCIPLINARY TEAM (MDT)

A multidisciplinary team determines whether a child is eligible for special education. In addition to the representatives required by law (e.g., a representative of administration, instructional representatives from special education and general education, assessment personnel, the child's parent, and the student if appropriate), it is important that the MDT includes representatives with expertise in the education of Latino students (Ortiz & Yates, 2001). If the student is in a bilingual education program, this teacher will likely participate in the team meeting as the general education representative. If the student is in an ESL program, the ESL teacher should be invited to participate, along with the child's general education teacher. If the student is being served in an alternative program (e.g., *Title I*, health services, or remedial reading), representatives from these programs should be included. An interpreter should attend so limited-English-proficient parents can participate meaningfully in team deliberations. These interpreters should have the same language skills and competencies as described previously.

The MDT decides whether the student has a legally defined disability and needs special education services. Team members must provide assurances that the problems are not the result of factors such as lack of academic support, limited English proficiency, cultural differences, or other background characteristics. In providing these assurances, the team should clearly describe the data used to reach these conclusions. Answering questions such as the ones that follow (adapted from Damico, 1991) can help the team rule out factors other than the presence of a disability as the source of difficulties (Ortiz & Yates, 2001). *In addition to the general education teacher, have others noted similar difficulties (e.g., the ESL teacher, remedial program personnel, or parents)? Does the problem exist across contexts (e.g., in the general education and the ESL classrooms, at school, and at home)?* For instance, regarding the student who acts out in class and whose parents report that the child demonstrates similar behaviors at home: *Are the problems evident in Spanish?* For native Spanish speakers who have difficulty understanding or who have not learned to read in Spanish, despite effective Spanish literacy instruction: *Does the student exhibit the same types of problematic behaviors in Spanish and in English?* For the student who cannot follow instructions in either language: *Is the student's progress in acquiring English as a second language significantly different from that of peers who started at essentially the same level of English language proficiency and have had comparable instruction in ESL? Is there evidence that difficulties can be explained according to cross-cultural or related cultural phenomena?* For example, the lack of eye contact, which the teacher interprets as defiance, may be considered appropriate behavior in the child's cultural group; the student's narratives may reflect patterns typical of storytelling in his or her culture. *Are there overt variables that immediately explain the difficulties?* Such variables might include that the student's school attendance has been inconsistent; that the student was tested in English but is limited-English-proficient; that language errors are typical of ESL acquirers or reflect dialectal variations; and that achievement was tested in the native language, but the student has not received native language instruction.

In addition, *is there evidence of extreme test anxiety?* This can occur when the child being tested has been in the country for only a brief period and has not had the opportunity to acclimate to the new environment and to the school and classroom cultures. *Were there procedural mistakes in the assessment process that might explain the problematic behaviors (e.g., the child's age was calculated incorrectly)? Can problematic behaviors be explained according to bias in operation before, during, or after the assessment?* Examples are that the child's teacher has referred all the Latino students in his or her classroom, that the instruments used are not normed for Spanish speakers and/or that the adaptations used were inappropriate, or that the assessor's low expectations for student performance influenced the interpretation of assessment instruments and procedures. *Do data show that the student was resistant to intervention in the context of general education (i.e., were clinical teaching, support team interventions, and alternative programs unsuccessful in closing achievement gaps)? Are the assessment results consistent with the teachers' and/or parents' concerns?* If the student's problems cannot be explained by factors such as those above, then the team is in a better position to conclude that the student has a disability.

Developing Individualized Education Plans

The MDT has other important responsibilities. Members develop the Individualized Education Plan (IEP) and decide the extent to which the student will participate in bilingual education, ESL, and/or the general education curricula. They also recommend whether the student will be exempted from district- or statewide assessments of achievement. Concepts about bilingualism, native language, and ESL instruction may be foreign to educators who work with Latino students with disabilities. In a study of IEP goals and objectives selected for limited English-proficient Latino students with learning disabilities or mental retardation, it was found that poor academic progress in general and poor progress in reading were the primary reasons for referring students to special education and that the most frequently specified IEP goals for these students were related to reading and language arts (Ortiz & Wilkinson, 1991). Yet, of the 203 IEPs examined, only 2% stated that some instruction would be carried out in Spanish. None included ESL goals and objectives. Students' language proficiency had little effect on the design of the special education services provided these students. In addition to the components required by law and state policy, IEPs should specify (a) whether goals and objectives will be delivered in Spanish and/or using ESL strategies; (b) the language to be used in delivering related services (e.g., speech therapy or counseling); and (c) specialized materials, programs, and recommended strategies and approaches that address students' Spanish and English proficiency and their disability-related needs.

Instructional Arrangements

Like their non-disabled peers, Latinos with disabilities who are also ELLs have the right to bilingual education and/or ESL services. The continuum of placement alternatives for these students should include instructional settings such as the following (Ortiz & Yates, 2001). In a *bilingual education classroom with special education consultation*, bilingual teachers take the lead in implementing IEP goals and objectives because they can provide native language instruction. However, teachers are supported by special education personnel so they can effectively integrate students with disabilities into their classroom routines. Otherwise, even the very best native language instruction is ineffective if instruction is not adapted to address disability-related needs.

In a *general education model with ESL instruction and special education consultation*, the special educator works with the general education teachers to ensure that the instruction accommodates the student's disabilities. The ESL teacher should also consult with the general education teacher to ensure that instruction delivered in English is understandable to the learner. The special educator should also work with the ESL teacher to ensure that second language instruction addresses disability-related needs. In addition, a *bilingual special education resource teacher* provides special education instruction in Spanish and/or using ESL strategies to address both language status and disability-related needs. On the other hand, *the special education teacher* uses ESL strategies and works with general education and ESL specialists to ensure the adaptation of instruction to meet disability-related needs. If the student is in a bilingual education classroom, the bilingual educator addresses native language goals, and the special educator provides instruction for those goals for which ESL was identified as the appropriate instructional approach. The special educator can work with ELLs with disabilities who are being transitioned from native language to English reading. Then, a *self-contained bilingual special education teacher* delivers special education instruction in the native language and/or uses ESL strategies, as appropriate; and a *self-contained special education/ESL teacher* provides special education instruction on a full-time basis using ESL techniques.

All too often, bilingual teacher assistants are given the primary responsibility for teaching ELLs with disabilities. These paraprofessionals are not certified teachers, nor do they have sufficient training in pedagogy, curriculum, or instruction to assume this responsibility. Instructional assistants should be closely supervised by the special education teacher, with the help of bilingual professionals, if the special educator is not bilingual. The assistant should preview lessons in the native language and provide advance organizers for lessons that will be taught in English (e.g., teach key vocabulary words and main ideas). The special educator then delivers the lesson in English, using ESL strategies, to make it comprehensible to the learner. After the teacher's sheltered lesson, the assistant can review important content in the native language. In this way, lessons taught in English are anchored by previews and reviews of important content in the native language. More importantly, though, the teacher retains responsibility for instruction, and the assistant serves in a support role.

Annual Reviews

The annual review is one of the most important components of the special education process in that it gives MDTs the opportunity to review progress toward attainment of IEP goals and objectives and to identify students who are not progressing as expected. Wilkinson and Ortiz (1986) found that after three years of special education services, Latino students identified as *learning-disabled* had actually lost ground. Their IQ scores were lower than at initial entry, and their achievement scores were essentially the same as at initial entry. Despite this, special education services were intensified. It is important to recognize that high expectations and academically rich programs can improve the academic achievement of ELLs, but only if students receive high-quality instruction designed to meet those expectations. When data indicate that students are not making anticipated progress, IEPs should be modified and alternative strategies recommended improving student performance.

The MDT is also expected to review existing evaluation data and to determine whether these data are sufficient to make decisions about continued eligibility (IDEA Amendments, 1997). If there are questions about progress, the team or the parent may request a reevaluation at that time. Even if a reevaluation is not required, because the language skills of ELLs may change dramatically over brief periods, native language and English assessment data should be updated at least annually. If students continue to qualify, IEPs are updated; if students are not progressing adequately, IEPs are modified and alternative strategies recommended to improve performance. Students who no longer meet eligibility criteria are exited from special education. For these students, it is important to monitor progress after exit to be sure that the integration into general education on a full-time basis is successful.

CONCLUSION

Because of the dramatically changing student demography, education systems must reform programs, policies, procedures, and practices to ensure that Latino students are successful in the context of general education and that students who are referred are placed in special education only if they truly have disabilities. The education of Latino students in general and of limited-English-proficient Latinos with disabilities specifically is a complex task requiring effective linkages between special language, general education, and special education programs. Bilingual education teachers must provide native language and ESL instruction. ESL teachers must help students acquire effective English skills but, to do so, must have the support of general education teachers. General educators must also use ESL strategies so that instruction is understandable to limited-English-proficient students. All teachers must be able to adapt instruction for struggling learners in order to reduce retention rates and inappropriate referrals to special education. When students are referred to special education, school psychologists, speech pathologists, and other assessment personnel must select instruments and procedures to ensure accurate diagnoses of disabilities, a goal that cannot be met if they rely solely on standardized tests whose norms were developed with monolingual White, middle-class samples. If students qualify for special education services, special education teachers and related services personnel must have the skills to implement programs that simultaneously address students' language-related and disability-related needs.

REFERENCES

Anderson, L. W., & Pellicer, L. O. (1998). Toward an understanding of unusually successful programs for economically disadvantaged students. *Journal of Education for Students Placed at Risk, 3*(3), 237–263.

Artiles, A. J., Rueda, R., Salazar, I., & Higareda, J. (2000, November). *Factors associated with English learner representation in special education: Emerging evidence from urban school districts in California.* Paper presented at the conference on Minority Issues in Special Education in Public Schools, Harvard University, Cambridge, MA.

Burke, M. D., Hagan, S. L., & Grossen, B. (1998). What curricular design and strategies accommodate diverse learners? *Teaching Exceptional Children, 31*(1), 34–38.

Chalfant, J. C., & Pysh, M.V.D. (1989). Teacher Assistance Teams: Five descriptive studies on 96 teams. *Remedial and Special Education, 10*(6), 49–58.

Cummins, J. (1989). A theoretical framework for bilingual special education. *Exceptional Children, 56*, 111–119.

Damico, J. S. (1991). Descriptive assessment of communicative ability in limited English proficient students. In E. V. Hamayan, & J. S. Damico (Eds.), *Limiting bias in the assessment of bilingual students* (pp. 157–217). Austin, TX: Pro-Ed.

Dunn, L. L. (1968). Special education for the mildly retarded—Is much of it justified? *Exceptional Children, 35*, 5–22.

Frymier, J., & Gansnedner, B. (1989). The Phi Delta Kappan study of students at risk. *Phi Delta Kappan, 71*(2), 142–146.

García, S. B., & Domínguez, L. (1997). Cultural contexts that influence learning and academic performance. In L. B. Silver (Ed.), *Child and adolescent psychiatric clinics of North America: Academic difficulties* (pp. 621–655). Philadelphia: W. B. Saunders Company.

García, S. B., & Malkin, D. H. (1993). Toward defining programs and services for culturally and linguistically diverse learners in special education. *Teaching Exceptional Children, 26*(1), 52–58.

García, S. B., Wilkinson, C. Y., & Ortiz, A. A. (1995). Enhancing achievement for language minority students: Classroom, school and family contexts. *Education and Urban Society, 27*, 441–462.

Goertz, M. E., Floden, R. E., & O'Day, J. (1996). *Systemic reform.* Washington, DC: Office of Educational Research and Improvement.

Heur, M. B. (1997). Culturally inclusive assessments for children using augmentative and alternative communication (ACC). *Journal of Children's Communication Development, 19*(1), 23–34.

Individuals with Disabilities Education Act. (1997). *Public Law 102–119, 20 U.S.C. § 1400 et seq.*

Kindler, A. (2002a). *What are the most common language groups for LEP students?* AskNCBE No. 5. Available: www.ncbe.gwu.edu.

Kindler, A. (2002b). *How many school-aged limited English proficient students are there in the U.S.?* AskNCBE No. 1. Available: www.ncbe.gwu.edu.

King-Sears, M. E., Burgess, M., & Lawson, T. L. (1999). Applying curriculum-based assessment in inclusive settings. *Teaching Exceptional Children, 32*(1), 30–38.

Knapp, M. S., Shields, P. M., & Turnbull, B. J. (1995). Academic challenge in high-poverty classrooms. *Phi Delta Kappan, 16*(10), 770–776.

Krashen, S. D. (1991). *Bilingual education: A focus on current research.* National Clearinghouse for Bilingual Education Focus: Occasional Papers in Bilingual Education. Available: http://www.ncbe.gwu.edu/ncbepubs/focus/focus.3htm.

Leinhardt, G. (1992). What research on learning tells us about teaching. *Educational Leadership, 49*(7), 20–25.

Leung, B. P. (1996). Quality assessment practices in a diverse society. *Teaching Exceptional Children, 28*(3), 42–45.

Madden, N. A., Slavin, R. E., Karweit, N. L., Dolan, L., & Wasik, B. A. (1991). Success for all. *Phi Delta Kappan, 72*(8), 593–599.

Mazzeo, J., Carlson, J. E., Voekl, K. E., & Lutkus, A. D. (2000, March). *Increasing the participation rate of special needs students in NAEP: A report on 1996 NAEP research activities.* Washington, DC: U.S. Department of Education.

Mercer, J. R. (1973). *Labeling the mentally retarded.* Berkeley: University of California Press.

Muñóz-Sandoval, A. F., Cummins, J., Alvarado, C. G., & Ruef, M. (1998). *Bilingual verbal ability tests: Comprehensive manual.* Itasca, IL: Riverside Publishing.

National Center for Educational Statistics. (1999). *Digest of education statistics.* Washington, DC: U.S. Department of Education.

National Clearinghouse for Bilingual Education. (1995). The changing face of America's schools. *Forum, 8*(4). Available: http://www.ncbe.gwu.edu/ncbepubs/forum/1804.htm.

Oakes, J. (1986). *Keeping track: How schools structure inequality*. New Haven, CT: Yale University Press.

Ortiz, A. A. (1997). Learning disabilities occurring concomitantly with linguistic differences. *Journal of Learning Disabilities, 30,* 321–332.

Ortiz, A. A. (1990). Using school-based problem-solving teams for prereferral intervention. *Bilingual Special Education Newsletter, 10*(1), 3–5.

Ortiz, A. A., García, S. B., Wheeler, D., & Maldonado-Colón, E. (1986). *Characteristics of limited English proficient students served in programs for the speech and language handicapped: Implications for policy, practice, and research*. Austin: University of Texas Press.

Ortiz, A. A., & Kushner, M. I. (1997). Bilingualism and the possible impact on academic performance. *Child and Adolescent Psychiatric Clinics of North America, 6*(3), 657–679.

Ortiz, A. A., & Wilkinson, C. Y. (1991). Assessment and Intervention Model for the Bilingual Exceptional Student (AIM for the BEST). *Teacher Education and Special Education, 14,* 35–42.

Ortiz, A. A., & Yates, J. R. (2001). Considerations in the assessment of English Language Learners referred to special education. In A. J. Artiles & A. A. Ortiz (Eds.), *English Language Learners with special needs: Identification, placement, and instruction*. Washington, DC: Center for Applied Linguistics and Delta Systems.

Rivera, C. (1994). Is it real for all kids? *Harvard Educational Review, 64*(1), 55–75.

Robertson, P., Kushner, M. I., Starks, J., & Drescher, C. (1994). An update of participation rates of culturally and linguistically diverse students in special education: The need for a research and policy agenda. *The Bilingual Special Education Perspective, 14*(1), 3–9.

Snow, C., Burns, M. S., & Griffin, P. (Eds.). (1998). *Preventing reading difficulties in young children*. Washington, DC: National Academy Press.

Wilkinson, C. Y., & Ortiz, A. A. (1986). *Characteristics of limited English proficient and English proficient learning disabled Hispanic students at initial assessment and at reevaluation*. Austin: University of Texas. (ERIC Document Reproduction Service No. ED 283314)

Chapter 8

A Shameful Subject: The Condition of Latino Students in Gifted Education

Valentina I. Kloosterman

> La interpretación de nuestra realidad con esquemas ajenos sólo contribuye a hacernos cada vez más desconocidos, cada vez menos libres, cada vez más solitarios. (The interpretation of our reality through patterns not our own, serves only to make us ever more unknown, ever less free, ever more solitary.)
>
> —Gabriel García Márquez

INTRODUCTION

The socio-educational condition of high-ability Latino students in gifted programs has proved a *shameful subject*. Although much discussion on *excellence* and *equity* in the field of gifted education in the United States has taken place during the last 15 years, culturally and linguistically diverse students in general and Latino students in particular continue to be systematically excluded from the benefits of gifted and talented programs. Socio-cultural and linguistic misconceptions and stereotypical assumptions about Latino students, narrow definitions of giftedness, biased assessment procedures and tools, insensitive socio-educational practices, lack of well-trained professionals, poor socio-political and legislative decisions, and limited research are some of the contributing aspects perpetuating this injustice in gifted education.

Latino families and communities, like any other socio-cultural group, value their children's potential talents and cognitive abilities that often remain unrecognized and undeveloped by the U.S. school system. What do we mean by *excellence* and *equity* in gifted education? It is not simply a matter of continuously fooling ourselves by trying to find the *magical* assessment tool, the *appropriate* program or strategy, the inclusion of one or two courses about diversity in teacher preparation programs, or even conducting the most sophisticated research. None of these approaches are enough, and none will solve the social injustice alone. Excellence and equity will be fully expressed *if*, and only *if*, moral education and social justice are placed at the top of the national gifted education agenda.

This chapter addresses the main causes for Latino students' underrepresentation in gifted programs. The chapter provides a brief overview of the most important events affecting the field of gifted education in regard to the inclusion of diverse learners. Definitions, assessments, and programming are presented in relation to Latino students, but it is not the intention and scope of this chapter to discuss the many assessments and programs. Rather, the core of the chapter is the discussion of the socio-cultural as well as educational aspects contributing to or hindering the development of talents in Latino students. For this purpose, the most significant findings from a study conducted on high-ability Latino students are presented.

GIFTEDNESS AND LEGISLATION

During the past 30 years theorists and researchers in gifted education and related fields have defined the concepts of *giftedness* and *talent development*. Definitions vary from a very narrow to a very broad or more liberal perspective of the terms (Passow, 1981). A definition of giftedness such as one measured mainly by IQ or other standardized tests narrows the spectrum of students being identified for a gifted program. Renzulli (1994) indicates that we should look into "the development of gifted behaviors in specific areas of learning and human expression rather than giftedness as a state of being" (p. 16). Furthermore, he advocates the use of *talent development* because this term provides the flexibility necessary for both identification and programming to encourage the inclusion of underrepresented student populations in programs for the gifted. In addition, there is no consensus about what is involved in giftedness and in the specific characteristics of the possessor of a gift or talent. Rather, several definitions may be combined by similar psycho-educational approaches using different educational paradigms that have guided the field. "[C]hildren who in a previous era would have been thought gifted no longer stand out, and others who would not have been noticed now appear to have talent" (Csikszentmihalyi & Robinson, 1990, p. 268).

Due to a gradual awareness of the absence of appropriate identification procedures and the lack of programs for culturally and linguistically diverse (CLD) students in the United States, aspects such as culture, ethnicity, and language differences have emerged and slowly begun to be addressed in theoretical and operational definitions of giftedness. As Csikszentmihalyi and Robinson (1990) explain, "giftedness is not an objective fact but a result jointly constituted by social expectations and individual abilities.

From this perspective it is obvious that the question, what proportion of the population is gifted? means what proportion of the population have we agreed to call gifted?" (p. 266).

In 1988, the Jacob K. Javits Gifted and Talented Education Act was passed by Congress. The act recognizes talent potential and outstanding achievement in CLD and economically disadvantaged students, including English language learners (Passow & Frasier, 1996). It provides funding for a federal office, a national research center, and model programs. This act establishes that "outstanding talents are present in children and youth from all cultural groups, across all economic strata, and in all areas of human endeavor" (p. 26). Seventy-one percent of 48 states and territories were supported by the Javits Act from 1992 to 1996 (Council of State Directors of Programs for the Gifted, 1996). In 1993, the *National Excellence: A Case for Developing America's Talent* report was issued by the U.S. Department of Education. This report emphasized the importance of school reform in order to identify and serve underrepresented groups in programs for the gifted. In this report, gifted students are defined as

[c]hildren and youth with outstanding talent [who] perform or show the potential for performing at remarkably high levels of accomplishment when compared with others of their age, experience, or environment. These children and youth exhibit high performance capability in intellectual, creative, and/or artistic areas, possess an unusual leadership capacity, or excel in specific academic fields. They require services or activities not ordinarily provided by the schools. (p. 3) (For more information of policy in gifted education and CLD students, see Díaz, 2002.)

ASSESSMENT AND PROGRAMMING

Currently, a scarcity of culturally and linguistically sensitive assessment procedures and tools exists to accurately identify the potential talents, cognitive abilities, and creative skills in Latino students (Kloosterman, 1997; Reyes, Fletcher, Paez, & Gilbert, 1996). Some of the major difficulties for the identification and nomination of CLD students in general have been "the low expectations educational professionals have for culturally and linguistically diverse students, their low levels of awareness of cultural and linguistic behaviors of potentially gifted [CLD] students, their insensitivity to the differences within and among groups, and their inability to recognize *gifted behaviors*" among these students (Frasier & Passow, 1994, p. 4). Lack of information and misconceptions about learning and cognitive style preferences among CLD students have also been mentioned (DeLeón, 1983; Hartley, 1987).

The measures used in most districts and schools in the United States are based on mainstream standards rather than by valid ethno-linguistic criteria. Traditional psychometric tests used for identifying gifted students, such as intelligence tests, have been proven to be culturally biased (Frasier,

García, & Passow, 1995). To minimize the effects of bias and provide culturally and linguistically fair assessments, flexible and multidimensional assessment procedures and tools should be implemented (DeLeón & Argus-Calvo, 1997; Kloosterman, 1999, 2002). Apart from using traditional school performance indicators, such as school grades and achievement data, multiple methods of assessments should be evaluated, selected, and implemented according to the unique needs of each student (e.g., parent surveys and interviews, student talent portfolios, autobiographies, student journals, performance-based products and writing samples, peer nominations, classroom observations, and enrichment activities). Any evaluation should be sensitive to the students' cultural background and linguistic preference.

There is limited updated demographic information regarding the ethnic and cultural student configuration in gifted and talented programs nationwide; however, it has been reported that 8th grade students enrolled in gifted programs are 17.6% Asians, 9% Whites, 7.9% Blacks, 6.7% Latinos, and 2.1% American Indians (Resnick & Goodman, 1997). More than ever before, we must develop and implement research-based socio-educational programs that meet the needs of high-ability Latino students by focusing on the dynamic interaction of culture, language, and talent development. For example, among the limited number of gifted programs specifically created for high-ability Latino bilingual students, those that provide enrichment and accelerated opportunities in two languages, English and Spanish, are highly recommended (Kloosterman, 2002). Although rare, these programs provide students the opportunity to advance their knowledge in a particular interest area while simultaneously utilizing their bilingual skills in an educational environment in which cultural and linguistic differences are present and nurtured. A recent report from the National Research Council (2002) was unable to provide policy recommendations for gifted programs regarding CLD students, due to the extremely limited accessible data on assessment and programming. Thus, much remains to be done in these two areas for high-ability Latino students.

STUDY OVERVIEW

In an attempt to address the above-mentioned issues, a case study using qualitative research methodology was developed to examine and describe factors contributing to or hindering the development of bilingualism and abilities in 12 Latino elementary students in an urban school. In particular, the study examined teachers' and parents' perceptions of the Latino culture and students' linguistic and academic performance. The following research questions guided data collection. *What factors in the home and school environment appear to support academic achievement, talent development, and bilingual acquisition in Latino bilingual students in an urban environment? What are teachers' perceptions of the socio-cultural background, bilingualism, and talents in Latino bilingual students in an urban elementary school?*

Table 8.1
Student Demographics for Sex, Age, Latino Subgroup, Grade Level, and ESOL
Level

Student	Sex	Age	Latino Subgroup	Grade Level	ESOL Level
Adrian	M	6	Peruvian	1	4
Emilio	M	6	Puerto Rican	1	N/A
Juan	M	7	Puerto Rican	3	5
Daniel	M	8	Puerto Rican	3	N/A
Julian	M	9	Puerto Rican	4	5
Kristian	M	10	Puerto Rican	5	N/A
Sonia	F	6	Puerto Rican	1	4
Nilda	F	6	Puerto Rican	1	N/A
Mercedes	F	8	Puerto Rican	4	N/A
María	F	9	Dominican	4	N/A
Jennifer	F	9	Puerto Rican	4	N/A
Carmen	F	10	Colombian	5	N/A

METHODOLOGY

Purposive sampling (Patton, 1990) was used to select the 12 students (six
girls and six boys) from an urban elementary school in the northeastern
section of the United States. For sampling purposes, participating students
needed to be of Latino descent, display a high level of interest in special
topics or subject area, and/or demonstrate superior performance in one or
more academic areas. In addition, students eligible for the study were in-
termediate or fluent bilingual speakers in Spanish and English or were presently in levels IV or V in the *English to Speakers of Other Languages*
(ESOL) program. All participants were born in the United States, and, with
the exception of one girl, all were first-generation-born in this country and
from different Latino subgroups. Demographic information about participants is included in Table 8.1. Pseudonyms are employed for the participants.

The school personnel included 15 certified classroom teachers, 1 school
principal, and approximately 22 additional professionals and staff personnel (only two CLD teachers). The school had an enrollment of 294 students
in grades K–5, 45% of the student population came from diverse backgrounds, and approximately 33% of the students received free or reduced-
price meals. The school offered an ESOL program and a gifted program.
The gifted program in the school provided advanced learning activities for
18 students—12 students were coming from a mainstream family, and 6

students were from CLD families. At the time of the study, no Latino students were nominated for the program. The three main criteria in the identification process for the gifted program were limited to classroom teacher nomination, gifted teacher nomination, and state academic test scores in language arts and math.

During the two-year period of this study, data were drawn from a variety of sources, including interviews, observations, document review, and photographs. In-depth, semi-structured interviews were designed and conducted in English or Spanish to gather data from participating students, their teachers, and their parents, as well as the school principal, ESOL teacher, and gifted specialist. Observations focused primarily on the description of settings, events, and behaviors as they related to students' home and school environments, and specific attention was given to the reflection of cultural and linguistic diversity in the school environment and teachers' practice. Participating students were observed in different settings, including the regular classroom, the playground, special classes (e.g., art, gym, library), and the cafeteria. Observations also took place in students' homes while parent interviews were conducted. In addition, several official and unofficial documents—including teacher curriculum plans, children's school files, children's writing samples and artwork, school assessment forms, as well as photographs—were collected, cataloged, and coded. During data collection, field notes were taken to augment data analysis and to primarily describe participants, events, behaviors, classroom activities, and interactions related to students and adults. The implementation of these multiple data gathering sources enhanced the accuracy of the collection, interpretation, and trustworthiness of the study (Anderson, 1999).

The analysis process was both linear and iterative. Multiple data collection methodologies and sources enabled the researcher to triangulate data to clarify meaning, verifying the themes through the repeatability of an observation or interpretation across data sources (Erlandson, Harris, Skipper, & Allen, 1993). Within-case and across-case analysis was used in the three-stage coding paradigm, open coding, axial coding, and selective coding (Strauss & Corbin, 1990). Data analysis continued until all categories of codes remained stable and participant checks were saturated (Niles & Huberman, 1994). The study design ensures methodological soundness in its control for biases and in the way it meets the criteria of credibility, transferability, dependability, and confirmability (Lincoln & Guba, 1985). During different stages of the study, audits examined the process of inquiry and the accuracy of the data and interpretation (Merriam, 1998). These steps ensured the methodological soundness of the findings and provided an accurate insight into the development of talents in Latino bilingual students.

RESULTS AND DISCUSSION

Research Question 1

What factors in the home and school environment appear to support academic achievement, talent development, and bilingual acquisition in Latino bilingual students in an urban environment? The home and school environments of the participating students played essential roles in their socio-emotional and cognitive development. However, the main relationships identified by the 12 students as encouraging their academic performance, talent development, and bilingualism were indicated within the family, not at school. Regardless of gender, age, or Latino subcultural group, the family characteristics identified as influencing students' academic and linguistic development were described as emotional support, family values, strong maternal role, Latino legacy, and maintenance of the Spanish language.

For many of the students, the emotional support came from their immediate family, parents, and siblings, as well as a close relationship with other family members, such as grandparents, uncles, and cousins. Relationships were sustained and meaningful for the students even if family members were not living in the United States. As a strong family value, respect, or *respeto*, was identified by many parents and was defined as being considerate of authority. Children understood that they were to care about and follow what adults, such as parents and teachers, said. Of particular importance for parents was that their children respect elderly people. *Being good* or *ser bueno* could be described as the caring, sharing, and humanitarian attitude of one human being toward another. For these families, *to be good* went beyond this conception, and it was intimately related with a more spiritual aspect, meaning to be a good person *in heart and soul*. Also, a strong maternal presence was evident in all the Latino families. A number of common personal characteristics were demonstrated by the students' mothers in this study, regardless of age, socioeconomic background, Latino subcultural identity, or educational level: affection, protection, perseverance, commitment, hard work, optimism, acceptance, and transference of rules, values, and traditions. These personal characteristics, among others, contributed to each family's preservation and influenced the emotional and cognitive development of the students. Parents consistently advocated for the preservation and development of the cultural and linguistic characteristics of their families. These aspects were the pillars of maintaining the Latino legacy and Spanish language in the family.

The school predominantly represented the values, norms, and traditions of the mainstream society. The school perceived these families as Latinos with no personal knowledge of students' cultural differences. For the families in the study, to be described or labeled as *Latino* did not adequately describe their traditions and values. María's mother expressed her disappointment by saying, "[Teachers] don't have any idea of the Hispanic culture. María's teacher has no knowledge of the Dominican culture. She does not even care about it. Thank God I have never felt myself discriminated" (translation from Spanish). Another parent concurred, "They only know that there are different cultures, but they don't try to understand the cultures. Here, when you go to school, you have to forget your own culture" (translation from Spanish).

School personnel claimed that Latino families did not participate actively in school matters. The families in this study were aware that their involvement in school was not as active as it should be. Five reasons were reported by the parents to explain this issue: (a) time constraints in visiting the school, (b) absence of information about the activities and events at school, (c) no invitation from or a feeling of being unwelcome at the school, (d) no appreciation of their culture, and (e) no inquiry about or acceptance of their opinions and ideas. One father claimed:

The Latino family doesn't approach the school because this one is not open to us. You came to our house and talked with us today. No teacher in that school would do that. I see how they treat us as [Latinos]. If they have to greet us, they keep their distance. I like to observe people's behaviors. Sometimes I take my children to the school, and I observe from the car how the teachers say hello. If it is an American person, they are cheerful and expressive, but if it is Latino or Black, they lower their eyes. (translation from Spanish)

Academic Achievement and Talent Development. Parents were proud of their children's academic achievement, and education was a high priority for them. They acknowledged that a good education would result in better careers and job opportunities for their children in the future. These parents were committed to providing the best education possible for their children, and they had high expectations for them. For example, Carmen's mother remembered joking with her daughter about her future and explained,

We are always making jokes. One day, Carmen told me that she wanted to work in the postal service as I do. I told her that if she wasn't going to be the boss, she could forget about it. I didn't go to the university, I wanted to be a psychologist, but Carmen will go. I told her she could study whatever she wants. I know it will cost me a fortune, but it is worth it. (translation from Spanish)

Many parents like Carmen's mother were dissatisfied with the school because they believed their children were able to achieve at a higher academic level or to participate in the gifted program, and the regular curriculum was not challenging the academic abilities of their children. Despite the frustration, in most cases, education had a broader meaning. Nothing was more valuable for these parents than to be able to say things like, "My child is a good one," "My daughter has very good principles," "She is growing very nice," or "My child is a good boy; he has a good heart." Education was considered beyond the boundaries of school. Far more important for these parents was to encourage their children to *be someone* in their community and to strive for a better way of life.

The main experiences that challenged the interests and abilities in the 12 Latino bilingual students in this study were primarily provided by the home environment and partially by the school. Positive enrichment opportunities, such as some sporadic enrichment activities, special classes, reading and math instructional-level grouping, fine arts, instrumental music, and dance, were organized activities that encouraged the development of interests and skills in students. None of the students in this study were identified as gifted by the gifted programs. Parents in this study did not nominate their own children for the gifted program, not because of their unwillingness but because of their unawareness of the possibility of doing so. Furthermore, they did not know what the gifted program was about.

Conflicting points of view between parents and teachers were specifically noted in relation to the development of the curriculum and students' academic achievement. Parents were, in many cases, dissatisfied with the academic standards of the school, and they perceived that teachers did not sufficiently challenge their children, especially in the content areas in which their children excelled. They had a sense that their children were not learning at their potential, especially in the area of math and language arts. However, from the teachers' point of view, students were given excellent opportunities, and an adequate, standard education was provided to all students.

The Development of Two Languages. Spanish maintenance was strongly present in most of the participating students. The decision, effort, and commitment of themselves and their parents exclusively maintained students' Spanish. Parents in this study acknowledged the importance of the linguistic aspect in their cultures and the positive connotations of being bilingual. However, it was clear that they had no information or assistance either from the school or from the community to enrich the linguistic abilities of their children, especially with reading and writing in Spanish. As a reflection of the limited value that school culture placed on bilingualism, the school principal commented:

I believe kids need to be immersed in English. I watch kids that come from other school districts; many of those children have been in bilingual programs for more than four years but still don't speak fluently in English. So, my opinion is the children come, you give them a lot of care, and you work with the ESOL teacher that works with them to teach them in English. Many of our kids do learn English really quickly, some of them faster than others. I think kids need to be taught in English.

In the 20 years that she has been principal of this school, it appears she was unable to connect the development of English as a second language and the benefits of continuing with students' first language. The importance of having an additive bilingual context, in other words, a context in which bilingualism carries prestige and second language acquisition develops in a positive atmosphere, was clearly lacking in this school.

Research Question 2

What are teacher perceptions of the socio-cultural background, bilingualism, and talents in Latino bilingual students in an urban elementary school? Neither the classroom teachers nor ESOL teacher and gifted specialist had substantial knowledge of students' bilingualism, interests, or abilities, especially of their socio-cultural characteristics. Throughout the conversations with the staff at the school, it became clear that most of the teachers, specialists, and administrators had little knowledge of the meaning of *cultural diversity*. It became more evident considering the fact that almost half of the student population came from a diverse cultural and linguistic background, the majority being Latinos. Yet, the school personnel remained unacquainted with the meaning of and the practices related to diversity and its reflection in the school and classroom environments, as well as in educational instruction and evaluation. A 4th grade teacher said, "I don't think my curriculum is multicultural. I have one book about it. I haven't had a chance to do anything about that yet." The school principal's best explanation was, "We do a little in the classroom, but I think part of the problem is not that we don't want to or we don't believe in [diversity], but it is just a matter of time."

Lack of Awareness of the Latino Culture and Families. Few teachers were able to describe students' families or give details of the things that the students enjoyed doing at home or the celebrations, values, and traditions of each family. For example, many teachers did not know that their students regularly visited their families abroad and that, during those trips, they mainly spoke in Spanish. Even teachers with fewer than 16 students in their classrooms were unaware that participants like Emilio and Juan had important economic needs; that Julian and Kristian had lost their two parents; that Carmen had a close bond with and admiration for her aunt; or that María had a strong relationship with her family in the Dominican Republic. These examples clearly indicate the educators' lack of awareness of key issues in the lives of the 12 Latino students.

Lack of Awareness of Students' Bilingualism. The school was unable to provide accurate information about the bilingual proficiency and development of all 12 Latino students in this study. In this respect, the proficiency in English and the scattered information in the students' files were the only two available resources at the beginning of this study. In formal and informal conversations, parents and staff were asked about the participants' proficiency and use of English and Spanish. Most teachers did not know or were *not sure* about the language or languages usually spoken by the families and the students at home. It appears that language development was not relevant to discuss with Latino families if students were fluent in English. None of the teachers in this study asked parents how their children were developing their home languages. Teachers had information only of the level of proficiency in English, although the students participating in this study were simultaneously bilingual speakers, and some of them were even biliterate. The ESOL teacher, for example, said, "I don't ask parents about their first language. I don't know what the parents are doing with them at home. I would say most of the parents don't do very much."

An interesting finding emerged about the teachers' appreciation for and knowledge about their students' bilingualism. Because most of the teachers were unaware of the Latino students' language development other than English, they appeared to believe that, if students were not in the ESOL program, they were not bilingual. Teachers' comments supporting this belief were indicated in expressions such as, "Oh, I don't think she is bilingual; her English is perfect," or "I have six ESOL students in my classroom. Juan is not ESOL, but do you consider him bilingual?" Juan not only was a fluent speaker in English and Spanish, but he also read in both languages.

Lack of Awareness of Students' Talents. When teachers were asked about gifted education, they demonstrated a weak knowledge and training in this particular area. Although none of the 12 Latino students were identified to participate in the gifted program, they displayed above-average ability, interests, and task commitment in specific topics and academic areas. However, teachers did not provide individually differentiated curriculum for them. Interests, abilities, and high academic performance were displayed in subject areas such as mathematics, language arts, music, dance, and drama. In language arts, for example, most students were strong readers in English, and some of them were also avid readers in Spanish. With no assistance, parents were stimulating and enriching their children's bilingual abilities by going frequently to the library, reading them books in both languages, and having permanent verbal communication in the family. When teachers were asked if they knew of activities, hobbies, or sports that their students enjoyed doing out of the school, almost all the teachers responded that they were unaware. In terms of learning styles, teachers were asked if they perceived differences in the way students preferred to learn. The majority of the teachers reported no differences in their students' learning styles. A 2nd grade teacher reflected, "I think they might, but I did not see it in the classroom. Honestly, I never really thought about it. I don't know."

Discussion

Research has identified several obstacles impeding equal access to gifted programs for Latino students. Many of these obstacles have been confirmed in this study as interfering in the identification and development of talents in the 12 Latino students. The overrepresentation of teachers from the mainstream society, an unchallenging curriculum, teachers' negative attitudes toward bilingualism, and lack of teacher training (National Center for Research on Cultural Diversity and Second Language Learning, 1994; National Research Council, 2002; Passow & Frasier, 1996) were found to be some of the major obstacles in the identification and development of Latino students' academic abilities in this school. More importantly, these aspects were obstacles in the awareness, value, and expression of students' cultural and linguistic backgrounds. Stereotypical assumptions were still ingrained in the faculty and interfered with the communication with families.

Studies have shown that Latino families often value high-ability skills, including linguistic skills, while going unrecognized by the majority culture (Stephens & Karnes, 2000). This study supports this finding; parents considered bilingualism an asset in their children's lives, because of the sociocultural benefits, while simultaneously teachers denied or were unable to recognize them. The *attitude* of the staff toward Latino students was one of the most significant factors that needed to change at this school in order to recognize and stimulate students' talents and academic skills. Regarding bilingualism, bilingual students like the ones participating in this study, who are fluent bilinguals, deserve an education that recognizes and encourages the development of both languages. Often, languages other than English have low status and prestige in American schools, and English remains the exclusive language that is fully developed (García, 1991; Milon, 1996; Stephens, 1994).

Findings in this study also suggest that values and educational perspectives between the home and the school were in conflict, mainly because of the unfamiliarity of the teachers with the students' families, culture, abilities, and bilingualism. Students adjusted and developed in two conflicting environments, and an unconscious rule seemed to govern the communication between the school and the home. When students were at home, the Latino traditions were nurtured and developed; while in school, the Latino identity appeared to be precluded and overshadowed by the values and traditions of the mainstream society.

Educators, students, and families need to have an awareness of their own culture and an understanding of the similarities and differences among their own sets of values and those of others. Conceptions of and approaches to *giftedness, talent development, bilingualism, learning style preferences,* and *education* should be discussed in a respectful and ongoing manner. Language and cultural differences in staff and families should prove enlightening and be reflected in the curriculum, in the environment, and, most importantly, in people's personal attitudes. The gifted program of a school is not excluded from this important endeavor.

CONCLUSION

Every society values and encourages the development of certain talents or cognitive abilities in its youngsters, while simultaneously overlooking others. High-ability Latino students come from homes in which special talents are traditionally valued but may not be recognized by the majority culture, usually represented by the school. In the event that Latino students are bilingual, they should be encouraged to use their languages throughout their lives because bilingualism, like talents, is a treasure to be discovered and fully developed.

Certainly, changing attitudes is difficult. Acceptance of differences—moreover, respect and integration—becomes *the* challenge for school systems in the United States. The quality of education for Latino students in particular and for all students in general will improve, and equitable educational opportunities will be provided, only when professional educators become aware, informed, and trained in the acceptance and expression of diversity. The field of gifted education has not yet made a thorough self-evaluation of its philosophical and theoretical underpinnings and its research and practice, especially regarding equity and socio-educational justice. The field may not be ready for such introspective analysis. The actual socio-educational paradigms in gifted education describe a reality in which opportunities are denied to children of cultural and linguistical backgrounds. We pay a high social price in keeping these paradigms alive. The identification and nurturing of talents in high-ability Latino students will benefit not only from new research, practice, and teacher training but also from a field that takes consistent note of its mistakes and neglectfulness in regard to diversity and equity. As Elbert Hubbard (1856–1915) once said, "It is a fine thing to have ability, but the ability to discover ability in others is the true test."

REFERENCES

Council of State Directors of Programs for the Gifted. (1996). *The 1996 state of the states gifted and talented education report.* Oklahoma City, OK: Author.

Csikszentmihalyi, M., & Robinson, R. E. (1990). Culture, time, and the development of talent. In R. J. Sternberg & J. E. Davidson (Eds.), *Conceptions of giftedness* (pp. 264–284). New York: Cambridge University Press.

DeLeón, J. (1983). Cognitive style differences and the underrepresentation of Mexican Americans in the programs for the gifted. *Journal for the Education of the Gifted*, 6(3), 167–177.

DeLeón, J., & Argus-Calvo, B. (1997). *A model program for identifying culturally and linguistically diverse rural gifted and talented students.* (ERIC Document Reproduction Service No. ED 388024)

Díaz, E. I. (2002). Framing a contemporary context for the education of culturally and linguistically diverse students with gifted potential: 1990s to the present. In J. A. Castellano & E. I. Díaz (Eds.), *Reaching new horizons: Gifted and talented education for culturally and linguistically diverse students* (pp. 29–46). Boston: Allyn & Bacon.

Erlandson, D. A., Harris, E. L., Skipper, B. L., & Allen, S. D. (1993). *Doing naturalistic inquiry: A guide to methods.* Newbury Park, CA: Sage Publications.

Frasier, M., García, J., & Passow, A. H. (1995). *A review of assessment issues in gifted education and their implications for identifying gifted minority students* (RM Series No. 95203). Storrs, CT: The National Research Center on the Gifted and Talented.

Frasier, M., & Passow, A. H. (1994). *Toward a new paradigm for identifying talent potential* (RM Series No. 94111). Storrs, CT: The National Research Center on the Gifted and Talented.

García, E. E. (1991). Bilingualism and second language acquisition in academic contexts. In A. N. Ambert (Ed.), *Bilingual education and English as a second language: A research handbook, 1988–1990* (pp. 97–137). New York: Garland.

Hartley, E. A. (1987). *How can we meet all their needs? Incorporating education for the gifted and talented into the multicultural classroom.* (ERIC Document Reproduction Service No. ED 336968)

Jacob K. Javits Gifted and Talented Students Education Act, 20 U.S.C. ¶ 3061–3068 (1988).

Kloosterman, V. I. (2002). The schoolwide enrichment model: Promoting diversity and excellence in gifted education. In E. I. Díaz & J. A. Castellano (Eds.), *Reaching new horizons: Gifted and talented education for culturally and linguistically diverse students* (pp. 175–199). Boston: Allyn & Bacon.

Kloosterman, V. I. (1999). *Socio-cultural contexts for talent development: A qualitative study on high ability Hispanic bilingual students* (Research Monograph 99142). Storrs, CT: The National Research Center on the Gifted and Talented.

Kloosterman, V. I. (1997). Building a bridge of success: A combined effort between gifted and bilingual education. *National Research Center on the Gifted and Talented Newsletter*, Spring, 3–7.

Lincoln, Y. S., & Guba, E. S. (1985). *Naturalistic inquiry.* Newbury Park, CA: Sage Publications.

Merriam, S. (1998). *Qualitative research and case study applications in education.* San Francisco: Jossey-Bass.

Milon, J. (1996). When language is not the issue. *National Association for Bilingual Education News*, 20(2), 25, 30.

Miles, M., & Huberman, A. (1994). *Qualitative data analysis: An expanded sourcebook* (2nd ed.). Thousand Oaks, CA: Sage Publications.

National Center for Research on Cultural Diversity and Second Language Learning.

(1994, February). *Funds of knowledge: Learning from language minority households*. ERIC Digest, ERIC Document Reproduction Service No. EDO-FL-94-08. Washington, DC: Center for Applied Linguistics.

National Research Council. (2002). *Minority students in special and gifted education*. Washington, DC: National Academy Press.

Passow, A. H. (1981). The nature of giftedness and talent. *Gifted Child Quarterly*, 25(1), 5–10.

Passow, A. H., & Frasier, M. (1996). Toward improving identification of talent potential among minority and disadvantaged students. *Roeper Review*, 18(3), 198–202.

Patton, M. Q. (1990). *Qualitative evaluation and research methods* (2nd ed.). Newbury Park, CA: Sage Publications.

Renzulli, J. S. (1994). *Schools for talent development: A practical plan for total school improvement*. Mansfield, CT: Creative Learning.

Resnick, D., & Goodman, M. (1997, Fall). Research review. *Northwest Education Magazine*. Available: www.nwcrcl.org/nwedu/fall_97/text6.html.

Reyes, E. I., Fletcher, R., Paez, D., & Gilbert, C. (1996). Developing local multidimensional screening procedures for identifying giftedness among Mexican American border population. *Roeper Review*, 18(3), 208–211.

Stephens, K. R., & Karnes, F. A. (2000). State definitions for the gifted and talented revisited. *Exceptional Children*, 66(2), 219–238.

Stephens, T. M. (1994). The role of English and Spanish (bi)lingualism in U.S. Hispanicity: Factors in constructing a collectivity. *The Bilingual Review/La Revista Bilingüe*, 19(1), 3–8.

Strauss, A., & Corbin, J. (1990). *Basics of qualitative research: Grounded theory procedures and techniques*. Newbury Park, CA: Sage Publications.

U.S. Department of Education. (1993). *National excellence: A case for developing America's talent*. Washington, DC: Office of Educational Research and Improvement.

Chapter 9

Ensuring Success for Latino Migrant Students

Velma D. Menchaca

INTRODUCTION

Each year, approximately 3 to 5 million migrant farmworkers and their families leave their homes to *follow the crops*, hoping to improve their financial situations (National Center for Farmworker Health, 2001). They "move for the purposes of obtaining seasonal or temporary work in agriculture or fishing" (U.S. Department of Education, 1994, p. 4). Approximately 92% of all migrants are culturally and linguistically diverse, of whom 85% are Latinos. The largest Latino subgroup is Mexican Americans (60%), followed by Puerto Ricans, Cubans, and Central and South Americans (Kissam, 1993). Migrants who have immigrated to the United States from Mexico and parts of Central America primarily harvest fruits and vegetables. In the summers, they may harvest tomatoes or broccoli in Texas or possibly apricots, peaches, or grapes in California. They tend to migrate along three known geographic routes: the East Coast Stream, the Mid-Continent Stream, and the West Coast Stream following seasonal crops.

This chapter addresses the educational experiences of Latino migrant students, culturally relevant teaching, migrant parental involvement, and the challenges of secondary schools. The chapter also provides an array of information on the lives of Latino migrant children and hardships they encounter in the fields. Also discussed are the challenges they encounter in schools because of their mobile lifestyles, the obstacles that keep them from graduating from high school, and the hurdles they must successfully negotiate to enter college.

PROFILE OF THE MIGRANT FAMILY

Over 80% of migrants and seasonal farmworkers are U.S. citizens or are legally in the United States (Fix & Passel, 1994). The average annual income for these families is less than $7,500 per year, far below the federal poverty level (Oliveira, Effland, & Hamm, 1993). Because the work of migrant farmworkers tends to be seasonal, it is often extremely inconsistent. The number of farmworkers needing housing exceeds the number of available substandard housing units, which are usually barracks-like structures, run-down farmhouses, trailer homes, or small shacks (National Center for Farmworker Health, 2001). Some migrants may be forced to sleep in tents, cars, or even ditches when housing is unavailable. Many migrant families live without adequate rest-room facilities and clean drinking water. Although agricultural employers recognize that lack of adequate housing is a serious challenge, they often resort to temporary housing such as labor camps, of which the construction and maintenance can be expensive, especially since the camps are occupied only during harvest season. In addition, the housing that is readily available for most migrant families may not meet even the minimum inspection standards, consequently contributing to serious health problems.

Many migrant families suffer occupation-related health problems such as risk of injury from farm machinery and equipment and also from pesticide poisoning (Menchaca & Ruiz-Escalante, 1995). Respiratory problems caused by pesticide poisoning, natural fungi, and dusts are common. Lack of safe drinking water contributes to dehydration, heat stroke, and heat exhaustion. Dermatitis is often intensified by overexposure to the sun, by sweat, and by lack of sanitary facilities. Some commonly reported health problems among migrant children include lower height and weight, respiratory diseases, parasitic conditions, chronic diarrhea, and congenital and developmental problems, among others. Poverty, hunger, fear, and uncertainty fill the lives of migrant children. Thus, the intensity of health problems for migrant farmworkers is far more frequent than for the general population (National Center for Farmworker Health, 2001).

Migrant Parental Involvement in Education

Historically, school districts have lacked coherent policies and practices that attend to the needs of migrant parents. Because their lives revolve around moving from workplace to workplace, the hardships migrant parents confront are much greater than what most other parents encounter. Migrant parents tend to be intimidated by and unresponsive to schools, particularly if they did not enjoy positive experiences as students. Many are unsure about how best to be involved in schools and the degree of involvement that is appropriate. Language barriers also play a major role in their lack of participation. In addition, some Latino migrant parents believe it is the school's responsibility to educate their children; therefore, parental participation is sometimes non-existent (Chavkin, 1991). Thus, it is critical for educators to understand how migrant parents define schooling and education and their perceptions of how schools operate (Martínez & Velásquez, 2000). Often schools limit parental involvement to open houses, parent–teacher conferences, monitoring children's homework, and reinforcing school discipline policies. These approaches are one-way communications from school to home, rather than respecting the home situation and recognizing that parents have something valuable to contribute. A directed, authority-based form of communication that lacks a sense of closeness and mutual interest intensifies feelings that lead to a lack of parental participation.

Parent involvement strategies should be adopted and incorporated to develop strong relationships between the school and community (Ruiz-Escalante & Menchaca, 1999); however, many current intervention programs tend to be *prescriptive* instead of inclusive (Valdes, 1996). A strong partnership between the family and the school can support and empower Latino migrant parents to become more involved in schools. Thus, educators should begin to rethink their communicative approach, include Latino migrant parents in schools, and respond to their specific needs.

EDUCATIONAL EXPERIENCES OF MIGRANT STUDENTS

Children of Latino migrants tend to be academically unsuccessful. Their mobility interrupts their education several times throughout the school year and puts enormous stress on them and their schools. The particular educational needs of Latino migrant students vary considerably; some lack the literary skills in Spanish, while English language abilities are limited for others. The quality of instruction for Latino migrant students could also be hampered if the curriculum does not adequately address their needs or provide supplemental instructional services to overcome academic difficulties that result from frequent disruptions in schooling. Most school personnel are not well prepared to adequately serve the academic needs of Latino students in general and Latino migrant students in particular (Menchaca, 1996).

Migrant students have the lowest graduation rate of any other population in the United States (Johnson, Levy, Morales, Morse, & Prokop, 1986); their dropout rate is almost twice that of children from non-migrant families. Approximately 50% of Latino migrant students are one or more years below grade level. Thus, half of all migrants could be at risk of leaving school early (Migrant Education Secondary Assistance Project, 1989). Poverty is another factor that leads to dropping out; the addition of another family member's income is welcomed. In addition, Latino migrant students tend to drop out of school if they are not proficient in English, and some teachers become disinterested in Latino migrant students due to their diverse academic, social, and economic needs.

In a study conducted by the Migrant Youth Program (1985) some students indicated that the school personnel did not meet their needs, although teachers and counselors believed the students' needs were met. Martínez (1994) reported that, according to principals and teachers, factors that influence the school performance of migrant children are: (a) social prejudice, (b) lack of communication, (c) mobility, (d) lack of educational continuity, (e) not valuing education, (f) inappropriate home environment, and (g) lack of knowledge of how educational systems operate. Yet, migrant advocates such as mentors, counselors, or advisers had a more holistic perspective on reasons migrant students leave school. Many indicated that poverty contributed to school absences because these students needed to work; and they often had to care for younger siblings or were absent due to illnesses (Martínez & Cranston-Gingras, 1996).

Because Latino migrant children can transfer schools as much as three times per year, schools must provide an environment for them to adjust as quickly as possible. The Jackson County Migrant Education Program (1981) in Medford, Oregon, produced a handbook titled *Migrant Education—Harvest of Hope*. This handbook covers several topics including knowledge of children for whom English is a second language (ESL) and how migrant students relate with teachers and provides suggestions for meeting the needs of ESL students. Most important is the message that the migrant students need teachers' care, respect, understanding, and encouragement. Another site that provides migrant children with rich learning experiences is Waitz Elementary in Mission, Texas; approximately 30% of its students are from migrant families and live in tar-paper shacks or in trailer homes along dirt roads. With a 99% Mexican American student population, Waitz Elementary annually places among the top 10% of all Texas schools in reading and mathematics achievement. The school "defies predictions of low achievement by a sustained focus on multiple factors" (Cawelti, 1999, p. 1) that remarkably improve student performance. The principal and teachers are committed to high expectations and make every effort to ensure high student achievement. For example, teachers use bilingual education approaches with students who enter with limited English skills, making sure that all students pass the state-mandated assessment. These two programs are good examples of how schools, with motivation and effort, can effectively serve the unique needs of Latino migrant students.

CULTURALLY RELEVANT TEACHING

Culturally relevant teaching is a pedagogy that empowers students intellectually, socially, emotionally, and politically (Ladson-Billings, 1990,

1995). It rests on three criteria: (a) academic success, (b) cultural competence, and (c) cultural consciousness (Ladson-Billings, 1995). It also utilizes students' home culture to help create meaning and understanding of their world. Thus, the culturally relevant teacher emphasizes academic, social, and cultural success and believes that academic success is possible for all students.

Making the connection between home culture and school allows migrant students to learn from a familiar cultural base that acknowledges their ancestors and develops understanding in their culture, thus empowering them to build on their personal backgrounds (Banks, 1994; Barba, 1995). Culturally relevant teachers believe that Latino migrant students have special strengths that need to be explored and utilized in the classroom. When needed, teachers encourage students to use their home language while acquiring English as a second language. Latino migrant students must have opportunities to make decisions and to take actions related to the topic, issue, or problem they are studying. In other words, when students identify a problem and are given the liberty to make decisions on what actions need to be taken to remedy the problem, they will have a sense of pride and satisfaction. It is important for teachers to communicate to students that they are being successful.

Teachers must direct, reinforce, and cultivate academic success and excellence in their migrant students. Culturally relevant teachers validate students' cultures by integrating culturally relevant content into the curriculum (Menchaca, 2000). Teachers legitimate Latino migrant students' real-life experiences as part of the formal curriculum. In a science lesson, for example, the use of culturally familiar plants, flowers, and fruits prevalent to the Latino culture could be presented along with the content in the textbook. Studying the production of plants, fruits, and vegetables gives teachers an excellent opportunity to introduce the mobile lifestyle of migrant students. In addition, when studying the food pyramid in a health lesson, the use of culturally familiar foods and examples enhances concept acquisition. Also, examples of foods and diseases that are prevalent in migrant family households should be presented along with the examples in the textbook.

In a language arts lesson, teachers can incorporate a variety of Latino children's books. Much of the Latino literature focuses on the life and experiences of migrant students. Nurturing ethnic affiliation helps migrant students learn about and respect cultural groups' heritage and histories while keeping their own culture instilled in their hearts and minds. Adolescent novels can be used at the middle or high schools with migrant students (e.g., *White Bread Competition*, Hernández, 1997; *Spirits of the High Mesa*, Martínez, 1997; and *Trino's Time*, Bertrand, 2001). These novels explore conflict, friendships, loyalties, romances, racial identities, death, and Latino traditions. With humor and sensitivity, the authors shed light on the lives of middle school and high school Latino adolescents. Migrant students can read about their own life experiences as they read about the mysteries, challenges, dreams, and conflicts of other young Latino adolescents. It is also important for White students to read about the successes, challenges, and dreams of Latino students to view different perspectives and to understand the ways in which the histories and cultures of our nation are inextricably bound.

Instructional Strategies for Migrant Students

Cooperative learning, metacognitive skills, positive educational environments, and extracurricular activities can help build on Latino migrant students' strengths and foster self-esteem. Cooperative learning lowers anxiety levels and strengthens motivation, self-esteem, and empowerment by using students as instructional agents for migrant students (Platt, Cranston-Gingras, & Scott, 1991). Students take responsibility for both their own learning and the learning of their peers. By becoming active group participants, they gain equal access to learning opportunities.

Metacognitive skills assist students in becoming independent learners by helping them comprehend concepts, monitor their success, and make the necessary adjustments when meaning is elusive. Students learn to recognize when they are approaching an obstacle, make necessary corrections, and proceed. Teachers instruct students to employ alternative strategies once they have recognized and determined a lack of comprehension. Because migrant students often find themselves in new and unfamiliar classrooms, the challenges of adjusting to strange, new learning and home environments often contribute to feelings of isolation and loneliness. Teachers can help students overcome these feelings by modeling respect and eliminating any form of threat or ridicule. A sense of safety and trust can be fostered by allowing students to share some of their own experiences and by assigning older students to act as mentors or buddies to new students.

Since schooling for migrant students is interrupted with each move, most are not involved in any form of extracurricular activity. Many of them do not participate in after-school activities because they lack transportation or have after-school responsibilities or because their parents are unaware of the extracurricular activities available. Yet, participating in these types of activities can provide enriched learning experiences to develop social skills and talents and promote positive attitudes. Some of these challenges can be overcome by providing after-school transportation. Parents should be informed of all before- and after-school activities. In some communities, after-school programs are sponsored by clubs, organizations, or local park and recreation departments. In Florida, for example, the Dade County Park and Recreation Department has activities specifically designed for migrant students, since the enrollment of these students has increased dramatically in that area. The facility, located close to a migrant camp, offers adult supervision and activities in which games and activities are planned in both English and Spanish. The goal of this facility is to contribute to the total well-being of children regardless of language or ethnicity.

THE CHALLENGES OF SECONDARY SCHOOLS

High dropout rates, low achievement test scores, poor attendance, mobility, cultural differences, and limited proficiency in English are among the challenges that many Latino migrant students encounter in secondary schools. These challenges are overwhelming for public schools and present difficult instructional problems to educators. Secondary schools have begun to seek assistance from external entities to respond to the needs of Latino migrant students by establishing, for example, bilingual or dual-language programs in elementary schools and ESL programs in secondary schools. Flexible instructional and support programs are needed to facilitate schooling through reading, writing, and critical thinking skills. Such support programs include tutorial services, counseling services, enrichment activities, career awareness, health services, and medical referrals. Because intervention must be provided to highly mobile students, placement in small classrooms, in which instruction is more personalized, is important.

Migrants who are high school seniors have needs that are numerous in nature, and schools must provide solutions for their success. There are more Latino seniors in vocational or general education programs than in the college preparation programs. There are fewer numbers of Latino seniors in senior-level courses such as trigonometry, calculus, physics, chemistry, or English. Fewer Latinos take the Scholastic Aptitude Test (SAT) and American College Test (ACT), examinations used for college admissions. These deficits exclude Latino migrant students from entering college. Schools should provide academic opportunities for making up credits, tutoring, taking appropriate courses, and developing test-taking skills. Also, school counselors should assist migrants in applying to and preparing for college. This type of involvement increases college attendance rates (Horn & Chen, 1998). Other more personal services that schools can provide migrant students are counseling, extended day/week/year programs, and special summer schools. Career awareness about work experiences and vocational education has also been successful for migrant students. Because even successful migrant students are at risk in high school, programs such as the College Assistance Migrant Program (CAMP) have been designed for continued support. CAMP is a *Title IV* program that provides tutoring, orientations, and counseling for migrants planning to enter college. Such programs are found on many university campuses and have been successful. They have lowered freshman dropout rates by offering academic support to students during their first year of college (National Commission on Migrant Education, 1992). In addition, College Bound is a summer program to assist seniors in the transition from high school to college. Students work, study, and receive assistance and counseling at a college campus. Approximately 90% of College Bound students enroll in colleges the following semester.

The U.S. Department of Education's Migrant Education Program has worked for more than 20 years with states to prepare migrant students for a successful transition to post-secondary education or employment (Morse & Hammer, 1998). To be admitted into college, migrant students need to have completed high school with the appropriate courses for post-secondary education and understand the application requirements and financial aid deadlines and strategies and skills to progress through a system that was not created for them. Factors that have contributed and facilitated migrant students' college attendance are (a) access to counseling centers that offer an array of options; (b) students' self-efficacy; (c) access to financial aid and scholarships, loans, and work-study programs; (d) support from family, friends, and educational personnel; and (e) parental involvement in decisions about their children's education. Thus, schools must take an active role in ensuring that migrant students receive assistance in preparing and applying for college.

CONCLUSION

This chapter has provided an array of information on the lives of migrant students in general and the condition of Latino migrant students in particular. These students encounter many hardships; the poverty and health aliments from which they suffer can be severe. These are among the many obstacles that prevent them from succeeding in school; thus, they require a supportive school environment. It is imperative that educators remember that migrant students dream of being successful and of transcending the lifestyles of their families. They understand what it means to work hard; they want to graduate and be successful. As educators, we must help them realize their dreams.

REFERENCES

Banks, J. A. (1994). *Multicultural education: Theory and practice.* Boston: Allyn & Bacon.

Barba, R. H. (1995). *Science in the multicultural classroom: A guide to teaching and learning.* Boston: Allyn & Bacon.

Bertrand, D. G. (2001). *Trino's Time.* Houston, TX: Arte Público Press.

Cawelti, G. (1999). Improving achievement. *American School Board Journal, 186,* 34–37.

Chavkin, N. F. (1991). *Family lives and parental involvement in migrant students' education.* Washington, DC: U.S. Department of Education, Office of Educational Research and Improvement. (ERIC Document Reproduction Service No. ED 335174)

Fix, M., & Passel, J. S. (1994). *Immigration and immigrants: Setting the record straight*. Washington, DC: The Urban Institute.

Hernández, J. Y. (1997). *White bread competition*. Houston, TX: Arte Público Press.

Horn, L. J., & Chen, X. (1998). *Toward resiliency: At risk students who make it to college*. Washington, DC: U.S. Department of Education Office of Educational Research and Improvement.

Jackson County Migrant Education. (1981). *Migrant education—Harvest of hope*. Medford, OR: Jackson County Educational Service District. (ERIC Document Reproduction Service No. ED 212441)

Johnson, F. C., Levy, R. H., Morales, J. A., Morse, S. C., & Prokop, M. K. (1986). *Migrant students at the secondary level: Issues and opportunities for change*. Las Cruces, NM: ERIC Clearinghouse on Rural Education and Small Schools. (ERIC Document Reproduction Service No. ED 270242)

Kissam, E. (1993). Formal characteristics of the farm labor market: Implications for farm labor policy in the 1990s. In Briefing of the Commission on Security and Cooperation in Europe, *Migrant farmworkers in the United States*. Washington, DC: U.S. Government Printing Office.

Ladson-Billings, G. (1995). But that's just good teaching! The case for culturally relevant pedagogy. *Theory into Practice, 34*(3), 159–165.

Ladson-Billings, G. (1990). Like lightning in a bottle: Attempting to capture the pedagogical excellence of successful teachers of Black students. *International Journal of Qualitative Studies in Education, 3*(4), 335–344.

Martínez, F. (1997). *Spirits of the high mesa*. Houston, TX: Arte Público Press.

Martínez, Y. G. (1994). Narratives of survival: Life histories of Mexican American youth from migrant and seasonal farm workers who have graduated from high school equivalency program. Unpublished. University of South Florida.

Martínez, Y. G., & Cranston-Gingras, A. (1996). Migrant farmworker students and the educational process: Barriers to high school completion. *The High School Journal*, 28–38.

Martínez, Y. G., & Velázquez, J. A. (2000). *Involving migrant families in education*. Charleston, WV: ERIC Clearinghouse on Rural Education and Small Schools. (ERIC Document Reproduction Service No. ED 448010)

Menchaca, V. D. (2000). Culturally relevant curriculum for Limited English-Proficient students. *The Journal of the Texas Association for Bilingual Education, 5*(1), 55–59.

Menchaca, V. D. (1996). The missing link in teacher preparation programs. *Journal of Educational Issues of Language Minority Students, 17*, 1–9.

Menchaca, V. D., & Ruiz-Escalante, J. A. (1995). *Instructional strategies for migrant students*. Charleston, WV: ERIC Clearinghouse on Rural Education and Small Schools. (ERIC Document Reproduction Service No. ED 388491)

Migrant Education Secondary Assistance Project. (1989). *MESA national MSRTS executive summary*. Geneseo, NY: BOCES Geneseo Migrant Center.

Migrant Youth Program. (1985). *Perceptions of why migrant students drop out of school and what can be done to encourage them to graduate*. Albany, NY: Upstate Regional Offices and Migrant Unit, State Education Department.

Morse, S., & Hammer, P. C. (1998). Migrant students attending college: Facilitating their success. Charleston, WV: ERIC Clearinghouse on Rural Education and Small Schools. (ERIC Document Reproduction Service No. ED 423097)

National Center for Farmworker Health. (2001). *About America's farmworkers.* Available: http://www.ncth.org/abouttws.htm.

National Commission on Migrant Education. (1992). *Invisible children: A portrait of migrant children in the United States.* Washington, DC: Author. (ERIC Document Reproduction Service No. ED 348206)

Oliveira, V., Effland, J. R., & Hamm, S. (1993). *Hired farm labor use of fruit, vegetable, and horticultural specialty farms.* Washington, DC: U.S. Department of Agriculture.

Platt, J. S., Cranston-Gingras, A., & Scott, J. (1991). Understanding and educating migrant students. *Preventing School Failure, 36*(1), 41–46.

Ruiz-Escalante, J. A., & Menchaca, V. D. (1999). Creating school–community partnerships for minority parents. *Texas Teacher Education Forum, 24,* 45–49.

U.S. Department of Education. (1994). *Improving America's schools act, 103–382 statute, Title 1, part C, (Migrant Education) Program purpose, Section 1301-(4).*

Valdes, G. (1996). *Con respeto: Bridging the distance between culturally diverse families and schools: An ethnographic portrait.* New York: Teachers College Press.

Chapter 10

Triumphs and Tragedies: The Urban Schooling of Latino Students

Theresa Montaño and Eloise López Metcalfe

INTRODUCTION

A dialectical and critical worldview of urban education would carefully reflect upon and analyze the development and implementation of educational practices and reform efforts as a series of contractions, a dichotomy of educational progress. The movement toward equity in education for urban Latinos in the United States can best be described as a mixture of modest progress and continued oppression. The dialectical relationship between the advancement of educational opportunities for Latino students and continued inequity remains.

This chapter describes Latino students' urban education experience from a critical perspective. It begins with a demographic description of urban Latinos and critiques current reform efforts in urban school districts throughout the nation. Although there is a particular focus on the Los Angeles Unified School District as the site of analysis, the political, social, and educational dynamics in Los Angeles are reflective of what is currently under way in major urban centers throughout the United States. The chapter is written from the perspective of a teacher educator and highlights the work of a social justice teacher education program that prepares teachers to teach in urban schools. It concludes with the recommendation for the development of a Latino educational initiative that would include the voices of parents, community members, teachers, and representatives of higher education.

PROMISES AND CHALLENGES FOR URBAN LATINO STUDENTS

In presenting the contradictory experience for Latinos in urban schools, one needs only to examine and interpret data on Latino student achievement. While urban school districts report incremental gains in test scores for Latino students, the test scores remain lower than the scores of their White and Asian counterparts (National Center for Education Statistics, 2002). It is true that the number of Latino students graduating from high school and entering colleges is steadily rising; however, not one Latino subgroup has reached parity with Whites or African Americans (National Council of La Raza [NCLR], 2001). The increasing rate of Latinos' attending colleges and universities is juxtaposed with the fact that Latinos continue to be the student population most likely to drop out of school (Delgado-Bernal, 1999). As Latino students increasingly fill the classrooms and hallways of urban schools, their teachers are overwhelmingly White and do not speak Spanish (National Education Association, 2002). In fact, as the nation becomes culturally and linguistically diverse, states like California enforce archaic and discriminatory practices, such as *Proposition 227*, that outlaw the use of the primary language of Spanish-speaking students for purpose of instruction. When examining the data for urban students in California, it is apparent that an increasing number of Latino students are being placed into special education classrooms, while the opportunity to enroll in Advanced Placement courses remains limited (Solórzano & Ornelas, 2002). These data expose the sad reality that Latinos in urban schools are *still* educated in the most poorly financed, segregated, overcrowded, and unsafe schools in America (Council of Great City Schools, 2001; Orfield, 1999).

Even under these conditions Latino parents in urban America continue to believe that access to a quality education can guarantee their offspring the economic stability of which many could only dream (Valencia & Black, 2002). Many pursue this dream for their children while laboring under the worst working conditions, earning relatively low wages, with little or no opportunity for advancement. While most urban Latinos are employed, they still live in poverty and struggle to pursue a life of economic stability and social mobility. The poverty rate for Latinos has declined, but the low level of educational achievement of Latino workers remains a major obstacle to employment mobility (McDonnell, 2001). Latinos continue to navigate a vicious cycle of educational and economic oppression.

The contradictions between the Latino community and the broader American society extend beyond the hallways and playgrounds of inner-city schools. Many of the comforts taken for granted by many Americans are a result of the hard work of this nation's Latino workers. In fact, if one were to take a quick tour of urban America, one would most likely buy produce picked by Latinos, eat meals cooked and served by Latinos, sleep in beds made by Latinos, and purchase clothing made by a Latina garment worker in New York or Los Angeles.

It is a demographic fact that many Latinos reside in urban America. The last U.S. Census places 91.5% of Latinos in metropolitan areas of the country, with 46.8% of Latinos living in the central city (U.S. Census Bureau, 2000). The five urban centers with the highest number of Latinos are New York, Los Angeles, Chicago, Houston, and Philadelphia. The cities of New York and Los Angeles each claims a Latino population of over 3 million (National Council of La Raza, 2002). Latinos also reside in the smaller cities of Phoenix, San Diego, Dallas, San Antonio, San Jose, and Miami, which all claim more than 250,000 Latinos each (Therrien & Ramirez, 2000). The impact of the Latino population is already being felt throughout America's urban centers; it is time this country pays attention to Latino youth, for if it does not, the economic, social, and political consequences of an uneducated Latino majority could have a tremendously negative effect on the future of this nation's economy.

EDUCATION IS POLITICAL

The educational policies currently in place in urban schools throughout this country are part of a hegemonic, linguistically and culturally insensitive, and racist and classist national policy intended to maintain the status quo and keep Latinos *in their place*. Moreover, educational practices in this country that have been carried out are part of the "systemic subordination of those cultural groups perceived as threatening to the core values of American Democracy" (Darder, 2002, p. 37). As they relate to Latino students, these practices have historically been translated to a reduction of their culture and the erasure of their language. At present Latino students are subjected to a rote curriculum that promotes cultural and linguistic discontinuity. Linguistic codes, approved and promoted by a state and district, are perpetuated in our classrooms via a suspect reading program that is ultimately rooted in a classist and racist society.

Almost half of all Latinos are under 18, and since most reside in urban centers, the number has doubled in the last 20 years, experiencing a growth rate from 8.6% in 1980 to 16.2% in 1999 (ERIC Clearinghouse on Urban Education, 2001). The majority of urban students are impacted by a myriad of social and economic ills that adversely affect academic achievement. The cause of school failure experienced by Latino children rests squarely in the hands of those who determine educational policy. The social and political reality in this country is that class and race directly impact the amount of educational progress a Latino student might attain, the educational achievement level of Latino parents directly influences the possibility of educational success for their children, the level of education received influences the opportunities for gainful employment opportunities, and employment influences economic stability (Becerra, 2002). Latino children in urban America will grow up in crowded and/or substandard housing, have no medical insurance, and often live in unsafe communities. Until this nation is willing to spend a significant amount of time and money on Latino urban education, the living conditions of Latino children will relegate them to last place in the race for educational success. Latino students will be subjected to the never-ending game of *catch-up* with their White and Asian American compatriots, who are more successful in school. It should never be thought that the inability of urban Latinos to succeed in school is rooted in the cultures of our children. It is not because they are poor or do not speak English or because Latino parents do not place education in high regard. Latino children and youth are in a race for the finish line, and while they may start further behind and while they may need to run faster and harder than their White and Asian counterparts, educators need to realize that our children can get to the finish line, on their own terms.

CALIFORNIA AND LATINO EDUCATION

The Council of Great City Schools (2002) reported that the common set of challenges impacting urban school districts include (a) poor academic achievement among its low-income students, specifically African Americans and Latinos; (b) an inexperienced teaching staff; (c) teachers who have low expectations of their low-income and culturally and linguistically diverse students and have an undemanding curriculum; (d) schools that have little or no instructional coherence; (e) a high student mobility rate; and (f) unsatisfactory business operations. In California, where 29% of the Latino population resides and where 42% of the student population is Latino, the above list reflects the educational realities of many attending urban schools (Guzman, 2001). California has experienced a continual rise in its immigrant population. The contributions of the Latino immigrant population to the state not only help sustain its economy but add to the cultural mosaic that makes California one of the most diverse states in the nation. Californians often brag about their liberal political tendency, laid-back attitude, appreciation of cultural diversity, and sunshine, but the sun does not always shine on the state's Latino population.

Instead of responding to the need to improve student achievement for Latino students by convening members of the affected communities to collectively design a Latino educational agenda, California instituted a set of repressive educational policies. The majority White electorate, officials in State Department of Education, and local school boards have mandated educational policy changes that are having devastating effect on the education of Latino children. Latino children and youth, for many of whom their primary language is not English, are subjected to mandatory testing, scripted reading programs, and more. The trend in education, the move toward sameness in curriculum, the use of standardized tests as a measure of student achievement, the deculturalization and subtractive schooling of Latino children present a troubling dilemma. This trend is contrary to the pronounced liberal politics California is reputed to possess: to promote justice, equality, and access to quality education; to create democratic, respectful, multicultural communities of learners; and to facilitate critical thinking, creativity, and intellectual growth in American students. Herein lies the dilemma: how can this nation's colleges and universities recruit, train, and mandate that social justice teachers work in urban schools, particularly inner-city schools, when the urban school districts insist on implementing educational policies that only promote the existing inequities, fail to adequately measure student achievement, and devalue the professional experiences of teachers? How does one prepare teachers to work for social justice, if the teacher's job will depend upon submissively teaching under unjust conditions?

As this chapter goes to press, the state of California is aggressively implementing a series of educational policies that, at best, will force school districts to reckon with a new agenda for improving the delivery of instruction for the state's children and, at worst, ram through a series of dubious and complex changes that will have a devastating effect on the educational landscape for several years—and Latino children and youth are caught in the cross fire. The increasing number of Latino students is the real reason that the state, its educational infrastructure, and its electorate have decided upon a number of educational projects that are unfriendly to Latinos, such as English-only instruction, measuring student achievement on the basis of scores on English standardized exams, and unequal distribution of qualified teachers. All of this is being done without soliciting the opinions of Latino parents, who constitute almost 30% of the California labor force (Gándara, 2000).

The Pervasive Role of Politics in California

Latino immigrant students arrive from countries such as El Salvador, Guatemala, Belize, Colombia, Puerto Rico, and Cuba. The highest numbers of legal immigrants in California come from Mexico, an immigration pattern that has persisted since 1984 (Tafoya, 2002). The Central American student population in California is the second largest Latino subgroup, and any attempts to define educational policy in California must consider the issues of this immigrant population. The treatment of immigrant students can determine the effectiveness of any school reform effort aimed at improving student achievement (Valdés, 2001).

As Latino educators and community activists strive to improve schooling for this nation's urban immigrant students, the xenophobic treatment of

Latinos in the state contributes to the persistent cycle of educational inequity and presents the community with a number of political and social
obstacles (Trueba & Bartolomé, 2000). In 1994, Governor Pete Wilson,
Save Our State, and other anti-immigrant zealots organized successfully to
place one of the most repressive and racist propositions on the California
ballot. *Proposition 187*, passed by the California voters, aimed at denying
education, health care, and social services to any undocumented worker.
The intended target of this legislation, as evident in television commercials
depicting hordes of immigrants crossing the California border, was the Latino immigrant population. The proposition was callously allowing no exception to this intended law. The children of undocumented workers were
its primary victims. Although the majority of Latinos voted against the
initiative, the voters of California passed it by 59% of the votes. The U.S.
Supreme Court justified the denial of health and social services to the undocumented, but the denial of education to children of undocumented
workers was ruled unconstitutional. However, the California electorate was
not finished with California's Latino children.

Currently almost half of California's students (45%) are immigrants
from Latin America or children of immigrants (Tafoya, 2002). In 1996,
Ron Unz, a Silicon Valley businessman; Gloria Matta Tuchman, an elementary school teacher and unsuccessful candidate for state superintendent;
and Jaime Escalante, a math teacher who was famously depicted in the
motion picture *Stand and Deliver*, campaigned on behalf of the *English for
the Children* initiative, *Proposition 227*. Again, the anti-immigrant zealots
were successful. While the majority of Latinos voted against the initiative,
the voters of California voted to eliminate primary language instruction for
California's English learners. In addition, any teacher who refuses to abide
by this law is subject to legal action. The targets of this initiative were
Latino students, who constituted 83% of California's English learners. The
passage of these two propositions sent a strong message to California's
Latino immigrant population: *you are not welcomed here, but if you are
here, speak English*.

The question of language and language rights is of primary importance
for urban Latinos. Since the passage of *Proposition 227* over 1 million
Spanish-speaking students in California have been denied access to instruction in their primary language. Although other federal court cases and
mandates are still policy in California, the state has selected to implement
the provisions in *Proposition 227* that contradict portions of *Castañeda v.
Pickard*, which mandated school districts to implement bilingual programs
based upon *sound educational theory* and to ensure the implementation
and evaluation of such programs (Crawford, 2002; Hakuta, 2002). Clearly,
the *English for the Children* initiative ignores this policy. For the moment,
California's education of its Spanish-speaking population is at best an ambiguous attempt to implement the will of the California electorate and at

worst linguicism, racism, and oppression loosely disguised as an English language development program.

Today, school districts and the media promote the fallacy that English-only instruction has helped increase student test scores. A critical examination of the data and research speaks against such an interpretation. The critical, dialectical perspective so aptly presented by Crawford (2002) and Krashen (2001) exposes substantial evidence of continued inequality and moderate progress; only about a third of English learners are considered English-proficient after one year in the program, and the elimination of bilingual education has absolutely nothing to do with the rise in test scores.

While the question of immigration and language inequity is crucial to the development of a democratic urban Latino educational agenda, we must also pay close attention to the majority of California's Latino students who are not immigrants, many of whom speak primarily English. The state has ignored the almost 50% of Latino students who are the second- and third-generation offspring of Latino parents. NCLR aptly implores political and educational leaders to consider fully all aspects of inequity in education for Latino students and calls upon policy makers to move *beyond the immigrant paradigm*, which is loosely defined as the development of educational, social, and political policy from the narrow standpoint that the racial, social, and economic disparity among Latinos is solely an immigrant question and nothing else. The tendency to consider the issues of urban Latinos exclusively from an immigrant standpoint promotes the idea that if Latinos would just assimilate into American society, all forms of oppression will dissipate. It also fails to recognize the historical legacy of Latinos in this nation, as well as the contributions made to this country by Latino intellectuals, cultural workers, and laborers. Focusing on America's discriminatory practices from an immigrant paradigm also fails to recognize the legacy of racism faced by Latinos, past and present. A focus on the *immigrant paradigm*, as explained by Yzaguirre and Kamazaki (1997), does not satisfactorily explain the Latino condition in the United States because it reinforces the notion that Latinos are foreign, and in many respects it also reinforces the legacy of conquest, the idea that Latinos are outsiders no matter how deep their roots in this country.

Educational policy makers must give considerable significance to the concerns of California's Latino parents, who in spite of the odds still place a high value on the education of their children (Valenzuela, 1999). Education is the last vestige of hope for Latino parents, and according to a recent poll by the California Teacher Association (2001), Latino parents still have faith in the state's public school system, believing that the schools in their communities are good to excellent. However, this faith is not without criticism. Many Latino parents are also frustrated with the system of education in California's central cities. Latino parents experience language and communication barriers that prevent them from participating in their children's schools; they believe that teachers are too quick to give up on their children and do not understand their children's culture and history. Nearly three in five Latinos believe that discrimination and racism are still a problem in our schools.

The Miseducation of Latino Students, Los Angeles Style

We find the image that others have about Los Angeles to be quite intriguing. Their visions are often of nicely tanned blondes along the beach, movie stars in Beverly Hills, or Valley girls speaking into cell phones at the mall. We often wonder what people think when they see dark-haired, naturally tanned mothers walking their *mijos* (my child) to school. Los Angeles is the urban capital of Latinos in the United States. There are more Latinos living in the greater Los Angeles area than any major urban center in the nation. Los Angeles has had a Chicano, who is a former Los Angeles Unified School District (LAUSD) student, run for mayor, elected its first Latino city attorney, and sent several Latinos to the California state legislature and the U.S. Congress. LAUSD is the second largest school district in the country, with the highest number of Latino students and over 60% of Spanish-speaking students. In addition, Los Angeles has the highest percentage of English language learners (Council of Great City Schools, 2002).

While there have been steady increases in student achievement, there are still fewer Latinos and Latinas in advanced math and science classes and fewer students meeting the A-G (college entrance) requirements. The educational environment for Latino children and youth of Los Angeles is hostile. Teachers do not have their own classrooms, and high school students are often deprived of courses not offered on their track. Students are often taught in classrooms that lack fundamental educational tools; thus, teachers are forced to purchase basic materials out of their own pockets. Social justice education believes that every child has the right to attend school in a well-equipped, air-conditioned classroom with the latest technology, an ample supply of paper and pencils, and the most current and up-to-date textbooks. A safe and comfortable classroom with plenty of room for either group or individualized instruction can only enhance student learning. This is a right, not a privilege. Yet the classrooms for most Latinos in Los Angeles do not fit this description. In fact, one bilingual fifth grade teacher described his school as follows:

I have three broken non-functional computers. We have Internet access, but our broken computers are not even connected. The teachers in my school have to beg, borrow, and steal easels for their writing centers. There is even a shortage of pencils and paper. We have to fight the office to order pencils. We are using science textbooks from 1970 and the resources we do have, teachers don't have access to them. The materials are locked in the basement and the lady with the key doesn't come in until ten. If you can find her at recess, you have to physically walk her down to the basement and say, "I am not leaving until you open it and get me some supplies." We have two textbook storage rooms, both locked.

Deculturalization, dehumanization, and subtractive schooling have become standard practices in urban Los Angeles, where instructional priorities are standardized tests (Valenzuela, 1999). Scripted reading programs and mathematical instruction cover a variety of mathematical concepts, but all with little regard for the depth and breath of student learning. Spring (1997) defines deculturalization as "the stripping away of a people's culture and replacing with a new culture" (p. 1). In Los Angeles, multicultural education is a distant memory, and the students' primary language is outlawed. Students are subjected to a dehumanizing curriculum that "perpetuates a process of schooling in which the majority of students are so domesticated with fragmented and disconnected knowledge that they are left virtually uneducated and with little access to the political and economic spheres of society" (Darder, 2002, p. 15). In a recent meeting, a Latino parent addressed the dehumanization and deculturalization of the curriculum and described her child's experience with state- and district-adopted reading program: "My child is a precious jewel that I send to school, to learn to read; and I worry that LAUSD is treating my child like a guinea pig. . . . They are forcing teachers to use a one-size-fits-all program, and no one size fits everybody."

The standardized tests given in English to Spanish speakers are an inaccurate measure of what students are learning. In fact, the test is also an inaccurate measure of an effective school. From the perspective of many teacher educators, the schools that spend more time on genuine learning, on integrating children's culture into the curriculum, and allowing the students to complete free writing, are schools that truly involve their children in the learning process. Teachers who teach students to love reading, who expose them to a variety of reading materials, and who teach their children to think critically and problem-solve have children who love to learn.

TEACHER PREPARATION: A KEY COMPONENT FOR IMPROVING URBAN EDUCATION

The question of recruitment and retention of new teachers should be a part of any Latino urban school agenda. According to Darling-Hammond (1999), "the effects of well-prepared teachers on student achievement can be stronger than the influences of student background factors, such as poverty, language, background, and minority status" (p. 38). However, consideration must be given to the preparation of those teachers who not only possess necessary content area proficiency but genuinely care about Latino students and their parents. For five years the University of California at

Los Angeles (UCLA) Teacher Education Program (TEP) has struggled to prepare its urban teachers to "embody a social justice agenda, collaborate across institutions and communities, and blend theory and practice" (UCLA TEP, 2000, p. 1). Part of this journey has been a great effort to develop political and ideological clarity on the issues our students face as they enter the urban schools and communities. Teachers in the UCLA TEP are told that they must adopt principles of social justice and commit to a radical transformation of the educational system.

The UCLA TEP has a partnership with six urban school districts in the greater Los Angeles area. It organizes students in cohorts that continue for two years. First-year students, novices, engage in formal inquiry sessions intended to integrate the content, themes, and questions presented in their educational psychology and cultural foundations classes. During the second year, the residents are full-time teachers in urban schools. They attend a seminar once a week and write a master's portfolio. During the seminar there are opportunities for students to reflect on their own teaching practices. The theoretical models discussed include theories of culture, race, gender, critical pedagogy, sociocultural learning, and second language acquisition. Preparing students to teach in an urban setting requires prospective teachers to do their classroom observations and student teaching in inner-city, hard-to-staff, and underperforming schools. Upon graduation, students are required to teach for two years in these schools. Looking at teacher preparation through this lens calls upon teacher education programs to move beyond a service-learning model to social justice actions that tackle issues of critical importance to the communities they serve. Students come to understand that learning about educational injustice must occur simultaneously with learning about the economic disparities, deplorable social conditions, and lack of adequate health and social services. These are problems that the parents and families of Latino children in our inner cities confront on a daily basis.

CONCLUSION

As Zeichner (1993) reminds us, "teaching cannot be neutral. Neither can teacher development. We as teacher educators at whatever level must act with greater political clarity about whose interests we are furthering in our daily action" (p. 15). Trueba and Bartolomé (2000) recommend that TEPs increase the political and ideological clarity of prospective teachers by recognizing "the existence of the political and ideological dimensions of education [for in doing so teacher education programs will] produce the type of intellectual practitioners we need to teach in the ever increasing culturally and socially diverse urban schools of today" (p. 279). It is critical for teachers to consider education as a political entity, one filled with contradictions. An inequitable educational system, if forced to by parents and community political action, will change. Teachers must not only know their subject matter and possess a strong desire to impart knowledge but love their students unconditionally; they not only must be devoted classroom teachers and possess an ideology that is socially just but must enact a social justice political agenda. They must be political activists, change agents, and child advocates committed to challenging the inequity in urban schooling. This is the dialectical relationship in teaching, knowing your subject matter and loving your students but never forgetting that education is political and that political systems respond only to societal pressure. They must recognize that teaching in urban schools will call upon them to teach one curriculum to the children of the poor and one to the children of the wealthy; and they must refuse to implement such inequitable practices. Teachers with political and ideological clarity coalesce with Latino educators, parents, and activists to create a Latino educational initiative that considers the root causes of inequity in urban America. However, it is not only necessary to recognize the origins of educational injustice but equally important to develop a democratic, educationally sound urban education agenda, an agenda that not only is limited to interpreting student achievement by using dubious test scores, knowing how quickly children learn English, or whether there is an increase in the graduation rate for urban Latino high school students but honors and respects the students' bilingualism, facilitates the development of student bicultural identity and voice, provides Latino student with equal access to the core curriculum, and grants decision-making power to Latino parents.

A cursory review of history shows that the development of such an agenda can occur only through social action. In the words of one teacher activist, "where there is injustice, there will be resistance." As teacher educators, it is important to learn from social and political movements, community organizations, and teacher activists who are engaged in the process of creating fundamental changes in the educational institutions. Kohl (2000) says, "It is not enough to teach well and create a social justice classroom separate from the larger community. You have to be a community activist, a good parent, a decent citizen and an active community member, as well" (p. 14). Given the current educational program for urban Latinos, we hope that the entire Latino community becomes engaged in the hard work ahead, to transform the schools in our communities, to construct meaningful and equitable learning in urban schools throughout this nation. Our children can no longer wait.

REFERENCES

Becerra, R. (2002, February). *Investing in California's Latino children under five.* UCLA Chicano Studies Research Center. Available: www.sscnet.ucla.edu.

California Teacher Association. (2001, August). *Latino speaking points on minority attitudes on public education.* Burlingame, CA: Author.

Council of Great City Schools. (2002). *Foundations for success: Case studies of how urban schools improve student achievement.* Washington, DC: Manpower Demonstration Research Corporation.

Council of Great City Schools. (2001, October). *Educating English learners in the nation's urban schools.* Washington, DC: Author.

Crawford, J. (2002). *A few things Ron Unz would prefer you didn't know about . . . English learners in California.* Available: ourworld.compuserve.com/homepages/JWCrawford.

Darder, A. (2002). *Reinventing Paolo Freire: A pedagogy of love.* Boulder, CO: Westview Press.

Darling-Hammond, L. (1999). *Teacher quality and student achievement: A review of state policy evidence.* Washington, DC: Center for the Study of Teaching and Policy.

Delgado-Bernal, D. (1999). Chicano education from the civil rights era to the present. In J. Moreno (Ed.), *The elusive quest for equality: 150 years of Chicano/Chicana education* (pp. 77–108). Boston: Harvard Education Review.

ERIC Clearinghouse on Urban Education. (2001, February). *Latinos in school: Some facts and findings.* Available: ericweb.tc.Columbia.edu/digests/dig162.html.

Gándara, P. (2000, February). *Latinos and higher education: A California imperative.* Paper presented at Chicano/Latino Public Policy Seminar and Legislative Day, Sacramento, CA. Available: www.sfsu.edu.

Guzman, B. (2001, May). *The Hispanic population: Census brief 2000.* Current Population Report C2KBR/01–3. Washington, DC: U.S. Census Bureau.

Hakuta, K. (2002). *Educating language minority students.* Available: www.stanford.edu/~hakuta/mp_bilingual.

Kohl, H. (2000). Teaching for social justice. *Rethinking Schools, 15*(2), 14.

Krashen, S. (2001). *Why did test scores go up in California? A response to Unz/Reinhard.* Available: ourworld.compuserve.com/homepages/jwcrawford.

McDonnell, P. J. (2001, March). The *Times* poll: Latinos recover optimism lost in the 90's. More than 40% say the quality of life in Los Angeles has improved in the last five years. However, a majority gave the city's race relations poor marks. *Los Angeles Times.* Available: pqasb.pqarchiver.com/latimes/main/doc/000000069545123.html.

National Center for Education Statistics. (2002). *The condition of education 2002.* Washington, DC: Office of Education Research and Improvement.

National Council of La Raza. (2002, March). *Hill briefing to discuss the effects on high-stakes testing and social promotion on Latino youth.* Media Advisory. Available: www.nclr.org.

National Council of La Raza. (2001). *Beyond the census: Hispanics and an American agenda.* Washington, DC: Author. Available: www.nclr.org.

National Education Association. (2002). *Recruitment and retention of minority teachers.* Available: www.nea.org/recruit.minority.

Orfield, G. (1999). Politics matters: Educational policy and Chicano students. In J. Moreno (Ed.), *The elusive quest for equality: 150 years of Chicano/Chicana education* (pp. 111–121). Boston: Harvard Education Review.

Ruiz de Velasco, J. R., Fix, M., & Clewell, B. C. (2000). *Overlooked and under-served: Immigrant students in U.S. secondary schools.* The Urban Institute. Available: www.urban.org.

Solórzano, D., & Ornelas, A. (2002). A critical race analysis of advanced place-ments classes: A case of educational inequity. *Journal of Latinos and Education, 1*(4), 215–229.

Spring, J. (1997). *Deculturalization and the struggle for equality* (2nd ed.). New York: McGraw-Hill.

Tafoya, S. M. (2002, February). *The linguistic landscape of California schools. California counts: Population trends and profiles.* Available: www.ppic.org.

Therrien, M., & Ramirez, R. (2000, March). *The Hispanic population in the United States.* (Current Population Report P2–535). Washington, DC: U.S. Census Bureau.

Trueba, H. T., & Bartolomé, L. (2000). The education of Latino students: Is school reform enough? *Clearinghouse on Urban Education Digest.* Washington, DC. (ERIC Document EDO0UD–97–4).

UCLA Teacher Education Program. (2000). Teacher education program: Program description. Unpublished manuscript, University of Los Angeles.

U.S. Census Bureau. (2000, March). *Population by metropolitan-nonmetropolitan residence, sex, Hispanic origin, and race, with percent distributed by metropolitan-nonmetropolitan residence.* Available: www.census.gov/population/socdemo/hispanic/p20-535/tab20-1.txt.

Valdés, G. (2001). *Learning and not learning English: Latino students in American schools.* New York: Teachers College Press.

Valencia, R., & Black, M. S. (2002). Mexican-Americans don't value education! On the basis of the myth, mythmaking, and debunking. *Journal of Latinos and Education, 1*(2), 81–103.

Valenzuela, A. (1999). *Subtractive schooling: U.S. Mexican youth and the politics of caring.* Albany, NY: SUNY Press.

Yzaguirre, R., & Kamazaki, C. (1997). *The Latino civil rights crisis: A research conference.* Available: www.law.harvard.edu/groups/civilrights/conferences/latino/papers/comment/comment.html.

Zeichner, K. (1993). Connecting genuine teacher development to the struggle for social justice. *Journal of Education of Teaching, 19*(1), 5–20.

Chapter 11

The Role of Preservice Teacher Education in Serving Latino Students

Keith J. Suranna

INTRODUCTION

Despite its rich history, stimulating debates, and colorful reform efforts, preservice teacher education in the United States lacks a deep and far-reaching discourse when it comes to addressing diversity or multiculturalism, whether it be manifested by race, ethnicity, culture, language, sexual orientation, physical and cognitive disabilities, gender, or religion. Granted the situation has certainly improved over the past 25 years, and most preservice teacher education programs now offer courses in multiculturalism, diversity, and the like. However, considering the over 100 years in the history of formal teacher education in this country, these strides are still relatively recent and come sorely short of what remains to be done. Courses that focus on diversity are often viewed simply as *add-ons*, electives, and used to fulfill state certification requirements. More importantly is the fact that even though many teacher educators strive to foster *awareness* of diversity and multiculturalism in their students, no deep transference of this awareness is widely apparent in the day-to-day practice of public school teachers. In fact, many teachers, even well-meaning ones, still view differences among students as a hindrance, not as a strength (Kozol, 1991; Trueba, 1999). This is so even as the ethnic and racial population of the country rapidly shifts and teachers, especially new ones, find themselves lacking in tools to address the diverse needs of their young charges. This is especially pertinent as we focus on the education of Latino students.

This chapter begins by presenting a brief history of preservice teacher education in the United States, as well as some of the more visible reform efforts in recent years. Especially highlighted is the fact that even though important and potentially far-reaching reform has been proposed and implemented in teacher education, the preparation of teachers for service in a multicultural society in general and for service of Latino students in particular has been glaringly and painfully absent. An overview of the disparity in demographics between teachers and students in the United States and what this means to Latino students is then offered. The remainder of the chapter is devoted to practical ways in which preservice teacher education programs can serve Latino students.

A BRIEF HISTORY OF PRESERVICE TEACHER EDUCATION IN THE UNITED STATES

Historically, earning a liberal arts degree in the United States was usually thought of as enough preparation for one to serve as an educator of children. In contrast, public school advocates such as Horace Mann believed that traditional colleges and universities were not prepared to train *professional* educators; this could be achieved only via specialized academies or *normal schools* in which the study of *education* emerged as a unique academic discipline. Although noble in its inception, from the outset formal teacher preparation has struggled to gain wide acceptance and respect (Herbst, 1989). Labaree (1995) notes that this societal attitude had taken root as early as the mid-nineteenth century, when "the insatiable demand for teachers . . . meant that the emphasis was on finding warm bodies to fill classrooms rather than on preparing qualified professionals" (p. 50). It is not difficult to understand the misgivings that some had toward a teaching career. Lucas (1997) writes, "All things considered, the prospect of expending time, money, and energy preparing for a part-time or temporary teaching position, one that promised few benefits and even less pay, could hardly have seemed attractive or compelling" (pp. 16–17). Thus, the lowly status of teaching as well as the lack of economic resources and remuneration have historically brought little respect to the process of preparing future teachers.

In recent years, approximately 500,000 new teachers are prepared annually in more than 1,200 public and private colleges and universities that offer teacher education programs (Doyle, 1990). Generally speaking, preservice teachers are required to possess a foundation of both liberal arts and education course work, as well as some type of student teaching experience. A variety of structural formats of teacher education programs are currently offered: traditional four-year programs that lead to a bachelor's degree; fifth-year programs in which one already in possession of a bachelor's degree studies education for two semesters and, after which, earns a Master of Arts in Teaching (MAT); integrated bachelor's/master's programs in which undergraduate work and graduate work in liberal arts and education are completed consecutively; and various alternative certification programs, for example, a summer program for those entering teaching as a second career. Although colleges and universities claim their preparation programs are thorough in their approach, considering the sheer number of programs and their diversity, there tends to be a disparity in the quality between programs (Morley, Bezuk, & Chiero, 1997). Hence, throughout its history, teacher education has been routinely and sometimes sharply criticized. As one of the more acerbic critics of teacher education, Koerner (1963) states, "Course work in Education deserves its ill-repute. It is most often puerile, repetitious, dull, and ambiguous—incontestably" (p. 18). It was in reaction to sentiments such as this that various reform efforts in teacher education in the United States have been attempted.

Recent Reform Efforts

In October 1957, when the Soviet Union launched *Sputnik I*, the U.S. education system almost immediately came under scrutiny. Many surmised that our students were ill prepared to compete with the Soviets; and subsequently, teachers and teacher education shouldered much of the blame. Although this was certainly an important chapter in the history of U.S. education, it seems that the real time of ferment regarding preservice teacher education reform proved to be the 1980s and early 1990s. What has come to be commonly known as the *first wave* of educational reform in the early 1980s was launched during the Reagan administration in the form of the National Commission on Excellence in Education's (1983) report *A Nation at Risk*. Among other things, the report brought teacher education to task and highlighted its lack of academic rigor. Specifically, it criticized preservice programs for overemphasizing courses in how to teach (teaching methods) at the expense of those in what to teach (the liberal arts). Many viewed *A Nation at Risk* as a *wake-up call* and joined the *education bashing* bandwagon. A September 1984 *Newsweek* article synthesized a common assumption of the time: "Teacher training is perhaps the biggest running joke in higher education" (Williams, Howard, McDonald, & Michael, 1984, p. 64).

Following *A Nation at* Risk, many responded to this widespread criticism and precipitated the *second wave* of educational reform. Organizations such as the National Commission on Excellence in Teacher Education (1985), the Carnegie Forum (1986), and the Holmes Group (1986) and individuals such as Theodore Sizer (1984), founder of the Coalition of Essential Schools at Brown University, and John Goodlad (1990), director of the Center for Educational Renewal at the University of Washington in Seattle, offered sweeping reforms in an attempt to promote teaching as a true profession. Some important products of these reform efforts have been the continued promotion of a strong foundation in the liberal arts, partnerships between preservice programs and local K–12 schools or professional development schools, reflective practice, preservice programs extending beyond the baccalaureate level, and teacher leadership.

However interesting and important these broad reform efforts in teacher education have proven, issues of diversity in general and the service of Latino students in particular have all but been ignored. As Neuharth-Pritchett, Reiff, and Pearson (2001) note, "Most preservice teacher education programs educate undergraduates to work effectively with only one socioeconomic group—the middle class—as well as with only one culture—the mainstream or dominant culture" (p. 257; see also Cannella & Reiff, 1994; Gollnick & Chinn, 2002).

THE DISCONNECT IN DEMOGRAPHICS

Latinos are the fastest growing *minority* group in the United States (U.S. Department of Education, Planning and Evaluation Service, 2000). Thus, the education of Latino students will prove to be the most challenging situation for teachers as we enter the new century (Trueba, 1999). In fact, by the year 2020, Latinos will make up 20% of all U.S. children (National Center for Education Statistics [NCES], 1998a); and by the year 2030, Whites will compose only 30% of the U.S. student population, whereas Latino students will prove the largest student group as 44% of the total enrollment (Trueba, 1999; Valencia, 1991). But even though the population of Latinos has been rising and will continue to rise in the foreseeable future, "this increase in population has not been accompanied by a proportionate increase in educational attainment, economic stability, or political power" (Pérez & De La Rosa Salazar, 1997, pp. 45–46). One of the major and arguably most important reasons for this disheartening incongruity is the lack of quality education offered to Latino students. As Trueba (1999) aptly emphasizes,

The historical academic underachievement of Latino students is attributed to the lack of cognitively, culturally, and linguistically appropriate teaching methods, and the remedy is often presented in terms of methodological and mechanistic tools dislodged from the sociocultural and historical circumstances of children's family and community. There is a lack of understanding of the fundamental differences between Latino and other children. (p. 48)

Furthermore, recent public elementary and secondary school student demographics by race/ethnicity are 64.2% White, 16.9% African American, 14% Latino, 3.8% Asian/Pacific American, and 1.1% Native American/Alaskan Native (NCES, 1998b). In contrast, recent public elementary and secondary school in-service teacher demographics by race/ethnicity are 87% White, 7% African American, 4% Latino, less than 1% Asian/Pacific American, and less than 1% Native American/Alaskan Native (NCES,

1995). There is no clear indication that this "overwhelming presence of whiteness" (Sleeter, 2001) in the teaching force will shift anytime soon. In fact, according to the American Association of Colleges for Teacher Education (1995), recent preservice teacher demographics by race/ethnicity are 80.5% White, 9% African American, 4.7% Latino, 1.7% Asian/Pacific American, and 0.7% Native American/Alaskan Native: no significant variation by any means. Table 11.1 provides a visual representation of the current dissimilarity in the demographics between White and Latino teachers and students.

In addition to this disparity in teacher/student demographics, we must consider the major role that language plays in the education of Latino students. According to the NCES (2000), (a) 25% of Latino students speak mostly Spanish at home, (b) Latino elementary students are more likely to speak Spanish at home than those in higher grades, and (c) those students who speak mostly Spanish at home tend to have parents who are less educated than those who speak mostly English at home. These facts are important for teachers to be aware of, particularly when considering the development of English language skills in young Latino students and in communicating with Latino parents. However, the NCES (1999) reports that only 20% of teachers feel well prepared to serve students whose first language is other than English. In addition, out of the 42% of all public school teachers who have at least one limited-English-proficient (LEP) student in their class, only 32% have ever received any form of training in serving LEP students (NCES, 1994). The situation becomes even more dismal when we consider that some teachers are unaware of whether their Latino students are bilingual or not, the language that their Latino students speak at home, and if the parents of their Latino students speak English (Kloosterman, 1999).

When we ponder these important and telling statistics, it is clear that preservice teacher education programs can no longer ignore the fact that their preservice teachers are entering a veritable fray, ill prepared to serve our nation's Latino population. This can have lasting negative effects not only on the beginning teachers themselves but also on the Latino students they are presumed to serve (Meier & Stewart, 1991; Sleeter, 2001; Trueba, 1999). These negative effects can manifest as a lack of learning, underachieving, truancy, mislabeling, involvement in crime, and dropping out. Educators cannot simply blame students and families for these heinous situations and shoulder none of the responsibility. It is truly a disgrace that an entire population, a valuable and rich resource, in this country has been and is going unserved. The burden now rests on preservice teacher education to expediently and deliberately begin to grapple with how to remedy this situation and prepare future teachers to adequately serve this country's Latino population.

Table 11.1
Disparity in Demographics between White and Latino Students and Teachers

Race/Ethnicity	Students	In-Service Teachers	Prerservice Teachers
Whites	64.2%	87.0%	80.5%
Latinos	14.0%	4.0%	4.7%

PRACTICAL WAYS IN WHICH PRESERVICE PROGRAMS CAN SERVE LATINO STUDENTS

One of the most important items on the agendas of preservice teacher education programs should be to prepare teachers to serve Latino students in a multicultural society. In fact, this should inform the philosophical underpinnings of their teaching. As a vital aspect of U.S. public education and society, it must be discussed in theory and manifested in practice. If teacher educators wish to adequately prepare future teachers to serve Latino students, it will be accomplished through both dimensions. Only then will the full potential of doing so be realized in our public schools.

For a teacher education program to be successful in serving Latino students, its commitment to doing so needs to be ingrained and explicit in every aspect of the program. This must begin with professors and administrators possessing a common vision and understanding of the unique characteristics and needs of Latino students. This point cannot be overemphasized; the entire program must be clearly committed to this end. This certainly does not mean that teacher educators' perceptions will remain stagnant. They must remain flexible and open to new ideas and challenges but should begin with a core understanding of what it means to prepare teachers to serve the single fastest growing culturally and linguistically diverse group in the United States. This emphasis must be embedded in the curriculum, modeled for preservice teachers by university and public school teachers and administrators, as well as put into practice by student teachers themselves.

Following are recommendations that preservice programs can begin implementing in order to prepare their students to serve the Latino population of this country. Six particular ways toward this end are offered: recruiting, course work, field experience, reflective practice, teacher leadership, and in-service support.

Recruiting

As discussed above, the disparity in teacher demographics is disheartening when considering the fact that, compared to Whites, so few Latinos are entering the teaching force. Eubanks and Weaver (1999) state, "Children of color need teachers who look like them, who share similar cultural experiences and who can be role models to demonstrate the efficacy of education and achievement" (p. 452). Mechanisms certainly need to be in place to draw more Latinos to the field, but a wide array of clear and practical ways to do so is lacking. One way to interest Latinos in teaching can begin by actively engaging them at the high school level. Teacher educators and current student teachers, along with in-service teachers and administrators, could implement *future teacher* clubs in secondary schools to attract young students into the profession. These clubs would allow young students not only to learn about aspects of teaching of which they may not be aware but also to reflect upon their own schooling and why they are or are not interested in a teaching career. Interested students could also serve as *assistant student teachers* or *paraeducators* in their own or other schools to gain a firsthand glimpse into the work of a teacher (González, 1997). High school students could also be invited to universities to tour the campus and/or participate in an education class to further experience the life of a future teacher. Perhaps, by offering experiential learning situations for high school students, these types of clubs can contribute to interesting not only Latinos but also a more diverse population in considering and pursuing a teaching career.

Further analysis at the state and local levels undoubtedly needs to be done to deepen both the discussion on recruiting diverse students into teaching as well as our understanding of their experience as they proceed from preservice preparation to in-service practice (Grant & Secada, 1990). It is clear that preservice teacher educators must implement ways of recruitment that will help assure that teachers graduating from their programs will be expressing the rich diversity currently present in the student population of the United States. However, when considering recruiting Latinos or any other racial/ethnic group into teaching, sensitivity needs to be exercised. As Gordon (1994) reminds us, "token representation of minority teachers will in and of itself not attract more students of color to the profession" (p. 352). Instead of dwelling on sheer statistics, teacher educators should focus on creating and sustaining preservice programs in which all future teachers, particularly students from culturally diverse backgrounds, take part in educational activities that expose them to a wide variety of individuals and experiences (Dillard, 1994). In the end, of utmost importance is recruiting those individuals who bring particular experiences, knowledge, and personalities that will assist them in serving in culturally diverse educational settings (Haberman, 1996).

Course Work

From the outset of their teacher education program, students should be made fully aware of its emphasis on service to Latino students. Again, this emphasis should be explicit in every aspect of the program, especially in course work. As previously mentioned, courses in multiculturalism or diversity in general are usually added on to the curriculum to fulfill some type of state or graduation requirement. These insufficient offerings do very little to engage student teachers in the realities of classroom practice and often even promote misconceptions and stereotypes. Furthermore, courses in diversity or multiculturalism should never be manipulated to simply appear *politically correct*. Much thought on the part of the instructor must go into such a course to make it a critical and integrated component of the preservice program. It must serve to deepen students' and, I dare say, professors' understandings of what it means to contribute to a rich and diverse society.

Courses that address diversity and multiculturalism then should clearly be offered, required, and pervasive throughout a program and should be tailored to allow students to reflect upon their own misconceptions and prejudices. Not only should these courses grapple with racial and ethnic issues, but they should also address culture, language, sexual orientation, physical and cognitive disabilities, gender, gifts and talents, and even religion. Much more can be done in offering these types of classes. However, a problem arises when we, as many do, hold the limited view that only specific courses that explicitly deal with issues of diversity should be used to address the phenomena. Issues of diversity should also be addressed in other classes throughout a preservice program. This remains an untapped and rich opportunity. For example, in an elementary science methods course the professor should not only discuss ways to teach elementary science but also model practices that inform student teachers of ways that reach all students, regardless of the teacher's preconceived notions about students' abilities. Most courses should also have some sort of field requirement attached. This could take the form of a case study of a diverse learner or teacher, an action research project addressing an important communal concern, or implementing an intervention in a struggling school.

These types of experiences need to be implemented in all courses in order to broaden student teachers' perceptions of diversity. Teacher educators need to make clear that issues of diversity are never *compartmentalized* in schools. As Kloosterman (1997) reminds us, "Multiculturalism [is] not a day or a parade" (p. 206). Teachers should not *do* multiculturalism only during allotted times of the school day; nor should student teachers view this in their preservice course work. Future teachers need to be made well aware of the fact that they will be facing and making vital decisions about a diverse body of students. Their course work is a primary resource that should be broadened to this end.

Field Experience

Field experiences for student teachers should begin as early as possible in the program. During these progressively complex field placements, pedagogical theory being learned in the university should be both modeled for the students as well as put into practice by them. As students move along in the program and gain a deeper understanding of theory and ways to serve Latino students, they should be given more responsibilities in their placements. This could begin by simply observing a fine cooperating teacher, one who expresses the kind of practice that serves all students in the classroom, and then progressively taking on all aspects of teaching. The chasm that sometimes exists between the university and the school must also be bridged. During field experiences, preservice teachers should be placed with those in-service teachers who not only concur with the university's approach to serving Latino students but are widely acknowledged as teachers who exemplify inclusive practice. Inclusive practice should be modeled by cooperating teachers who serve as advocates for students not only inside the classroom but outside the classroom as well.

A most important consideration, usually neglected by preservice programs, is the opportunity for student teachers to spend time in the community, outside of the school setting (DeAcosta, 1994). This is vital if teacher educators wish to prepare student teachers to serve the *whole child*. An understanding must be gained about students' backgrounds, communal opportunities or lack thereof, and, of course, familial relationships. This will undoubtedly help student teachers see that there exist many subgroups in the Latino community with different countries of origin; diverse immigration, familial, educational, linguistic, and socioeconomic experiences; as well as various values and beliefs. As Stachowski and Mahan (1998) assert,

Given the documentation that most students entering teacher education programs are from non-minority backgrounds, possess a narrow cultural worldview, and have had limited exposure to cultural diversity, a growing sense of urgency characterizes the preparation of this relatively homogeneous group of future educators who will be facing increasingly heterogeneous classrooms. (p. 155)

Following formal classroom teaching placements, student teachers could be involved in internships at such diverse sites as a state department of education, an educational theater company, a camp for inner-city youth, or a child advocacy group. This will further help them in seeing students as well as the teaching profession in a much broader context than classroom teaching alone. In this way, they will be able to reflect on the ways in which they could best serve both their profession and a diverse student population.

To realistically prepare teachers to serve in multicultural schools, they must be placed in diverse educational contexts in which they can gain an understanding of and practice in serving a diverse body of students. By serving both inside and outside the school, student teachers will be immersed in the cultures of their students. This is so especially considering that most in-service and preservice teachers have such little experience with multiculturalism. Thus, a deep insight has the potential to further the education of new teachers and to help them gain a sense of empathy with their students.

Reflective Practice

Much has been written regarding the importance of teachers to, as Socrates said, "know thyself" through reflection and objective self-analysis (Hole & McEntee, 1999; Montessori, 1939/1966; Palmer, 1993). Oberg and Underwood (1992) write, "Each teacher's development is unique, affected by his or her history, insights, talents, and desires. To move consciously towards a fuller sense of what it means to be a teacher, this unique human story must be told" (p. 163). Through gaining self-knowledge as a teacher one can reflect upon one's heritage; ethnic, racial, and familial background; as well as personal thoughts, values, and perhaps prejudices toward one's fellow human beings and the process of education. In this way, student teachers will become active participants instead of observers. Preservice teacher education programs are certainly in a strong position to foster this in their students. As with all best practices, reflection should be modeled by teacher educators themselves. Seminars and reflective journals can be utilized as tools for collaborative and personal reflection as students undertake new and challenging situations, such as a particular course or field experience. For example, a student teacher may be placed in a setting that he or she has never experienced, such as an urban multicultural or a rural homogeneous environment. It is vital for the neophyte teacher to be guided to articulate his or her experiences. Through collegial reflection, student teachers may find that others are experiencing similar thoughts and feelings. These collaborative and problem-solving opportunities can have positive effects on new teachers as they discover and participate in the collegial nature of teaching. As Collier (1999) states, "[Preservice teachers] learn to access their personal beliefs through the important questions and answers needed for assimilating their role as teacher and the characteristics contributing to the effectiveness of a teacher" (p. 173).

Teacher Leadership

Teacher leadership is a concept that entails empowering classroom teachers, those directly involved in the educative process, to play vital roles in what actually occurs in schools. Katzenmeyer and Moller (2001) write, "Teachers who are leaders lead within and beyond the classroom, identify with and contribute to a community of teacher learners and leaders, and influence others toward improved educational practice" (p. 5). Teacher leaders are thought of as excellent classroom practitioners who work with their principals in collaborative decision making, professionals who take part in developing colleagues and mentoring new teachers and, when the occasion warrants, "take a stand" to advocate for students, even when it proves an unpopular notion at a particular time (Suranna, 2000). Because the Latino student population needs strong and vocal advocates who are informed about its unique experience, teacher leaders can take an active role in educating the community on vital issues facing Latino students. This can include, but is by no means limited to, leading parent seminars and addressing boards of education.

One way to foster teacher leaders in preservice programs is to offer a particular course that addresses the concept. The University of Connecticut is an example of a preservice program that requires its preservice teachers to enroll in such a teacher leadership course called *Teacher Leadership and Organizations*. This course primarily focuses on the dynamics of the culture and climate of schools, and discussions revolve around the idea of teachers serving as influential and ethical leaders in the creation of effective learning environments within schools. In such a course, in-service teachers who are identified as teacher leaders can be invited to address the class and discuss the importance of teacher leadership and how it can positively impact Latino students. In the end, teacher leadership is a concept that is just beginning to be widely manifested in public schools; thus, the possibilities that are available for teacher leaders to have a profound effect on Latino students are far from being exhausted.

In-Service Support

Upon graduating from their preservice program, new teachers must not be made to feel abandoned in their beginning practice. Many researchers have discussed the difficulty in dealing with the realities of classroom practice that beginning teachers experience when taking the step from preservice education to in-service practice (Armstrong, 1984; Corcoran, 1981; Veenman, 1984). Unfortunately, it has been noted that many gifted neophyte teachers become frustrated and leave the profession before their talents are fully realized (Johnson, 1990). Furthermore, research has also shown that teachers do not begin to take on teacher leadership roles until their first two to five years of teaching (Baker & Andrew, 1993). Thus, if some of the more talented new teachers leave the profession before they are able to emerge as teacher leaders and advocates for Latino students, these students will be denied the kind of service they otherwise might receive from these young teachers.

It has been noted that there often exists a lack of quality in in-service teacher education, especially as it relates to cultural diversity (Solomon, 1995). However, to facilitate its graduates in their transition to in-service practice and thus facilitate continued in-service development, teacher educators must reach beyond the academy walls to assure that their students are prepared for the demands and struggles of serving Latino students in our country's diverse schools. Teacher educators should be open to supporting graduates in practice; in effect, this is an opportunity to *put their money where their mouths are* and nurture the seeds that were sown in their preservice programs. This may entail visiting graduates in their new classrooms to observe and offer constructive criticism, model a lesson, or contribute to a combined action research study. Professors could also invite graduates to speak to current students about the realities of classroom practice in a multicultural society. Although it certainly takes effort to implement this bridge building between universities and public schools, especially on the part of preservice programs, its potential is far-reaching. If preservice programs are in fact preparing their students to be fine classroom practitioners, who are aware of and have had personal experience working with Latino students and families and who have the potential to emerge as teacher leaders, there is no reason that teacher educators cannot continue to deepen this education for new in-service teachers. The potential certainly exists; teacher educators themselves must be willing to take the first step.

In this section, six specific ways in which preservice teacher education programs can begin to prepare new teachers to effectively serve Latino students in a multicultural society have been identified. They are, of course, not exhaustive. It is hoped that this chapter has piqued the interests of both teacher educators and public school practitioners to begin the all-important journey of addressing the needs of the very large and growing Latino student population in the United States.

CONCLUSION

Although this chapter has specifically focused on ways in which preservice teacher education programs can serve Latino students in the United States, these suggestions are also valuable for serving all students. In the end, educators at all levels have the awesome responsibility to help bring about an equitable and peaceful society in which all students are valued as individuals and offered the kind of education that allows them to explore their unique interests, talents, and gifts. In this way our children will grow to be informed and critical-thinking citizens who are well equipped to carry on the democratic experiment that is the United States. Epictetus said, "Only the educated are free." If this is so, teachers must consistently guard against rigidity of thought and misconceptions about groups of individuals, whether regarding race, ethnicity, culture, language, sexual orientation, physical and cognitive disabilities, gender, or religion. Instead, we must remain open to the mysteries of the individual learner and to the organic nature that is inherent in the classroom. In this way, we will assist our students in agreeing with Walt Whitman: "I exist as I am. That is enough."

REFERENCES

American Association of Colleges for Teacher Education. (1995). *SCDE enrollments by race and ethnicity, 1989, 1991, and 1995*. Retrieved March 27, 2002, from http://www.aacte.org/Multicultural/enrollment_ethnicity_yr89-91-95.htm.

Armstrong, D. G. (1984). New teachers: Why do they leave and how can principals retain them? *NASSP Bulletin, 68*(460), 110–115.

Baker, T. E., & Andrew, M. D. (1993). *An eleven institution study of four-year and five-year teacher education program graduates*. (ERIC Document Reproduction Service No. ED 355224)

Borrowman, M. L. (1965). Liberal education and the professional preparation of teachers. In M. L. Borrowman (Ed.), *Teacher education in America: A documentary history* (pp. 1–53). New York: Teachers College Press.

Cannella, G. A., & Reiff, J. C. (1994). Preparing teachers for cultural diversity: Constructivist orientations. *Action in Teacher Education, 16*(3), 37–45.

Carnegie Forum. (1986). *A nation prepared: Teachers for the 21st century. A report of the task force on teaching as a profession*. New York: Carnegie Forum on Education and the Economy.

Collier, S. T. (1999). Characteristics of reflective thought during the student teaching experience. *Journal of Teacher Education, 50*(3), 173–181.

Corcoran, E. (1981). Transition shock: The beginning teacher's paradox. *Journal of Teacher Education, 32*(3), 19–23.

DeAcosta, M. (1994). *Preparing teachers for home-school-community partnerships: A foundational approach*. (ERIC Document Reproduction Service No. ED 380430)

Dillard, C. B. (1994, January/February). Beyond supply and demand: Critical pedagogy, ethnicity, and empowerment in recruiting teachers of color. *Journal of Teacher Education, 45*(1), 9–17.

Doyle, W. (1990). Themes in teacher education research. In W. R. Houston, M. Haberman, & J. Sikula (Eds.), *Handbook of research on teacher education: A project of the Association of Teacher Educators* (pp. 3–24). New York: Macmillan.

Eubanks, S. C., & Weaver, R. (1999, Summer). Excellence through diversity: Connecting the teacher quality and teacher diversity agendas. *Journal of Negro Education, 68*(3), 451–459.

Gollnick, D., & Chinn, P. (2002). *Multicultural education in a pluralistic society* (6th ed.) Upper Saddle River, NJ: Prentice Hall.

González, J. M. (1997, April). Recruiting and training minority teachers: Student views of the preservice program. *Equity & Excellence in Education, 30*(1), 56–64.

Goodlad, J. I. (1990). *Teachers for our nation's schools*. San Francisco: Jossey-Bass.

Gordon, J. A. (1994, November/December). Why students of color are not entering teaching: Reflections from minority students. *Journal of Teacher Education, 45*(5), 346–353.

Grant, C. A., & Secada, W. G. (1990). Preparing teachers for diversity. In W. R. Houston, M. Haberman, & J. Sikula (Eds.), *Handbook of research on* teacher education: A project of the Association of Teacher Educators (pp. 403–422). New York: Macmillan.

Haberman, M. (1996). Selecting and preparing culturally competent teachers for urban schools. In J. Sikula, T. J. Buttery, & E. Guyton (Eds.), *Handbook of research on teacher education: A project of the Association of Teacher Educators* (2nd ed., pp. 747–760). New York: Macmillan.

Herbst, J. (1989). *And sadly teach: Teacher education and professionalization in American culture.* Madison: University of Wisconsin Press.

Hole, S., & McEntee, G. H. (1999). Reflection is at the heart of practice. *Educational Leadership*, 56(8), 34–37.

Holmes Group. (1986). *Tomorrow's teachers.* East Lansing, MI: Author.

Johnson, S. M. (1990). *Teachers at work: Achieving success in our schools.* New York: Basic Books.

Katzenmeyer, M., & Moller, G. (2001). *Awakening the sleeping giant: Helping teachers develop as leaders* (2nd ed.). Thousand Oaks, CA: Corwin Press.

Kloosterman, V. I. (1999). *Socio-cultural contexts for talent development: A qualitative study on high ability Hispanic bilingual students* (Research Monograph 99142). Storrs, CT: The National Research Center on the Gifted and Talented.

Kloosterman, V. I. (1997). *Talent identification and development in high ability, Hispanic, bilingual students in an urban elementary school.* Unpublished doctoral dissertation, University of Connecticut, Storrs.

Koerner, J. D. (1963). *The miseducation of American teachers.* Boston: Houghton Mifflin.

Kozol, J. (1991). *Savage inequalities: Children in America's schools.* New York: HarperCollins.

Labaree, D. F. (1995). The lowly status of teacher education in the United States: The impact of markets and the implications for reform. In N. K. Shimahara & I. Z. Holowinsky (Eds.), *Teacher education in industrialized nations: Issues in changing social contexts* (pp. 41–85). New York: Garland Publishing.

Lucas, C. J. (1997). *Teacher education in America: Reform agendas for the twenty-first century.* New York: St. Martin's Press.

Meier, K. J., & Stewart, J., Jr. (1991). *The politics of Hispanic education: Un paso pa'lante y dos pa'tras.* Albany, NY: SUNY Press.

Montessori, M. (1966). *The secret of childhood* (M. J. Costelloe, Trans.). New York: Ballantine Books. (Original work published in 1939.)

Morley, A. I., Bezuk, N., & Chiero, R. (1997). Preservice teacher preparation in the United States. *Peabody Journal of Education*, 72(1), 4–24.

National Center for Education Statistics. (2000). *Condition of education: Language spoken at home by Hispanic students.* Retrieved March 27, 2002, from http://nces.ed.gov/programs/coe/2000/section1/indicator06.html.

National Center for Education Statistics. (1999). *Teachers' feelings of preparedness.* Washington, DC: Department of Education, Office of Educational Research, and Improvement.

National Center for Education Statistics. (1998a). *Issues in focus: The educational progress of Hispanic students.* Washington, DC: U.S. Department of Education.

National Center for Education Statistics. (1998b). *Digest of education statistics,*

1998. Retrieved March 27, 2002 from http://www.aacte.org/Multicultural/
    enrollment_ethnicity_yr86-93-96.htm.
National Center for Education Statistics. (1995). *Digest of education statistics,
    1995*. Retrieved March 27, 2002 from http://www.aacte.org/Multicultural/
    enrollment_ethnicity_yr93-94.htm.
National Center for Education Statistics. (1994). *Bilingual education/limited
    English proficient students*. Retrieved March 27, 2002 from http://nces.ed.
    gov/fastfacts/display.asp?id=96.
National Commission on Excellence in Teacher Education. (1985). *A call for
    change in teacher education*. Washington, DC: American Association of Col-
    leges for Teacher Education.
National Commission on Excellence in Education. (1983). *A nation at risk: The
    imperative for educational reform*. Washington, DC: U.S. Department of
    Education.
Neuharth-Pritchett, S., Reiff, J. C., & Pearson, C. A. (2001, Spring/Summer).
    Through the eyes of preservice teachers: Implications for the multicultural
    journey from teacher education. *Journal of Research in Childhood Educa-
    tion, 15*(2), 256–269.
Oberg, A., & Underwood, S. (1992). Facilitating teacher self-development: Reflec-
    tion on experience. In A. Hargreaves & M. G. Fullan (Eds.), *Understanding
    teacher development* (pp. 162–177). London: Cassell.
Palmer, P. J. (1993). *To know as we are known: Education as a spiritual journey*.
    New York: HarperCollins.
Pérez, S. M., & De La Rosa Salazar, D. (1997). Economic, labor force, and social
    implications of Latino educational population trends. In A. Darder, R. D.
    Torres, & H. Gutiérrez (Eds.), *Latinos and education: A critical reader*
    (pp. 45–79). New York: Routledge.
Sizer, T. R. (1984). *Horace's compromise: The dilemma of the American high
    school*. Boston: Houghton Mifflin.
Sleeter, C. E. (2001, March/April). Preparing teachers for culturally diverse schools:
    Research and the overwhelming presence of Whiteness. *Journal of Teacher
    Education, 52*(2), 94–106.
Solomon, R. P. (1995, September/October). Beyond prescriptive pedagogy: Teacher
    inservice education for cultural diversity. *Journal of Teacher Education,
    46*(4), 251–258.
Stachowski, L. L., & Mahan, J. M. (1998, Spring). Cross-cultural field placements:
    Student teachers learning from schools *and* communities. *Theory into Prac-
    tice, 37*(2), 155–162.
Suranna, K. J. (2000). *The nature of teacher leadership: A case study of elementary
    school teachers from a five-year teacher education program*. Unpublished
    doctoral dissertation, University of Connecticut, Storrs.
Trueba, E.(H.)T. (1999). *Latinos unidos: From cultural diversity to the politics of
    solidarity*. Lanham, MD: Rowman and Littlefield.
U.S. Department of Education, Planning, and Evaluation Service. (2000). *Helping
    Hispanic students reach high academic standards: An idea book*. Washing-
    ton, DC: Author.
Valencia, R. R. (1991). The plight of Chicano students: An overview of schooling

conditions and outcomes. In R. R. Valencia (Ed.), *Chicano school failure: An analysis through many windows* (pp. 3–26). London: The Falmer Press.

Veenman, S. (1984). Perceived problems of beginning teachers. *Review of Educational Research, 54*(2), 143–178.

Williams, D. A., Howard, L., McDonald, D. H., & Michael, R. (1984, September 24). Why teachers fail. *Newsweek, 104*(13), 64–70.

Index

About the Editor and Contributors

VALENTINA I. KLOOSTERMAN is a Research Associate in the Center for Children & Families at the Education Development Center, Newton, MA. Dr. Kloosterman has focused her research and practice on talent development, bilingualism, and cultural diversity, particularly regarding the socio-emotional and educational needs of Latino students. She serves as a consultant to several educational associations and has written extensively in her areas of expertise. In 1997, Dr. Kloosterman was recognized with the Hollingworth Research Award.

MARGARITA ALICEA-SÁEZ is Management Associate and Center Technologist in the Center for Children & Families at the Education Development Center in Newton, MA. Her professional goals include improving the quality of education for Latinos, especially young Latinas. Ms. Alicea-Sáez believes that to reach these goals, Latinas need to be empowered in their education in order to achieve personal success in a competitive and unequal society.

LILIA I. BARTOLOMÉ is an Associate Professor in the Applied Linguistics Graduate Program at the University of Massachusetts. Her research interests include critical pedagogy, teacher education, and classroom discourse acquisition patterns of linguistic minority students in U.S. schools. Dr. Bartolomé's recent publications include *The Power of Culture: Teaching across Language Differences*.

LEAH C. FABIANO is a doctoral student in Communication Sciences at Temple University. She is currently a Research Assistant examining bilingual Spanish-English-speaking children, specifically those with speech and language disorders. Ms. Fabiano is a certified speech-language pathologist and has extensive experience working with the Latino population.

LUIS A. HERNANDEZ is presently an Early Childhood Education Specialist at the Region IV Head Start Quality Improvement Center at Western Kentucky University. Mr. Hernandez is working on a number of national and regional initiatives in early literacy and learning outcomes for children, with a special focus on the needs of English Language Learners.

AQUILES IGLESIAS is a Professor in the Department of Communication Sciences, College of Allied Health Professions and Acting Dean of the Graduate School at Temple University. His area of research is language acquisition in bilingual (Spanish-English) children. In 1994, Dr. Iglesias was awarded the first Multicultural Achievement Award by the American Speech-Language-Hearing Association for his service in the area of multicultural populations.

VELMA D. MENCHACA is Chair and Associate Professor in the Department of Educational Leadership at the University of Texas Pan American. She has published extensively in the areas of English Language Learners, migrant education, multicultural education, and culturally relevant content. Her research has provided teachers with strategies for teaching diverse students.

ELOISE LÓPEZ METCALFE has extensive public school experience in Los Angeles County public schools. Dr. Metcalfe has been the Director of the University of California in Los Angeles Teacher Education Program since 1997. The preparation of teachers for urban schools and the diversity of the teaching workforce are two of her research interests.

THERESA MONTAÑO is an Assistant Professor of Chicano Studies at California State University Northridge. Her professional experience includes serving as a professional development specialist for the Los Angeles teachers union and as teacher educator in the University of California in Los Angeles Teacher Education Program. Her areas of interest are critical pedagogy and issues of educational equity for Latino students.

ALBERTO M. OCHOA is a Professor in the College of Education at San Diego State University and Chair of the Policy Studies in Language and Cross-Cultural Studies Department. His work focuses on the resolution of equity problems confronting social and educational institutions and broad-based community participation that affect the quality of life of school communities.

ALBA A. ORTIZ is Professor in the Department of Special Education and Director of the Office of Bilingual Education at the University of Texas at Austin. She is also the holder of the President's Chair for Education Academic Excellence. Dr. Ortiz is a nationally recognized expert on the education of English Language Learners with disabilities.

GUADALUPE SAN MIGUEL, JR. is currently a Professor in the Department of History at the University of Houston, TX. He is an authority on the struggle of Chicanos for educational equality in the United States and on Texas Mexican music. Dr. San Miguel is the author of *Quest for Educational Equality* and *Brown, Not White: School Integration and the Chicano Movement*.

KEITH J. SURANNA is currently a Research Associate in the Center for Science Education at the Education Development Center in Newton, MA. A former elementary school teacher and college professor, Dr. Suranna's professional interests include qualitative research, teacher leadership, and the nature of classroom practice. Dr. Suranna is also a published children's book author.

ALANA M. ZAMBONE is on the faculty of North Carolina Central University. Dr. Zambone has over 22 years' experience in higher education and has served in Latin America and Asia for six years. She has been engaged in systems change in school districts around the United States on issues of equity, special education, and policy.